Thinking

Directed, undirected and creative

Thinking

Directed, undirected and creative

Second edition

K.J. GILHOOLY

*Department of Psychology, University
of Aberdeen, Aberdeen, Scotland*

1988

ACADEMIC PRESS

Harcourt Brace Jovanovich, Publishers
London San Diego New York Berkeley
Boston Sydney Tokyo Toronto

ACADEMIC PRESS LIMITED
24/28 Oval Road,
London NW1 7DX

United States Edition published by
ACADEMIC PRESS INC.
San Diego, CA 92101

British Library Cataloguing in Publication Data

Gilhooly, K.J.
Thinking: directed, undirected
and creative. — 2nd ed.
1. Thought processes
I. Title
153.4'2

ISBN 0-12-283483-6
ISBN 0-12-283484-4 Pbk

Phototypeset by Colset Pte Limited, Singapore
Printed in Great Britain by T.J. Press (Padstow) Ltd,
Padstow, Cornwall

Preface

As with the First Edition, this book is intended to be an introduction to recent research and theory concerning thought processes in normal human adults. The major topics dealt with are (i) thinking directed at solving problems, (ii) less directed forms of thinking such as are found in daydreaming and (iii) creative thinking. While these topics are largely considered from the perspective of the information processing approach, which is currently dominant in cognitive psychology, some historical background is also provided (particularly in the first chapter). In the final chapter, an attempt is made to assess the progress achieved within the information processing approach to thinking and to indicate promising directions for future research. To help the interested reader go more deeply and widely into the various topics raised in the book, I have made suggestions for further readings at the end of each chapter.

The major changes in this edition are the addition of chapters on expertise in problem-solving and on decision making. Throughout, there has been a general updating of material to reflect some of the many developments over the six years or so since the first edition appeared. To make space for new material, there has also been some pruning. Among the new topics and approaches discussed in this edition are: cognitive science; connectionism; analogical reasoning; insight; search in chess; expertise; decision making; reasoning schemata; training in creativity; and simulation of scientific discovery.

The level of treatment is pitched at students who already have some background in psychology. As well as students and teachers concerned with courses on the psychology of thinking, I hope that the book will also be of interest to researchers, teachers and practitioners in other areas of psychology and in related disciplines, such as education, cognitive science and artificial intelligence.

While preparing this edition, I benefitted greatly from discussions of issues in the study of thinking with many fellow psychologists and cognitive scientists. Among those who helped me in this way, I would particularly like to thank Alison Green, John Maule and Norman Wetherick for their contributions to my thinking about expertise, decision making and reasoning respectively. Of course, it should not be assumed that they agree with my final treatment of the topics concerned.

Production of this book was greatly facilitated by the good working environment provided by my Head of Department, Professor Eric Salzen, whom I am pleased to acknowledge here. I should also like to thank very much our Departmental typists, particularly Elaine Duncan, who worked cheerfully and quickly on the manuscript.

April 1988   K J Gilhooly

Contents

1

Introduction

Thinking is an activity that has long intrigued and puzzled psychologists and philosophers – and continues to do so. Since all valuable innovations in the arts and sciences originate from fruitful thinking, it is a process of evident importance. At a more prosaic level, thought is frequently required to deal effectively with the various frustrations that arise in everyday activities. Even when not dealing with any pressing problems, thinking is always occurring during periods of wakefulness, albeit often in a free-floating daydreaming fashion. It is desirable to obtain a good theoretical understanding of thinking, not only for the sake of pure knowledge, but also with a view to helping people to think more effectively. This book, then, aims to review recent attempts, involving new approaches, techniques and experiments, to increase our understanding of thinking. The focus will be on thinking in normal adult humans, particularly problem-directed thinking, undirected thinking (daydreaming) and creative thinking.

I. PRELIMINARIES

A. Characterizing thinking

The term 'thinking' will be taken as referring to a set of processes whereby people assemble, use and revise *mental models*. For example, thinking directed toward solving a problem may be regarded as exploring a mental model of the task to determine a course of action that should be the best (or at least be satisfactory). A mental model often enables the thinker to go far beyond the perceptually available information (Bruner, 1957), and to anticipate the outcomes of alternative actions without costly overt trial and error. The first psychologist to describe thinking explicitly in terms of model-using, appears to have been Kenneth Craik (1943; see also, Zangwill, 1980). To illustrate his analysis, Craik used the example of a bridge builder determining a viable design by exploring symbolic models of possible bridges, rather than by overt and costly trial and error with real bridges.

More recently, the notion of thinking as mental modelling has been explored in the areas of deductive reasoning (Johnson-Laird, 1983), problem solving (Holyoak, 1984) and inductive reasoning (Holland *et al.*, 1986). A general discussion of thinking as mental modelling is given in Gilhooly (1987).

The view of thinking adopted here is 'reflexive' in that it encompasses the activity of psychologists as well as the activities of psychologists' subjects. Psychologists seek to assemble symbolic models of how humans (including themselves) assemble and utilize models. As Wetherick (1979, p. 105) has put it, "cognitive psychology seeks to model man's model-making capacities". To aid in the development of models of thinking, psychologists present experimental tasks to their subjects and record the resulting behaviour in varying degrees of detail. The psychologist's interpretation of the behavioural data should, on the approach presented here, take account of the way in which the subjects model (or interpret) the experimental task. As will emerge in later chapters, it is frequently the case that behaviour which seems unintelligible or irrational becomes clear and sensible when an understanding is achieved of how the task has been interpreted by the subjects.

As well as varying in degree of *directedness* (problem solving *v.* daydreaming), thought is also often considered to vary in *modality*. Subjectively, thinking often seems to involve inner speech or visual, auditory, or other forms of imagery. For example, reporting the 6th letter in the alphabet after 'E' would generally involve the experience of inner speech. On the other hand, deciding whether an irregular shape was the same as another irregular shape at a different orientation (Shepard and Metzler, 1971) would generally involve an experience of visual imagery. Subjective experience, then, suggests the existence of different internal 'languages', or distinct sets of symbols (verbal, visual, etc.), with their own rules of combination. Some translation rules must also exist to enable one to go from a word to an image and vice versa. Although the *experience* of imagery is not denied by current theorists, the *functional role* of imagery has been questioned. Imagery might merely be epiphenomenal, i.e. like factory noise, a non-functional by-product of the important processes. For instance, it has been argued strongly (Pylyshyn, 1973) that the *meaning* of both verbal and non-verbal representations is conveyed by an underlying abstract, conceptual code. On this view, a visual image is generated on the basis of a symbolic description of the object being imaged, but it is the symbolic or propositional description that is important, rather than the image itself. To use one of Pylyshyn's examples, two images of a chessboard might be *pictorially* identical, but one image might be based on an abstract encoding that includes the relationship 'Black Queen attacks White Bishop' while the other image might not. On Pylyshyn's view, the important thing about an image is the propositions that it is derived from, rather than any 'pictorial' properties. The opposing point of view is that images can convey 'appearance' information better than propositions. The obtained patterns of reaction times to tasks that would appear to involve image comparing, rotating and scanning have been taken as supporting this latter view (Kosslyn and Pomerantz, 1977). But interpretations in propositional terms always seem possible and, since it is not yet clear which position is correct (Pylyshyn, 1981, 1984; Kosslyn, 1981) or even whether the question is empirically decidable (Anderson, 1978), the issue will be left open in this text.

B. Characterizing problems

Given the strong emphasis on problem solving in this text and in the general literature on thinking, the question arises 'what is a problem?' The definition offered by the Gestalt psychologist Karl Duncker (1945, p. 1) is still serviceable. He wrote that "a problem arises when a living organism has a goal but does not know how this goal is to be reached".

This is a useful initial formulation that signals a number of points. First, that a 'task' set by an experimenter, is not necessarily a problem for a given individual. Whether it is a problem or not, depends on the subject's knowledge and on his ability to locate relevant knowledge, should he have it. Secondly, a problem may vanish or be dissolved if the person changes his goals. A third point is that a problem does not effectively exist until the person detects some discrepancy between his goals and the situation he finds himself in.

Most psychological studies of problem solving (especially, as we shall see, those within the information processing framework) have dealt with *well-defined* problems. If we accept Reitman's (1965) useful proposal that problems in general can be viewed as having three components (viz. a starting state, a goal state and a set of processes that may be used to reach the goal from the starting state), then a problem is well-defined if all three components are completely specified. Problems in mathematics, in logic and in various board games tend to be well defined. Although well defined, such problems can be very difficult and the psychologist is faced with the task of explaining how we humans, with our various limitations, manage to solve geometry, chess and similar scale problems in reasonable times. Of course, it will be still more difficult to explain how we tackle those *ill-defined* problems that are more typical of real life than the well-defined variety.

Ill-defined problems leave one or more components of the problem statement vague and unspecified. Problems can vary in degree of definedness (Reitman, 1965, Ch. 5); for example, from 'make a silk purse out of a sow's ear' (which leaves possible methods unspecified), to 'make something useful from a sow's ear' (which has a vague goal and unspecified methods), to 'make something useful from some part of a pig' (which leaves vague the goal, the starting state and the methods available).

It seems a reasonable strategy for psychologists to start by studying people's ways of handling apparently well-defined problems and then to move on to consider ill-defined tasks. Perhaps people tackle ill-defined tasks by seeking a well-defined version of the problem, which they then work within until the problem is solved or a new definition is tried. If this is so, then studies with well-defined problems will be relevant to part of the process of solving ill-defined problems. Indeed, processes of defining, or interpreting, the problem are also important in well-defined tasks and some attention has recently been given to task interpretation processes that must play a role in both well- and ill-defined tasks (Kochen and Badre, 1974; Simon and Hayes, 1976). Some studies relating to task interpretation processes will be discussed in later sections.

Another useful distinction is that between *adversary* and *non-adversary* problems. In an adversary problem the person is competing with a thinking opponent, whereas in non-adversary problems the struggle is with inert problem materials (real or symbolic) that are not reacting to what the person does with a view to defeating him or her (despite what the problem solver may feel!). Both of these sorts of problem will be dealt with in future chapters.

A third distinction that has become increasingly important in problem-solving research is that between *semantically rich* and *semantically impoverished* problems (Chi *et al.*, 1982). To a large extent, this distinction refers to the solver's view of the problem. A problem is semantically rich for solvers who bring considerable relevant knowledge to the problem. For example, if someone has just been told the basic rules of a game that they have never encountered before, then a problem in that game would be semantically impoverished for that person, but the same problem would be semantically rich for an expert player of the game. Many artificial puzzles used in studies of problem solving are semantically impoverished for most subjects. Until relatively recently, most studies of problem solving focussed on semantically impoverished puzzles, particularly in the case of non-adversary problem solving. More recently, there has been considerable interest in the study of semantically rich non-adversary tasks such as computer programming and physics problem solving. Such studies frequently involve contrasts between the behaviour of subjects for whom the problems concerned are semantically rich (experts in the area) with subjects for whom the problems are semantically impoverished (novices in the area). See Chapters 3 and 4 for further discussion of semantically rich problems.

II. APPROACHES TO THINKING

Historically a number of theoretical approaches have been taken to the topic of thinking. The principal early approaches were those of classical introspectionism, behaviourism, Gestalt theory and neo-behaviourism. More recent work has been dominated by the information processing approach. Although this text is written largely from the point of view of the currently dominant information processing approach, a brief historical overview will now be given to help set recent developments in perspective.

A. Early approaches

1 Introspectionism

In the late nineteenth and early twentieth centuries the classical introspectionists, such as Wundt and Titchener, took conscious experience to be their subject matter and attempted to analyse consciousness into elementary sensations. A good analogy for the introspectionist endeavour is with chemistry. As chemists analyse complex compounds into chemical elements, so the introspectionists sought to analyse complex experiences into elementary sensations. Such analyses were to be made by means of the classical introspective report. To produce a classical introspective report the subject was required to adopt a special attitude or 'set' such that the 'meaning' of the experience was to be ignored in favour of the component sensations. So, instead of a report, for instance, that one saw 'a large red book', a report of 'an experience of a red coloured slightly trapezoidal shape' was expected. At this point, it is worth distinguishing between 'classical introspectionism', with its emphasis on reporting in the language of sensations, and 'ordinary' introspective reporting in everyday terms. The latter form of introspection is used quite widely in the current study of thought (Ericsson and Simon, 1984), as will be seen in future chapters. Classical introspectionism, by contrast, has fallen into disuse. One reason for the decline of the method of classical introspection was that it led to conflicting reports which could not easily be reconciled. In particular, the question of thinking without images aroused considerable controversy between the introspectionists of Wurzburg (who reported imageless thought under certain circumstances) and those of Leipzig and Cornell who adamantly insisted that thought was always accompanied by imagery even although it might be very faint.
    As well as the difficulty of resolving conflicts on such basic matters as imageless thought, the introspectionist approach was, in any case, limited in its scope to the consciousness of specially trained, sane, adult human

subjects. To tackle unconscious thought processes or those of children, the insane, untrained subjects and animals would require very different approaches (Miller, 1960). The early behaviourists offered a radical alternative to classical introspectionism and this alternative was eagerly adopted by many psychologists.

2 Behaviourism

The early behaviourists (e.g. Watson, 1913) changed the focus of psychology from conscious experience to observable behaviour. Their dominant theoretical notion was the 'stimulus–response link'. As a topic of study, 'thought' was displaced from its centre stage position by 'learning'. Thorndike (1898), an important precursor of Watson, had paved the way for this development through his studies of trial-and-error behaviour during problem solving in cats. Cats placed in puzzle boxes displayed considerable trial-and-error behaviour before escaping, and on being returned to the boxes after each trial, they were only a little faster at escaping on each successive trial. There was no sign of 'insight' leading to sudden solutions that could then be repeated without error when the cats returned to the puzzle boxes. Ruger (1910) found similar patterns of results in studies of humans working with manipulation puzzles. Thorndike and Ruger suggested that thought in problem solving could be described as *covert* trial and error similar to the *overt* trial and error observable in their subjects' behaviour. Notions of 'insight' or 'understanding' were felt to be unnecessary.

3 Gestalt

A contrasting view was put forward by the Gestalt psychologists who objected to the different forms of 'elementarism' represented by the classical introspectionists and the early behaviourists. Gestalt theory focussed especially on perception, rather than on thinking or learning, and the importance of perceptual organization was particularly stressed. Thus, in dealing with thinking and problem solving, the Gestalt theorists emphasized the way in which the problem was perceived as a determining factor in task difficulty. The solving process was described as one of perceptual restructuring in which the problem comes to be seen in such a way that the solution is obvious. Examples of purely perceptual restructuring would include suddenly seeing the alternative interpretation of an ambiguous drawing or coming to see a face hidden in a puzzle painting. In the problem-solving area, 'restructuring' may be illustrated by the following anecdotal example (discussed by Wertheimer, 1945, Ch. 4). When the famous mathematician Gauss was a 6-year-old schoolboy he amazed his teacher by being able to give immediate answers to problems requiring the sum of successive whole numbers from 1 to N. Gauss was able to do this, not by rapid addition, but by restructuring the task. In the case of adding the following series of numbers (1, 2, 3, 4, 5, 6, 7, 8, 9, 10), Gauss noticed that each number from the left increases by one and each number from the right decreases by one. Thus the numbers can be regrouped into pairs that all have the same sum [(1, 10), (2, 9), (3, 8), (4, 7), (5, 6)]. There are five pairs in this example, each of which sums to 11, and so the answer to the original question is 55. In general, the number of pairs will be $N/2$ and the sum of each pair will be $N + 1$; hence the formula that the sum of such a series ending in an even number is given by $(N/2) \times (N + 1)$.

For the Gestalt theorists, then, problem solving involved 'insight', which was an appreciation of how the solution was necessitated by the nature of the problem, and this insight would come through a restructuring of the subject's perception of the problem. Some important early Gestalt research on problem solving was carried out with animal subjects. Presumably, if insight could be convincingly demonstrated with animals, then its occurrence in humans could scarcely be denied. So, Kohler (1925), on the basis of his famous series of studies with apes, claimed that his animal subjects suddenly solved manipulation problems, after periods of overt inactivity (interpreted as periods of thought).

Behaviourist critics argued that trial and error was evident in Kohler's behavioural records and that the results could be explained simply by trial and error. They also pointed out that prior experience with the tools (sticks) used in the tasks was necessary for solution (Birch, 1945). To Gestalt replies that, even if trial and error had occurred, it was not blind or random, the behaviourist retort was that *random* trial and error had never been postulated, but rather trial and error biased by prior learning. The issue of trial and error *v.* insight was also taken up within the more constrained area of discrimination learning. Krechevsky (1935) reported data apparently showing sudden solutions by rats of discrimination learning tasks together with response patterns that could be interpreted as evidence of hypothesis testing. The response patterns in question showed consistent responding to some irrelevant cue, such as position or size of the stimulus when brightness was the relevant cue. However, Spence (1936) showed that these response patterns could be produced by gradual accretions and reductions of response strength to the cues in the task and so could be explained in simpler, less mentalistic terms than those proposed by Krechevsky.

Studies of human problem solving were not neglected by the Gestalt school. Karl Duncker (1945) examined in detail solution attempts to a range of problems involving mathematical or practical contents. The task known as the 'X-ray' or 'radiation' problem was particularly closely studied by Duncker.

The radiation problem was posed as follows (Duncker, 1945, p. 1): "Given a human being with an inoperable stomach tumour, and rays which destroy organic tissue at sufficient intensity, by what procedure can one free him of the tumour by these rays and at the same time avoid destroying the healthy tissue which surrounds it." The subject was usually also given a sketch (see Fig. 1.1) and told that someone had visualized the situation in that way, but that this simple approach of sending a beam of rays straight through to destroy the tumour would not do, since the rays would destroy healthy tissue on the way to the tumour.

Fig. 1.1 Sketch given to subjects working on X-ray problem (Duncker, 1945). The oval represents a cross-section through the body with the tumour in the centre. The radiation apparatus is on the left, sending a beam through the tumour.

Subjects were asked to think aloud as they worked on the problem and the resulting records or protocols indicated a tendency to work backwards from the overall goal to subgoals which, if achieved, would lead to solution. So, for instance, the major goal of 'treating the tumour by rays without destroying healthy tissue' could be achieved if the subgoal of 'avoiding contact between rays and healthy tissue' could be attained. In the most thoroughly discussed protocol, this particular subgoal governed much of the subject's efforts. However, solution was not obtained until an alternative subgoal was set up of 'lowering the intensity of the rays on their way through healthy tissue'. This subgoal led to the solution of using a lens to focus the rays on the tumour so that lethal intensity is only reached at the focal point.

While Duncker investigated the development of insight, the opposite phenomenon of problem 'blindness' or ('misleading sets') was studied by Luchins (1942) in a series of experiments using water jar problems. In these tasks the subject was asked to say how one could get exactly a specified amount of water using jars of fixed capacity and an unlimited source of water, e.g. given three jars (A, B and C) of capacities 18, 43 and 10 units respectively, how could you obtain exactly 5 units of water? The solution may be expressed as $B - A - 2C$. After a series of problems with that same general solution, subjects had great difficulty with the following problem: given 3 jars (A, B and C) of capacities 28, 76 and 3 units respectively, how could you obtain exactly 25 units of water? In fact, the solution to this problem is very simple (i.e. $A - C$), but when it comes after a series of problems involving the long solution (B – A – 2C) many subjects fail to solve or are greatly slowed down compared to control subjects.

A related block to effective problem solving, known as 'functional fixity', was also identified by work in the Gestalt tradition. Functional fixity tends to arise when an object has to be used in a new way in order to solve some problem. The classic study of functional fixity was carried out by Duncker (1945) using the 'box' (or 'candle' problem). In this task subjects were presented with tacks, matches, three small boxes and three candles. The problem was to put the candles side-by-side on a door, in such a way that they could burn in a stable fashion. For one group of subjects the boxes were empty, but for the other group (experimental group) the boxes were used as containers and held the matches, tacks and candles. The solution is to use the boxes as platforms and fix them to the door using the tacks. It was found that the solving rate was much higher in the control group than in the experimental group. Duncker explained this result in terms of a failure to perceive the possible platform function of the boxes when they were presented as containers. Functional fixity has been independently demonstrated and further investigated in a number of later studies (e.g. Birch and Rabinowitz, 1951; Adamson and Taylor, 1954; Glucksberg and Weisberg, 1966; Glucksberg and Danks, 1968). Glucksberg has proposed an alternative interpretation of the effect, in terms of failure to notice the boxes as separate units when they are presented as containers. Whatever the detailed explanation, the phenomenon appears to be a robust one and is doubtless one source of difficulty in real-life problem solving.

4 Neo-behaviourism

The Gestalt investigators helped keep the study of thought processes alive in the 1920s and 1930s while behaviourists focussed on associative learning in man and the white rat. In the face of studies such as Duncker's on the X-ray problem, the simple S–R approach to extended chains of thought appears quite inadequate. Even in the case of maze problem solving by rats, it was becoming evident that richer internal processes would have to be postulated within behaviourist theory. Thus the notion of a 'mediating response' (r_m) was introduced into neo-behaviourist analyses. 'Mediating responses' are seen as implicit, covert responses that generate 'mediating stimuli' (s_m), which can elicit further mediating responses or overt behaviour. Chains of mediating stimuli and responses are taken to represent thought sequences. In many problems, various alternative sequences of actions might lead to the desired goal and such alternatives could be explored via mediational chains without overt trial and error. To take Berlyne's (1965) example, a resident of Boston may have many possible ways of travelling to New York involving different routes and different forms of transport. In thinking of how to make this journey the Bostonian subject would, on the neo-behaviourist analysis, 'embark' (covertly) on one mediational chain out of those available. The alternative chains may be assumed to vary in strength of association to the problem stimulus, i.e. they form a hierarchy, ordered from strongly associated to weakly associated chains. If the person is told that his dominant chain (air route, say) is blocked (e.g. airport closed), the next most dominant chain would tend to be evoked. Such a hierarchy of mediational response sequences is an example of a *habit-family hierarchy* (Hull, 1934).

Maltzman (1955) proposed an extension of the habit-family hierarchy notion which would permit hierarchies of habit-family hierarchies. Thus a problem stimulus could be associated in varying degrees of strength with a number of different habit-family hierarchies. Furthermore, the 'nesting' of hierarchies within hierarchies could continue to many levels. These elaborate structures of mediating stimuli and responses are known as *compound* habit family hierarchies. As Berlyne (1965) points out, when stimulus–response associations are organized in this way, the actual course of action followed will result from selection of a hierarchy at the highest level, then from selection of a sub-hierarchy within the first hierarchy, and so on. At each stage, 'selections' would automatically be made on the basis of habit strength. This kind of scheme could, albeit in a cumbersome way, represent results such as those of Duncker on the X-ray problem, that show subjects following one general direction (corresponding to a selection at a high level of the compound hierarchy) down to a fair degree of detail (corresponding to selections at lower levels). Duncker's subjects abandoned directions and selected different ones when success was not obtained. In neo-behaviourist terms, continued failures within a given hierarchy of responses would reduce the relevant habit strengths and thus increase the probability of alternative hierarchies being evoked. Berlyne (1965) developed such ideas in an ambitious book (*Structure and direction of thinking*) that attempted to demonstrate how neo-behaviourist theory could account for directed thought. However, by the time Berlyne's work appeared, the information processing 'revolution' that still dominates cognitive psychology had begun [see, e.g. Miller *et al.*'s (1960) *Plans and the structure of behavior* for an important early manifesto of the new approach], and Berlyne's neo-behaviourist notions had little impact.

Although precursors of the modern information processing approach can be identified in researchers active before the Second World War, such as Selz (see De Groot, 1965; Frijda and De Groot, 1981), it appears to have taken developments in cybernetics and computer technology before psychologists in general felt secure in ascribing 'goal directedness' and complex internal processes to people. Such concepts were felt to be open to charges of 'mentalism', until implemented on machines such as guided missiles and computers. The information processing approach that is now dominant in cognitive psychology, will be discussed in the next section.

B. The information processing approach

1 Basic ideas

The main stimulus for the development of the *information processing* approach to thinking was the arrival of the computer. The basic idea of the information processing approach is that in his cognitive aspects, man can be regarded as a computer-like system that codes, stores, retrieves and transforms information. Computers work by following *programs*, which are essentially lists of step-by-step instructions. The instructions can be conditional, that is, can involve simple decisions so that the computer can be instructed to jump from one part of the program to another, depending on the outcome of intermediate operations – thus making the system very flexible. Furthermore, complete groups of instructions (sub-routines) can be given labels and activated by those names. This facility for creating and using sub-routines increases greatly the ease and flexibility of programming. Since both computers and humans flexibly manipulate symbols it is tempting to seek computer analogies and metaphors for human processes. Such analogies span a continuum of detail from vague verbal similarities between man and machine at one end to working computer programs that are intended to *simulate* (i.e. mimic) human processes at the other end. At an intermediate level of detail are outlines of the organization and sequencing of major processing steps and decisions (e.g. flow charts). Many information processing analyses are at this level.

Broad verbal analogies between man and computer provide an orientation for thinking about human processes. Within the loose constraints of this orientation, models of greater specificity can be constructed. If a model is at the outline level, then at least a definite sequence of broad steps has been specified and it may be possible to derive predictions from the outline itself. Furthermore, the outline may be used to guide construction of a model at the most detailed and completely specified level, viz. that of a running program. Thus, the outline is a useful summary of the main features of the program. Indeed, it can be argued that the outline level is the most fruitful one (not too vague and not too detailed) for making comparisons between human and computer processes. However, having a running program corresponding to a given outline is a reassuring guarantee that the outline describes something that works.

2 Simulation

The virtues and problems of simulation level models will now be considered in more detail. First, it may be noted that computer simulation is a general method that can be applied in all fields that involve the study of complex processes. For instance, the economy could theoretically be represented by a large number of variables (wages, prices, employment levels, balance of payments, exchange rates, etc.) which are all related to one another. An economist might speculate that a particular pattern of relationships holds among the main economic variables and this hunch could be tested by programming a computer to behave in accord with the economist's model. Many predictions could then be generated and checked against subsequent events (or degree of fit to past events could be assessed) and the simulation model could be revised to improve its predictions and ultimately provide a better understanding of the process being modelled.

In a similar way simulation can be used to explore and test ideas about human information processing. If we thought that humans solved, say logic problems, by going through a certain sequence of decisions and operations, we could program a computer to go through the same sequence on a number of such problems and compare the computer's performance with that of a sample of human subjects. If the computer tended to take more steps on the problems that humans found more difficult or to make the same patterns of mistaken conclusions as humans, then the theory would gain support from such results. Furthermore, the computer could be made to print out every operation and decision that it makes and the resulting record could then be compared with the records produced by humans 'thinking aloud' as they work on the problems. Comparison of human 'thinking aloud' records and the computer's report of the steps taken by the program can be used in attempts to assess the degree of detailed match between computer and human processes. However, in practice, there are many difficulties in assessing the degree of match between two such multidimensional records.

3 Capacity limitations

Whatever process is to be simulated, a clear and unambiguous model is required, since a computer program cannot work unless it is completely specified. So, one benefit of simulation is that it forces the theorist to be clear and unambiguous – properties that have sometimes been felt lacking in psychological theories and models! (see Broadbent, 1987, for a recent relevant discussion). Of course, a simulation model should not invoke processes that exceed human capabilities. Knowledge of human limitations is derived from studies of basic information processing tasks (e.g. recognizing familiar symbols, comparing symbols, reproducing previously presented symbols and so on). The following broad picture seems to emerge from such studies. Humans have a vast *long-term memory* capacity which is so organized as to permit generally rapid recognition of familiar symbols and retrieval of information associated with recognized symbols. Familiar symbols representing both presented information and associated, retrieved information, can be held temporarily in a small capacity *working memory system*. Memory span studies initially suggested a capacity of about 5–9 symbols for this system (Miller, 1956).

Detailed research and theorizing on human memory has led to more elaborate models in which both long-term and working memory systems are seen as involving a number of interrelated components. So, long-term memory has been analysed into semantic and episodic memory (Tulving, 1983), with semantic memory being decomposed further into lexical and encyclopaedic memory (Lachman, 1973). Working memory in turn, has been analysed into three main sub-systems comprising a central executive, an articulatory loop and a visuo-spatial scratchpad (Baddeley, 1986). However, from the point of view of research on thinking, it has rarely seemed necessary to consider the fine structure of memory; a general distinction between unlimited long-term and limited short-term storage systems has usually proven adequate. Of course, this may not continue to hold as analyses of thinking become more fine-grained.

It may be noted that many studies in the memory literature have focussed on the transfer of information from temporary storage in working memory to permanent storage in a long-term memory. From the point of view of problem-solving studies, the reverse traffic is more relevant. Problem solving may often be viewed as involving the application of rules which take inputs from working memory, locate appropriate symbols in long-term memory and place those symbols in working memory, displacing old symbols if working memory capacity is exceeded.

In addition to storage capacity limitations, an important processing limitation is also generally acknowledged on the number of operations that can be carried out simultaneously. At the level of problem solving, the human information processing system is assumed by most workers in the field to be *serial*, i.e. only one operation is carried out at a time. This is a convenient assumption for computer simulation, since virtually all current computers are serial devices. Also, there is little solid empirical evidence that humans can explore more than one line of problem development at a time. However, the notion of unconscious work progressing in parallel with the single conscious mainstream of thought has been invoked (e.g. Neisser, 1963b), especially in connection with creativity, and the possibility cannot be ruled out *a priori*. Recently, there has been increased interest in parallel processing schemes in both computing science (Hillis, 1985) and psychology. Within psychology, there has been particular interest in massively parallel *connectionist* models (Rumelhart *et al.*, 1986a). Connectionist approaches postulate information processing by vast networks of simple, densely interconnected units that mutually excite and inhibit each other. While such schemes have achieved clear successes in accounting for certain basic learning, perceptual and memory processes, their application to sequential thought is less evident (Norman, 1986). The connectionist approach will be discussed further in the final overview in Chapter 10.

The assumptions of (a) separate long-term and short-term working memories, and (b) of serial symbol processing, jointly serve to define a model that has been widely accepted within the information processing approach to thinking. Borrowing from Murdock's terminology for models of memory (1971), I will refer to the model, so defined, as the *modal model* of thinking. Although the modal model for thinking may well prove insufficient to cover all aspects of the topic, performance in a number of task areas has been successfully analysed within its confines and many examples will be found in the following chapters of research based on its assumptions.

4 Artificial Intelligence

Before going on to discuss applications of the information processing approach, it should be pointed out that simulation programs are by no means the only ones that tackle problems hitherto the preserve of humans. Within the area of computer science there is a thriving sub-discipline known as *artificial intelligence* (AI) that attempts to construct programs capable of such achievements as playing master level chess, interpreting pictures and understanding natural language, among other undoubtedly intelligent activities. However, unlike simulation programs, AI programs are not restricted to processes that humans might conceivably use. Many chess programs, for example, are greatly superior to humans in their ability to look ahead exhaustively for a number of moves and cannot be considered to be simulations.

However, AI research has been a very useful source of ideas about possible human processes and of terminology for describing problems and methods. For example, the General Problem Solver program (Newell and Simon, 1972) was a valuable source of ideas about human methods in problem solving (e.g. Egan and Greeno, 1974), and the 'production system' approach to programming in AI has been very influential in computer models of cognition, such as Anderson's (1983) ACT* model, discussed in Chapter 4.

5 *Cognitive science*

As has been noted in previous sections, both psychological analyses of human problem solving and AI syntheses of computer problem solving view problem solving as a form of information processing. Thus, both humans and suitably programmed computers are seen as flexibly manipulating symbols in order to solve problems. Viewing natural and artificial information processing as essentially similar is the perspective of the emerging discipline known as cognitive science (Gardner, 1985). Cognitive science takes as its topic *knowledge acquisition and use – in general –* whether by artificial or natural systems.

In the case of problem solving the focus of cognitive science is on real-life, complex, knowledge-rich problem areas, in which extended effort is required for solution. A typical cognitive science study will examine in detail the performance of a small number of subjects on a complex task and will often lead to a computer program model of the processes underlying performance. Thus, a combination of psychological and computational skills are brought to bear on understanding the task performance. (Also, since the task is usually complex, task expertise is an additional requirement among the experimenters.) Thus cognitive science is typically an interdisciplinary enterprise and is generally regarded as representing a promising fusion of inter-related subject areas (principally, psychology, computing, linguistics and philosophy). It has, however, been criticized on general methodological grounds by Skinner (1985) and on philosophical grounds by Searle (1984). Some of these criticisms will be considered more fully in the final chapter, in the context of the examples of cognitive science work discussed in the intervening chapters.

III. SUMMARY AND CONCLUDING COMMENTS

In this chapter thinking has been characterized as an internal symbolic activity. This activity may be tightly directed to specific goals, as in problem solving, or it may be free-floating, as in daydreaming. Thinking directed towards problem solving involves exploring a model of the task to determine a useful course of action without overt and possibly costly trial and error. Following Duncker, problems were defined as arising when an organism has a goal which it does not know how to reach.

Problems can vary in the degree to which they are well- or ill-defined. Most research has focussed on well-defined problems (drawn from puzzles, games, logic, maths) but it is hoped that results from these studies will be relevant to ill-defined problem solving to the extent that people tackle such problems by first converting them into well-defined variants.

A second useful distinction is between adversary and non-adversary problems. In non-adversary problems the solver has to manipulate inert materials (concrete or symbolic) to reach a goal, whereas in adversary problems there is an additional layer of complexity caused by having to counter a rational opponent whose goals are contrary to those of the solver. A third distinction was drawn between semantically rich problems in which the solver brings a large mass of relevant knowledge to bear and semantically impoverished problems in which little or no prior knowledge is available to aid in solving. After a long period of neglect, the solving of semantically rich problems has become an area of intense study over the last few years.

A variety of approaches have been taken to the topic of thinking in the history of psychology. The principal approaches have been those of classical introspectionism, early behaviourism, Gestalt, neo-behaviourism and information processing. Although the field has been dominated by the information processing approach since the early 1960s, the earlier approaches were reviewed above in order to give some historical perspective. To summarize, the introspectionists focussed on the analysis of consciousness into elementary sensations, while the early behaviourists stressed observable behaviour and the importance of learning. The Gestalt school emphasized organization in thought and perception and argued strongly for the role of insight and restructuring in problem solving. The neo-behaviourists attempted to explain the internal processes of thought in terms of covert chains of mediating responses and (response-produced) mediating stimuli. The resulting analyses could be stretched to deal with extended problem solving, as in Duncker's X-ray problem, but only in a rather cumbersome fashion.

The currently dominant information processing approach takes the computer as its key metaphor for the mind. In their cognitive aspects, this approach sees people as computer-like systems that code, store, retrieve and transform information. Within this approach, models for thinking in particular tasks have been proposed in greatly varying degrees of detail. An intermediate level of analysis in terms of broad steps and decisions has probably been the most prevalent and useful.

Most information processing models for various tasks accept certain limitations on cognitive capacities. More specifically, it is generally accepted that processing is serial at the problem-solving level and that while long-term memory is vast, working memory is very limited. These memory and processing limitations are key elements of what may be referred to as the "modal model" for thinking. According to this modal model, thinking involves serial symbol manipulations between long-term and working memory, in accord with rules or programs stored in the long-term memory. Throughout this text, the modal model assumptions will be considered against the data resulting from recent psychological research on thinking. The theoretical challenges to the modal model from connectionism and other parallel processing schemes will be discussed in the final chapter.

IV. FURTHER READING

Simon, H.A. (1981). Cognitive science: the newest science of the artificial. In D.A. Norman (Ed.), *Perspectives on cognitive science*, pp. 13–26. Norwood, N.J.: Ablex. This paper gives a very clear founder's view of cognitive science.

Gardner, H. (1985). *The mind's new science: A history of the cognitive revolution*. New York: Basic Books. Gardner offers a very readable account of the development of cognitive science from the concerns of psychology, philosophy, linguistics, anthropology, computing and neurology.

2
Solving puzzles

What mental processes are involved in solving, or attempting to solve problems? Since there are indefinitely many problems, varying greatly in content and form, the question, as it stands, is too broad and needs to be divided up into more specific questions to be manageable. This 'splitting up' has been reflected in research practice, and efforts have been directed at mental processes involved in tackling *particular* problems, or classes of problems. It is, of course, hoped that similar processing limits will emerge over a variety of task areas. In Chapter 1 distinctions were drawn between well- and ill-defined problems, between adversary and non-adversary problems and between semantically rich and semantically impoverished problems. These distinctions will help organize the discussion of research in this and following chapters.

Within the field of problem solving, certain methodological tendencies are quite marked and deserve some consideration at this point, before going on to deal with studies of particular topics. For instance, much research has focussed on well-defined problems in which the goal, starting state and permissible actions are all clearly specified. A major reason for using such problems is to increase the chances that all subjects will interpret the tasks concerned in the same way. Such unanimity would be useful in that it would simplify the theoretical task of explaining problem-solving behaviour if all subjects could be assumed to start with a similar model of the task which is to be worked on. Even if there is some variation in interpretation, the degree of variation is likely to be less for well-defined than for ill-defined tasks. A further tendency, until relatively recently, was for studies of non-adversary tasks to be limited to unfamiliar and rather artificial puzzles. The main reason for using artificial material was to equate degree of familiarity with the task over subjects. The effects of familiarity (or expertise) in the task area were initially studied in connection with adversary problems, such as chess, in which people vary widely in skill levels. An additional tendency has been to use small-scale tasks that are usually solvable within one hour or less. This tendency probably grew up for the very practical reason that subjects often cannot spare longer times to take part in experiments. Thus, studies of non-adversary problem solving have often focussed on puzzles that are well-defined, small scale, artificial and unfamiliar. As indicated already, there are some advantages in using such materials, but there are also drawbacks, particularly in that generalization to problems not fitting the typical description (well-defined, small scale, etc.) must be somewhat uncertain. However, even within the typical methodological constraints, problem content and structure vary widely. So, it is not obvious, in advance, whether similar processes and limitations will show up across the various different, but typical, laboratory tasks. The current chapter includes consideration of this issue and focusses on well-defined, non-adversary puzzles.

The contents of the remainder of this chapter will now be indicated. First, I will introduce some terminology and approaches (largely from outwith psychology), that have proved useful in describing well-defined problems and solving processes. In broad terms, on one approach (state-action representation), the possible manipulations of the problem material are seen as generating an often vast network of possible paths leading to numerous intermediate states, and the solver is regarded as searching the resulting mental 'maze' or 'tree' of possibilities for a path to the goal. A second approach (problem reduction) involves attempting to divide problems up into more manageable sub-problems. Again, this leads to a "tree" of possible divisions of the problem. How these notions have been used in the analysis of human problem solving will be discussed with reference to a range of laboratory tasks ranging from very well-defined examples (e.g. missionaries-and-cannibals puzzles) to less well-defined cases (e.g. cryptarithmetic). The issues of task interpretation processes, analogy and insight will then be addressed. Finally, the chapter closes with a brief summary and some concluding comments.

I. STATE-ACTION REPRESENTATIONS

A. Graphs and trees

Many well-defined problems can be represented as involving a search for a suitable series of operations that will transform the starting state of the problem into a state that meets the goal requirements. In general, the possible sequences of actions and intermediate states can often be represented by diagrams composed of points (or 'nodes'), which represent the actions that transform one state into another. Such structures of 'nodes and arcs' are known in mathematics as 'graphs' and can be used to represent many phenomena.

A special form of graph which is frequently useful is the *tree*. In a tree graph the connections are directional and there are no loops or returns to earlier nodes. The appearance of such graphs is reminiscent of an upside-down tree with the starting node at the top of the page and its descendants branching out down the page. The possible sequences of actions and inter-mediate states in well-defined problems can often be represented by this special form of graph and the resulting diagrams are known as *state-action trees* (Wickelgren, 1974). Take, for example, the 8-puzzle (Nilsson, 1971) as shown in Fig. 2.1. The numbers are on tiles in a 3 × 3 frame. One cell of the frame is always empty, so that an adjacent tile can be moved into the empty cell, thus also moving the empty cell. The possible sequences of moves in this 8-puzzle can be represented by a state-action tree (Fig. 2.2) in which states of the puzzle generated by making the possible moves are depicted.

Fig. 2.1 An example 8-puzzle. The tiles are to be moved so that the goal state is reached from the given starting configuration.

The first three levels of the tree are shown in Fig. 2.3 (assuming that no move is immediately 'undone'). There are over 100,000 states that can be reached from the start. One of these is the goal. You may find it instructive to seek the solution path for the puzzle shown in Fig. 2.3.

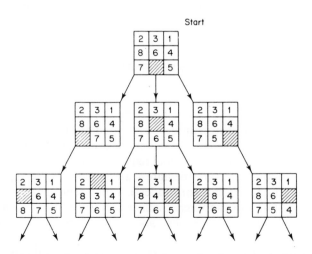

Fig. 2.2 First three levels of the state-action tree for the example 8-puzzle.

A major characteristic of state-action trees is the rapid way in which they grow. If there are m alternative actions per state, then there will be m^n possible sequences of n actions; in other words, with n actions one could reach any one of m^n states. So, for example, with four alternative actions (moves) available from each state, one could reach any of $1\,024$ (= 4^5) different states in just five steps. The difficulty is in finding a short path to a goal state with little search of the state-action tree.

In the fields of AI and operations research, ideas have been developed about searching state-action trees that are useful for discussing problem solving both by people and by machines and a sample of these notions will be outlined in the following sections.

B. Basic search methods

In principle, paths from starting states to goal states can often be found by systematic searches. The two main search schemes are known as *'depth first'* and *'breadth first'* searching. Depth first searching follows up just one state from each state examined until either the goal or a dead end is reached. (A 'dead end' would be a state which could not be developed further). On encountering a dead end, depth first search would 'back up' to the preceding state and follow up another hitherto unexplored branch. In terms of the 8-puzzle example a depth first search could develop as indicated in Fig. 2.3.

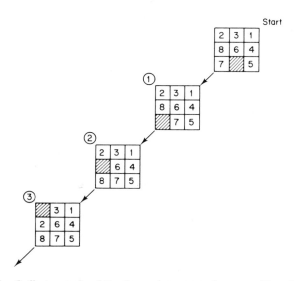

Fig. 2.3 A depth first search of the 8-puzzle state-action tree. The circled numbers indicate the order in which states are examined.

There are no dead ends in the 8-puzzle search tree and so depth first search would never back up, but would continue indefinitely or until the goal was reached. Order of examination of the states is indicated by the circled numbers in Fig. 2.3.

As depth first search proceeds, the memory load grows relatively slowly, by just one intermediate state per level of depth. Breadth first search is much more stressful in terms of memory load.

In breadth first search, all states at a given level are examined before using the moves from each state to check all the next level states. The resulting pattern of search is illustrated for the 8-puzzle example in Fig. 2.4. The circled numbers in the figure indicate the order in which states would be examined in a breadth first search.

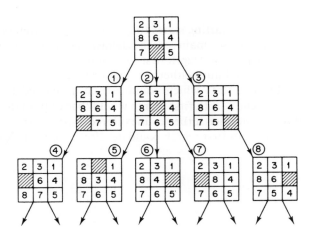

Fig. 2.4 A breadth first search of the 8-puzzle state-action tree. The circled numbers indicate the order in which states are examined.

Breadth first searches involve ever increasing memory loads as search progresses downwards through ever expanding trees of possibilities. In return for high memory loads, breadth first search is *algorithmic*, that is, it will always find a goal state and, furthermore, it will be a goal state that is a minimum number of moves from the start. (An algorithm is a procedure, possibly inefficient, that is guaranteed to solve all members of a given class of problems.) By contrast, depth first searches will not necessarily find the goal. They can be diverted down infinitely long by-ways and so fail to solve. Also, any solutions reached by depth first are not necessarily the best ones in terms of number of moves from start to goal.

A compromise form of search that mixes depth and breadth first methods is known as *'progressive deepening'*. This method consists of searching depth first up to some limit, then backing up and continuing search down all branches up to the depth limit until the entire tree has been searched to the depth limit or the goal has been located. If the goal has not been found within the first depth limit, the limit is increased by some fixed amount and search continues in the same way until the new depth limits are encountered or a goal state is located. This method is of additional interest because rather similar strategies have emerged from studies of human search processes in chess (Charness, 1981b; De Groot, 1965; Holding, 1985; Newell and Simon, 1972; Wagner and Scurrah, 1971; see Chapter 3 for further details).

C. Selective search

Search of a state-action tree can often be made more efficient by selecting promising states for further development on the basis of an evaluation of how close the states are to the goal.

In the classical 'hill climbing' method, the exact value of the goal state is not known and the solver tries to find the best state in the state-action tree. The task is rather like that of a real climber in thick fog, who wishes to reach the highest spot in the area. He or she can certainly find a peak by first testing out one pace in the four main directions and taking a pace in the direction that moves to the highest spot of the four tested, and then repeating this process until a spot is reached from which no move yields an improvement. This method is sure to find a peak, but there is no guarantee that it will be the highest peak, if there are foothills around. If the climber has an altimeter and knows the height of the highest peak then he or she could backtrack from any mistakenly climbed foothills and keep trying until the desired peak is reached.

Hill climbing can be useful but it does have its hazards. Apart from the 'foothill' problem just alluded to, there are also the 'plateau problem' and the 'ridge problem'. If a plateau is reached then no steps (actions) lead to any marked improvement and much wandering results. On a ridge, it might be that none of the four principal directions lead to improvement, although some other intermediate direction might (Winston, 1984, Ch. 4).

A better procedure than hill climbing is known as *'best first'*. In this method, forward motion is from the best state encountered so far, no matter where in the search tree. For such a procedure to work the solver must remember the evaluations that have been made of previously encountered states.

For any selective search method to work, a useful *'evaluation function'* must be developed which expresses the 'promise' of an intermediate state as a function of its characteristics, e.g. in attempting the 8-puzzle, a simple evaluation function would be to calculate the average distance of the pieces from their target positions. This should be better than nothing, though certainly sub-optimal and poorer than those functions that Doran and Michie (1966) developed for their Graph Traverser program that successfully tackles 8- and 15-puzzle tasks.

II. PROBLEM REDUCTION APPROACH

State-action approaches to problem solving involve direct attempts to mani-pulate the problem materials (mentally or in reality) in worthwhile directions. A more roundabout, but often more useful approach, is known as '*problem reduction*'. The basic idea is to convert a single complex problem into a number of (easily) solved sub-problems. 'Factoring' or dividing a problem into sub-problems, each of which can be solved separately, is generally a very useful procedure when it can be applied. Newell *et al.* (1962) give the example of safecracking. If 10 dials each with two possible positions have all to be set correctly before a safe will open then one try in 2^{10} (i.e. 1024) will be correct and on average you would need around 500 trials to find the correct combination (assuming sampling without replacement from the possi-bilities). If, however, each dial clicked when it was in its own correct position, one would need on average only 1.5 trials per dial, i.e. around 15 trials for the whole set. So when this problem is reduced from a single task to 10 small ones, the savings in terms of expected search effort are dramatic (a 97 per cent reduction in the number of trials required).

Of course, problems do not always yield to such a simple 'factoring' approach. In the 8-puzzle, for example, one would not get far by trying to set the 8 pieces separately because getting one piece correct may disrupt those that have been set previously. Also, a more complex problem – sub-problem structure may be required in which the sub-problems themselves need further reduction.

A rather general method for developing sub-problem structures is '*means–end*' analysis. In this, the solver compares the goal with the starting state and selects one of the ways in which they differ as a goal for the first sub-problem. The solver then selects from memory an action or 'operator' relevant to reducing this difference. If the first selected operator cannot be applied, because its preconditions are not met, then a new sub-problem is generated, viz. to reduce the difference between the current state and the operator's preconditions. This new sub-goal causes a relevant operator to be selected and so on. The 'means–end' process develops a tree of sub-problems and, as in state-action trees, some backing up will often be necessary.

Making travel plans provides a real-life example of means–end analysis. If the problem is to travel from London to New York, the difference between the starting state and the goal is a large distance. Large distances can be reduced by using aeroplanes (the first operator). But to use a plane one needs to have a ticket and to be at the airport. That is, the preconditions of the first operator have to be met. These preconditions define two sub-problems. The 'ticket' problem may be solved by using a travel agent, but to use a travel agent the would-be traveller must be in communication with one and, therefore, a new 'communication' sub-problem arises . . . and so on, until the solving of the subsidiary problems resolves the overall problem. Means–end analysis is especially useful when the number of alternative actions is very large – because it offers rules for selecting actions for further exploration. Only actions relevant to approaching closer to the goal are selected on this method.

The usefulness of the means–end approach was demonstrated by the successes of Newell and Simon's *General Problem Solver* (GPS) program. This program incorporated means–end analysis and achieved a fair measure of success with a range of problems including integral calculus, symbolic logic, missionary-and-cannibal puzzles and the Tower of Hanoi (Ernst and Newell, 1969). Comparison of the steps taken by the GPS program and the thinking aloud record of a human subject when both tackled a symbolic logic task, indicated a promising degree of match between the problem-solving processes of humans and GPS. Other evidence for means–end analysis in human problem solving may be found in Duncker's (1945) thinking aloud records from subjects attempting the X-ray problem (discussed in Chapter 1).

III. EXPERIMENTAL STUDIES

In this section I will review experimental studies of human puzzle solving in which there is no element of competition or conflict with another rational being. We will consider first of all tasks, such as 'missionaries-and-cannibals' and water jug problems, to which the state-action approach can be applied quite directly, then a task that lends itself to a problem reduction approach (the Tower of Hanoi), next an example of a task in which the ''space'' that the solver works in is less obvious (i.e. cryptarithmetic) and, finally, studies of how task representations are constructed from problem descriptions and the roles of analogy and insight in problem solving.

While considering the experimental studies discussed in this chapter, it might be useful to keep the following questions in mind.

(1) Under what conditions do humans adopt state-action as against problem reduction approaches? What factors of problem structure or prior experience are relevant?

(2) Both state-action and problem reduction methods require search. What factors shape human search patterns? What affects the depth and breadth of search? Can limits of working memory be related to the search strategies adopted in various tasks? What factors of problem structure or prior experience are relevant?

A. Move problems

The two main examples of problems that can easily be described in state-action terms and that have been studied extensively are the 'missionaries-and-cannibals' and 'water jars' tasks. These are also referred to as 'move' problems, in which movements of units or materials are required to transform the starting state into the goal state.

1 Missionaries-and-cannibals tasks

The first study of the 'missionaries-and-cannibals' problem that used a state-action approach seems to have been carried out by Thomas (1974). He used a variant of the task in which 'hobbits' replaced the missionaries and 'orcs' replaced the cannibals. The 'hobbits-and-orcs' problem requires that the solver produce a sequence of moves to transport three hobbits and three orcs across a river. The only way to cross the river is by using a boat, and the boat can carry one or at most two creatures. At least one creature must be in the boat for it to cross. The major constraint in the problem is to avoid having the hobbits ever outnumbered by orcs on the same side of the river, since, as is well known (Tolkien, 1966), the orcs will gang up and devour the hobbits at the slightest opportunity.

   This problem can readily be represented as a 'state-action' graph in which states of the problem are specified by (a) the numbers of hobbits and orcs on the starting (left) side and (b) the position of the boat (on the right or left bank). Actions consist of moving one or two creatures from where the boat is to the opposite bank. At each state a number of actions are conceivable – some are 'illegal', i.e. result in consumption of hobbits, some take the subject backwards to a state already visited and one or at most two, advance toward the solution state. The 'legal' search space is represented in Fig. 2.5 and the solution can be read from the diagram. Each state is specified by a three-digit code: (1) the number of hobbits on the starting side, (2) the number of orcs on the starting side, and (3) the location of the boat – '1' if on the starting side, 'O' if on the other side.

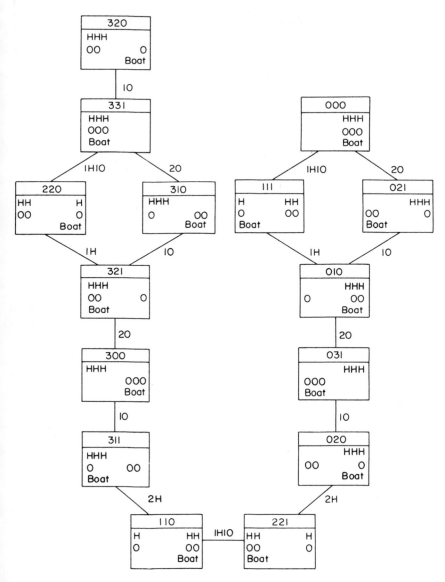

Fig. 2.5 State-action graph of hobbits–orcs problem. See text for further explanation. Reproduced with permission from Thomas, J.C. (1974). An analysis of behavior in the hobbits–orcs problem. *Cognitive Psychology* **6**, 257–269.

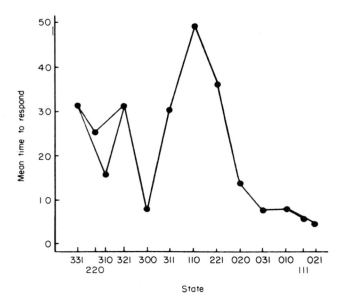

Fig. 2.6 Mean time to respond at each state. Reproduced with permission from Thomas, J.C. (1974). An analysis of behavior in the hobbits–orcs problem. *Cognitive Psychology* **6**, 257–269.

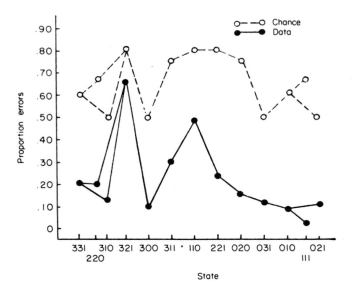

Fig. 2.7 Proportion of errors at each state. Reproduced with permission from Thomas, J.C. (1974). An analysis of behavior in the hobbits–orcs problem. *Cognitive Psychology* **6**, 257–269.

The transitions are labelled to represent corresponding actions, e.g. 1H1O means that one hobbit and one orc were transported on the move.

In Thomas's study subjects tackled the problem on a computer display which showed the current state of the problem. The computer changed the display in accord with the subject's decisions about moves if the moves were legal, otherwise the computer informed the subject of the error and invited another try.

The relative difficulties of decisions are indicated by the graphs of times to choose and error rates per state (Figs 2.6 and 2.7). The greatest difficulties were experienced in states 321 and 110.

Thomas notes that these states may be difficult for different reasons. It may be pointed out that state 321 does have three legal moves, of which one is helpful. There are also two illegal moves possible in this state. Furthermore, at state 321 there is the possibility of 'cycling' from 321–310–331–220–321. So there are more alternative responses at 321 than at other states. The difficulty at 110, however, may be due to the apparent reversal of progress that is required at that point. This conflicts with the general 'hill climbing' approach of moving to ever closer approximations to the goal. In going from 110 to 221 the solver actually appears to be getting further from the goal rather than closer. Wickelgren (1974, pp. 85–88) puts this problem into a general class of 'detour' problems that pose difficulties for 'hill climbing' methods.

As well as a (control) group of subjects who worked through the problem from the normal starting state, a part-whole group first solved the problem from the halfway state, 110 to 000. Then the part-whole group were given the whole problem from the normal starting state (331).

Table 2.1 Average moves in each half of the hobbits–orcs problem (Thomas, 1974)

	First half of task	Second half of task
Control group ($n = 71$)	13.0	15.5
Part-whole group ($n = 44$)	10.8	14.3 (First attempt = 12.0)

The part-whole group had prior experience of the second half and then tackled the whole problem. The control group worked through the whole problem in the normal way, without prior training.

The results (Table 2.1) indicate that the part group learned something from doing the second half that helped in tackling the first half. Interestingly, the control group do not appear to have benefited from the first half when they tackled the second half. Furthermore, when the part group repeat the second half while attempting the whole problem, they do *worse* than on the first time through. Apparently, a strong context effect occurred when subjects reached state 110 while solving the whole problem. This seems to support the idea, based on Wickelgren's analysis, that people tackling the whole problem are reluctant to reverse the apparent flow of moves in the direction of solution, but the 'detour' is less apparent without the background of progress through the earlier states.

Finally, from an analysis of the distributions of total times to solve, using a statistical technique devised by Restle and Davis (1962), Thomas inferred that some three or four major cognitive steps were involved in solving.

These steps would be decisions about whole blocks of moves, blocks that were then run off with increasing speed. At the end of each preplanned block of moves a longer pause would be evident while the next major decision was taken. The plot of latencies over states was consistent with about three such major decisions points (Fig. 2.6). However, subsequent studies, some of which will be described next, suggest that subjects tackle this problem by making only very 'local' move-by-move decisions, rather than higher-order strategic decisions.

Simon and Reed (1976) examined a more complex version of the hobbits-orcs or missionaries–cannibals task than that studied by Thomas. In the Simon and Reed study, subjects were required to solve a problem involving five missionaries and five cannibals (known as the 5MC task from now on). In this problem the boat can hold up to three people. The state-action graph for this problem is shown in Fig. 2.8. There are 27 legal states and, although there are only a few possible moves per state, subjects find the task quite difficult. For example, although it can be solved in 11 moves, one of Simon and Reed's naive groups averaged 30.6 legal moves to solution.

Simon and Reed put forward a model involving *strategy shift* during solving. According to their model, people start out with a 'balancing' strategy that leads them to try to have equal numbers of missionaries and cannibals on each side, but then they switch at some point to a 'means–end' strategy in which legal moves that maximize the number of people on the target side are preferred (as long as missionaries are not outnumbered). Additionally, the model assumed that subjects performed a local 'anti-looping' test to avoid reversing the move made on the immediately previous trial. This was suggested because at each step it is possible to go back to the preceding state. Some randomness was built into the model by an assumption that people would sometimes make random moves and would not always check for loops.

The model was tested against data from two experiments. In Experiment 1 a control group tackled the problem without any special hints, while an experimental 'sub-goal' group were told that on the way to solution, a state would be reached in which three cannibals were on the target side, on their own, and without the boat (state L in Fig. 2.8). In Experiment 2, subjects

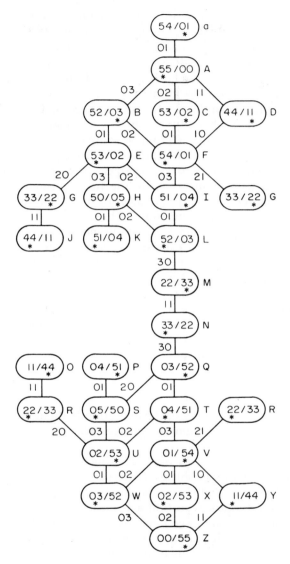

Fig. 2.8 State-action space for the five missionary–five cannibal (5MC) problem. The four-digit code for each state represents the number of missionaries and cannibals on the left and right banks. The position of the boat at each state is marked with a small star.

solved the same problem twice, thus producing data on training effects.

In each condition, estimates were made of the model's five parameters. These parameters were the probabilities of (1) shifting strategy, (2) checking for loops, (3) making a random move, (4) the rate of increase in the probability of loop checking and (5) the rate of decrease in the probability of moving at random. It was found that providing a sub-goal (Experiment 1) facilitated performance of the experimental subjects and this was reflected in an increase in the probability of shifting strategy from 'balance' to 'means–end' in the experimental group as compared with the control group.

Similarly, a second attempt at the task (Experiment 2) led to an improved performance which was reflected in a larger estimated strategy shift parameter on the second attempt than on the first. Furthermore, the model predicted quite closely the average number of times, within each condition, that subjects made each possible move. Thus, the data can be interpreted reasonably well within the framework of this model – a model that involves only local decisions with no extensive forward planning or look ahead beyond the immediate alternatives. It may be that this is the case for the 5MC problem, while the 3MC problem that Thomas (1974) studied, may permit more strategic planning; or it may be that Simon and Reed's analysis was not sensitive enough to uncover features of performance not consistent with their model. Thomas used latency and error data in his analysis, whereas Simon and Reed ignored error trials (which were approximately 20 per cent of all trials), and did not use latencies.

2 Water jugs tasks

A somewhat similar style of model exploration is found in Polson et al.'s studies of water jug and missionaries-and-cannibals tasks, to which we now turn.

Atwood and Polson (1976) have developed a model for solving the following sort of water jug problems. Given three jugs (A, B, C), where A can hold 8 units, B 5 units and C 3 units; A is initially full, and B and C are empty. The subject's task is to find a sequence of pourings which would divide the contents of the largest jug evenly between the largest and the middle size jug. In pouring, water is transferred until the jug the subject is pouring from is empty or the jug being poured into is full. Water cannot be added or flung away during the course of solving the problem. Such problems can be succinctly represented by state-action graphs, as in Fig. 2.9.

As can be seen from the state-action graph there is ample scope for 'looping'. Of course, the subject only sees the current state at any one time and has to envisage the successor states and evaluate them mentally. Under such conditions these problems are generally found to be difficult, e.g. the

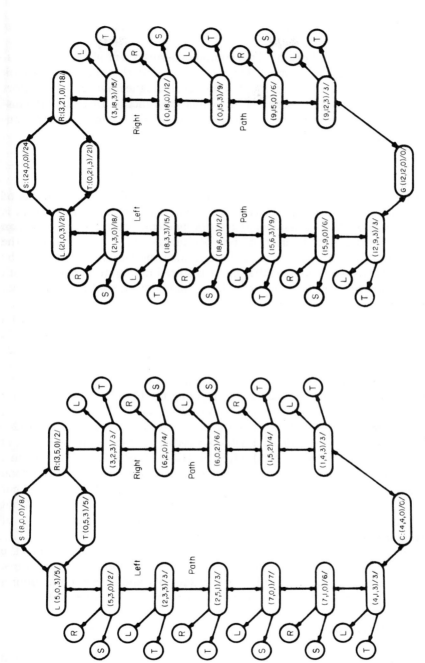

Fig. 2.9 State-action space for water jugs problems. Each state has a three-digit code showing the amount of water in each of the three jugs.

(8, 5, 3) problem can be solved in 7 moves yet it took a naive group 26 moves on average.

The Atwood and Polson model combines assumptions about state evaluation, look ahead and memory processes. It assumes that subjects only look ahead to a depth of one step and that they evaluate the immediate successors of the current state by means of an evaluation function that sums the discrepancies between the target (goal) quantities in jugs A and B and the quantities in each successor state considered.

The actual evaluation function is:

$$e_i = c_i(A) - G(A) + c_i(B) - G(B)$$

where $c_i(A)$ is the number of units in jug A in state i, $G(A)$ is the number of units in jug A in the goal state. The smaller e_i is, the more the evaluated state is like the goal state. It is assumed that working memory can hold information up to some small number, r, of possible moves. At the beginning of the problem all moves are *new* and the one with the best evaluation will be selected. Information about that move is stored in long-term memory with some *probability s*. In future decisions, 'old' moves tend to be avoided, unless there are no 'new' moves.

Experiment 1 involved two conditions. In condition 1, subjects solved a practice problem (6, 4, 1), then the (8, 5, 3), the (24, 21, 3) and the (8, 5, 3) task. The (24, 21, 3) problem could be solved by applying the 'means–end' evaluation heuristic already outlined whereas (8, 5, 3) requires a 'detour' (i.e. a move to an 'unacceptable' state with a much poorer evaluation than the current state). It was predicted that tackling the (24, 21, 3) problem first would strengthen reliance on the means–end strategy, and so make the (8, 5, 3) problem more difficult, and that the (8, 5, 3) would be harder than the (24, 21, 3) problem. In Experiment 2, all subjects did the practice problem (6, 4, 1) followed by one of the (8, 5, 3), (4, 9, 5), (12, 7, 4) or (16, 10, 3) problems.

As the model predicted, (8, 5, 3) was considerably more difficult than (24, 21, 3), but there was no order effect, in that doing (24, 21, 3) first did not hinder performance on (8, 5, 3). Analysis of both experiments indicated that the *number of acceptable looping moves* was the main determinant of problem difficulty.

The numbers of visits per problem state were quite well predicted by the model when the parameters were set such that information about three possible moves could be held in working memory and information about a visited state entered long-term memory with a probability of $P = 0.90$.

3 A general model?

Jeffries *et al.* (1977) described and tested an extension of Atwood and

Polson's water jug model that can handle missionaries-and-cannibals problems. The extended model assumes that moves are selected on the basis of state evaluation processes and memory processes. Possible moves are evaluated in terms of how close they come to the goal state. The following general evaluation function is proposed.

$$e_i = aM_i + bC_i + cP_i$$

where M is the number of missionaries, C is the number of cannibals and P is the number of MC pairs, on the target side in all cases.

By varying the parameters (*a, b* and *c*), pure means–end, balancing, cannibals- or missionaries-first strategies can be represented, as can mixed strategies. The proposed memory processes are the same as in the water jug model. Information about a small number of moves (*r*) currently being considered is stored in working memory. Information about actually visited states is stored in long-term memory with some probability (*s*).

It is assumed that move selection may involve up to three stages. First, all 'acceptable' moves are considered. These are moves that do not lead to 'worse' states than that already occupied.

Moves to new 'acceptable' states are more likely to be taken than moves to 'old' states (i.e. states recognized as having been already entered). If a move is not selected at this stage, the subject then seeks any moves leading to new states ('acceptable' or not). If all immediate successor states are 'old', the next stage begins and the subject simply selects the best one of the *r* states that he is considering. Finally, once a move is selected it may or may not be screened for *illegality*. If illegality is detected, the selected move is dropped and the process returns to the point where the illegal move was selected and continues from that point. So, this model permits illegal moves as well as legal ones.

A total of 25–35 subjects tackled four variants of the missionaries-and-cannibals problem. These variants had the same structure but were couched in terms of (1) hobbits and orcs, (2) elves and men I (elves disappear if outnumbered by men), (3) elves and men II (custom requires elves and men to be paired or for three elves to be together), and (4) silver and gold (a monk must convey six talismans through a forest. Gold talismans must never outnumber silver talismans on either side of the forest).

Quite good fits to the state-to-state transition frequencies were obtained using the following parameter values over all problems:

$$\alpha = 0.70, \beta = 0.15, s = 0.85, r = 2$$

where α is the probability of picking a new move at stage 1, β is the probability of picking an old move at stage 2, *s* is the probability of storing information about a visited state in long-term memory, and *r* is the number of successor states about which information is held in working memory.

The evaluation function was

$$e_i = 3M_i + C_i + 2P_i$$

(*Note*: A wide variety of functions would lead to similar results.)

The illegal move detection parameters varied across problems. However, the general pattern of results was very similar over task variants.

The model was supported by reasonable fits between its predictions and the data, including illegal move data over all conditions. It is an attractive model in that it relates missionaries-and-cannibals tasks to water jug tasks and so reduces the fragmentation so prevalent in the problem-solving area. More critically, the model has a rather large number of free parameters (9) and has only been fitted to the three missionaries-and-cannibals task. It would be interesting to see an extension to the five missionaries-and-cannibals task, in which it could be compared directly with Simon and Reed's 'strategy shift' model. Also, the model deals only with the move data and not with latencies (cf. Thomas, 1974). Again, it would be interesting to see extensions in that direction. Finally, the model does not seem to offer a ready explanation for the effects of hints and prior experience – effects which are dealt with by Simon and Reed's model.

A subsequent study (Atwood *et al.*, 1980) focussed on the question of the degree of planning used by subjects in the water jar task. The Jeffries *et al.* (1977) model proposes that people only look one move ahead. Subjects were given a number of water jug problems under different memory aiding conditions. For some subjects the immediately available successor states were presented on each trial, for others the successor states were shown and were also marked to indicate whether they had been visited before. This manipulation should help reduce looping moves. Control subjects worked under normal conditions of problem presentation. Analysis indicated that very good fits to move data could be obtained without assuming any look ahead beyond one level. These data then support the Jeffries *et al.* model. However, we must note that a large number of free parameters are involved and that the subjects were naive with respect to the task.

4 Puzzle solving with partial understanding

Polson and Jeffries (1982) report a further extension of their general model to more complex tasks in which subjects are likely to detect major sub-goals and organize their problem solving accordingly. In particular, Polson and Jeffries consider the 'hobbits, orcs and gold' task. As the name suggests, this is a hobbits and orcs task combined with the concurrent task of moving some bags of gold across the river, one at a time. Two main versions of this problem were explored, viz. a non-interaction and an interaction version. In the interaction version, if all three orcs and all the bags of gold are left alone on the same side of the river, the orcs will steal the gold. Three strategies were distinguished. First, there was a gold-first strategy in which some combination of travellers is used to move the gold across the river, before then moving the travellers. Secondly, there was a travellers-first strategy, in which the travellers sub-problem was solved first and then the gold sub-problem. Finally, there was a combined strategy in which subjects attempt to solve both sub-problems simultaneously. The combined strategy is the most efficient. The travellers-first approach was extremely rarely used and the combined strategy was a little more prevalent than the gold-first approach (which led to a need for detouring in the interaction versions of the problems).

Data obtained from variations of the problems, with differing numbers of bags of gold, were well fitted by assuming (a) that subjects did recognize two sub-goals and pursued these independently and (b) that there was a probability that subjects would realize that (in the interaction problems) a single bag of gold had to be left on the starting side until near the end of the task. Generally, deciding on the gold move is not a problem, and the model combines such decisions with decisions on the travellers' movements which are made in the same way as in the model already outlined for the simple 'hobbit and orc' problems. Polson and Jeffries thus indicate how the solving of complex puzzles with a clear and easily appreciated goal structure may be modelled by modest extensions of models developed for simpler tasks.

5 Tower of Hanoi problem

In the classic Tower of Hanoi (or Tower of Brahma) problem the subject is presented with three vertical pegs on one of which are n discs piled up in order of size, with the largest on the bottom. The task is to transfer the entire stack of discs from the starting peg to a target peg, moving only one disc at a time and never placing a larger disc on top of a smaller disc. The spare peg may be used as a temporary holding place. If there are n discs, then the minimum

Starting peg   Target peg

Fig. 2.10 A Tower of Hanoi problem. The stack of discs is to be moved from the starting peg to the target peg, moving only one disc at a time and never placing a larger disc on a smaller one.

number of moves required is $2^n - 1$. Thus the four-disc version in Fig. 2.10 would require a minimum of 15 moves.

According to legend (Raphael, 1976) some monks near Hanoi are working on a 64-disc puzzle, and when they complete it the world will end. However, even if they make no mistakes or wasted moves it will take them nearly a trillion years to finish, at one move per second!

Research with small versions of this puzzle suggests that subjects come to impose a goal–sub-goal (or problem–sub-problem) structure on the task (Egan and Greeno, 1974; Luger, 1976). For example, the four-disc task may be structured as follows:

(1) Solve the three-disc puzzle of moving the top three discs from peg 1 to peg 2, so that disc 4 can be moved to the target peg 3. (8 moves)
(2) Now solve the two-disc puzzle of moving the top two discs from peg 2 to peg 1 so that disc 3 can be moved to the target peg 3. (4 moves)
(3) Now solve the one-disc puzzle of moving the top disc on peg 1 to peg 2 so that disc 2 can be moved to peg 3. (2 moves)
(4) Finally, move disc 1 from peg 1 to peg 3. (1 move)

Following the above structure the problem is solved in the minimum of 15 moves – and the solution was guided by splitting up (reducing) the task into sub-problems. A possible 'problem reduction' tree for the four-disc task is shown in Fig. 2.11.

Egan and Greeno (1974) report a study in which some subjects had prior experience with three-disc problems before tackling five- or six-disc puzzles. Other subjects attempted the difficult tasks without prior experience. The error profiles for all groups indicated that they performed better as important goals were near accomplishment. Also, they tended to perform worse (i.e. make more moves off the best solution path) when they were at points in the task that were remote from satisfying important goals.

Further evidence that a goal–sub-goal structure is commonly induced by this problem comes from studies by Luger (1976). The state-action graph for Tower of Hanoi problems clearly shows sub-spaces corresponding to the sub-problems (see Fig. 2.12).

By tracing subjects' paths through such state-action graphs, Luger has found that subjects generally (1) follow goal-directed paths, in that each successive step tends to approach a goal or sub-goal, and (2) whenever a sub-goal state is reached the preferred path exits from the space of the just-completed sub-problem to enter a new sub-problem space. However, Luger's analysis is not conclusive regarding strategies, since as Simon (1975) has shown, a number of rather different strategies could produce minimum solution paths.

Simon considers three main alternative strategies. The first, 'goal recur-

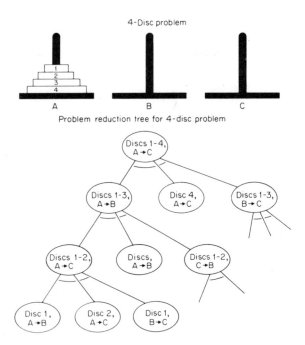

Fig. 2.11 Part of the problem reduction tree for the four-disc Tower of Hanoi problem. The overall task is successively reduced into sub-problems until sub-problems solvable in one move are reached.

sion', is essentially the one already outlined. As he points out, this strategy requires a list of goals and sub-goals to be kept in working memory and the list grows with the number of discs so that by the time 10 discs are tackled, the list would be completely unwieldy. For large numbers of discs at least, a different strategy is needed. The second strategy, the 'perceptual' strategy, is much less demanding on memory. The main steps are: (a) identifying the largest disc (label it k) not yet on the target peg; (b) identify the largest disc obstructing movement of k to the target peg; (c) if there is no obstructor, make the move; (d) if there is an obstructor, establish the goal of moving the obstructor to the other peg (neither the source nor the target of k), then recurse, for the obstructor, through steps (b) and (c). This strategy involves perceptual tests but a much more limited load on memory – only one goal need be in working memory at any one time, no matter how large the stack.

Finally, Simon describes a 'move pattern' strategy, that also involves very little memory load, that could be used with large versions of the Tower of Hanoi problem, but whose rationale is obscure. This strategy can be described as follows:

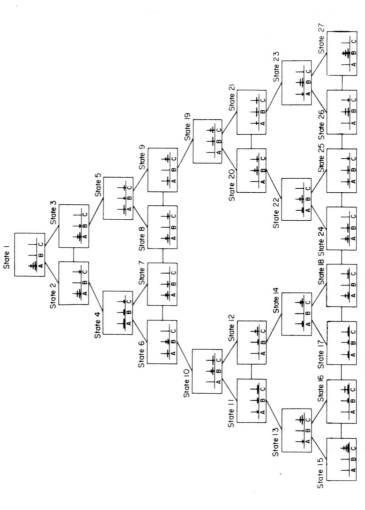

Fig. 2.12 Part of the state-action graph for a three-disc Tower of Hanoi problem. The upper nine states correspond to two-disc problems (the left-hand side to one such sub-problem and the right-hand side to another). On leaving the upper nine states, further two-disc sub-problem spaces are entered. Reproduced with permission from *Cognitive psychology: Learning and problem solving* (Part 3), Unit 28, D303. Milton Keynes: The Open University Press.

(1) On odd-numbered moves, move the smallest disc.
(2) On even-numbered moves, move the next-smallest disc that is exposed.
(3) If Peg S is the initial, source peg, T, the target peg and O the other peg, then if the total number of pegs is odd, the smallest disc is always moved from S to T to O to S and so on, while if the total number of pegs is even, the smallest disc is always moved in the opposite cycle: from S to O to T to S, and so on.

While people can follow such a strategy, if they are told about it, it seems unlikely that it would be discovered spontaneously. The strategy makes very small demands upon either pattern recognition or on working memory and can be applied to any number of discs.

Simon's analysis alerts us to the existence of alternative strategies (even within this very well-structured task) that can produce identical patterns of moves but involve very different demands on memory and perceptual processes. Clearly, further data on reactions to task variants (increasing number of discs, for instance), further response measures (e.g. latencies) and verbal protocols would be useful in determining which strategies actually tend to be followed under which conditions. Karat (1982) used move latencies as well as move patterns and task variants to test a model for naive performance in the Tower of Hanoi. The model derives from Polson and Jeffries's analyses of puzzle solving discussed in the previous section of this chapter. Karat assumed that subjects searched the problem space guided by two strategies. These are, first, to have as a sub-goal moving the largest disc to the goal peg and, secondly, to avoid returning to just-visited problem states. A model incorporating these assumptions about decision latencies yielded good fits to move and latency results from three-, four- and five-disc problems.

An important factor in performance is the degree of experience that the solver has with the task. Anzai and Simon (1979) allowed a single subject four attempts at a five-disc version of the Tower of Hanoi problem. The instructions urged the subject to seek a good solution procedure. Over the four attempts, distinct strategies evolved. The earliest was a form of forward search from the starting state, with a check against repetitions of previously obtained positions. Thus, a form of state-action representation seems to have been used initially. Subsequently, a strategy similar to Simon's (1975) 'perceptual' strategy was evolved and this in turn gave way to a 'pyramid' strategy in which the subject saw the task as one of moving sets and subsets of discs. This final strategy is essentially the same as Simon's (1975) 'goal recursion' strategy. These results are suggestive of an order of acquisition of alternative strategies with task experience. Anzai and Simon propose some plausible mechanisms for strategy improvement. For example, if a short sequence of moves leads to a desired sub-goal, then remember that sub-goal–sequence association and use it next time the same sub-goal is sought. However, since this experiment involved but a single subject, the results are suggestive only and do not allow confident generalization. The study does serve as a reminder that strategy change within subjects exists, and indicates how it might be examined further.

B. Cryptarithmetic

The missionaries-and-cannibals, the water jugs and the Tower of Hanoi tasks have clear, simple structures. In such tasks subjects were successfully represented as working with state-action or problem reduction representations that followed, quite directly, from the problem statements. In the case of *cryptarithmetic* tasks, the permissible actions and the problem states are relatively more open to differing definitions (and so such problems represent a step toward less well-defined types of problem).

Newell and Simon (1972) attempted a detailed analysis of behaviour on the following cryptarithmetic task. (The solution is on page 44. You may find it instructive to attempt the task at this point.)

$$\text{DONALD} + \text{GERALD} = \text{ROBERT}$$

Given $D = 5$ and that each letter stands for a different digit from 0 to 9, find the assignment of digits to letters that makes the sum correct.

This problem could, in principle, be tackled by trying out all possible mappings of nine digits to nine letters in a pure trial-and-error manner. However, there are 9! (= 362,880) such mappings and so a serial processor testing five mappings per minute would require about a month to solve. Since human subjects can solve in 15–20 min, we can rule out pure trial-and-error on their part.

Whatever human subjects do, Newell and Simon claim that they work within some definite *problem space* and that attempts to solve can be seen as searches through the problem space. By a 'problem space' is meant the set of possible states of knowledge that a solver can be in with respect to the problem. The problem space is essentially defined by the distinctions and relationships that the solver uses while working on the task. Clues about the problem space used by a particular subject can be gained by examining thinking aloud records or "protocols" obtained while the problem is worked through.

The beginning of a thinking aloud protocol from this task is shown in Fig. 2.13. The subject concerned here (S3) makes use of information he has inferred about in equalities, parity (i.e. oddness or evenness of numbers) and whether there are carries or not from column to column. He also makes assignments by calculation and, later on, by hypothesis. Hypothesized assignments are rejected if they lead to contradictions. Newell and Simon conclude that S3 is working within what they call the 'augmented problem space' for cryptarithmetic. This may be contrasted with a 'basic space' that deals only in assignments and contradictions and does not use information about parities and carries.

There are ten different letters and each of them has one numerical value.

Therefore, I can, looking at the 2D's – each D is 5; therefore, T is zero. So I think I'll start by writing that problem here. I'll write 5, 5 is zero.

Now, do I have any other T's? No, but I have another D. That means I have a 5 over the other side.

Now I have 2 A's and 2 L's that are each – somewhere – and this R – 3 R's. Two L's equal an R. Of course, I'm carrying a 1 which will mean that R has to be an odd number because the 2 L's – any two numbers added together has to be an even number and 1 will be an odd number. So R can be 1, 3, not 5, 7 or 9.

(The experimenter asks at this point, "What are you thinking now?")

Now G – since R is going to be an odd number and D is 5, G has to be an even number.

I'm looking at the left side of this problem here where it says D + G. Oh, plus possibly another number, if I have to carry 1 from the E + O. I think I'll forget about that for a minute.

Fig. 2.13 Beginning of thinking aloud record (protocol) from subject working on the DONALD + GERALD problem. Reproduced with permission from Newell, A. and Simon, H.A. (1972). *Human problem solving*, pp. 230–231. Englewood Cliffs, N.J.: Prentice-Hall.

Newell and Simon propose that a person's movement through the problem space can be represented by a *Problem Behaviour Graph* (PBG). The subject is envisaged as moving through a series of 'states of knowledge' (some of the knowledge may be of provisional assignments or hypotheses). Movement from state to state is mediated by operations that modify the current knowledge state into a different knowledge state. It is possible to return to previously visited knowledge states (though the subject may not realize that this has happened). Four broad operations were distinguished in S3's protocol.

(1) *Process column* (PC): extract whatever information can be inferred from a given column in view of other information available in the current knowledge state.
(2) *Assign value* (AV): assign a digit to a letter.
(3) *Generate* (GN): generate possible values for a given letter, in view of available information in the current knowledge state.
(4) *Test digit* (TD): check whether a particular digit could be assigned to a

given letter, in view of information available in the current knowledge state.

Part of the PBG for S3 is shown in Fig. 2.14. The PBG for the complete protocol involved 238 states. Note that there is no automatic procedure for producing a PBG for a given protocol, despite some preliminary proposals (Bhaskhar and Simon, 1977). Deriving PBGs from such protocols is largely a matter of judgement. The major pitfalls in PBG construction are that the graph will be (a) too superficial (will miss important details), (b) too disaggregated (over-detailed), or (c) be epiphenomenal (will be in terms of the wrong problem space).

At the various states in the PBG, alternative operations would often be possible and the question arises of the strategy by which operations are chosen. The order in which letters are solved provides a clue to strategy. Newell and Simon report that those subjects who solve tend to substitute numbers for letters in approximately the same sequence, i.e. first, $T = \emptyset$ then $E = 9$, $R = 7$, then $A = 4$ and $L = 8$, then $G = 1$, then $N = 6$, $B = 3$ and finally $O = 2$.

The structure of the task allows subjects to concentrate on the column whose entries are most constrained by virtue of previous information or by the nature of the column, e.g. $O + E = O$ is constrained and very informative. Processing the most constrained columns first in this way greatly cuts down the amount of trial and error and leads to the observed order of solving.

Newell and Simon propose a fine grain analysis that is intended to account for the state-to-state transitions in the PBG and to be a specific implementation of the general strategy of 'focussing on the most constrained

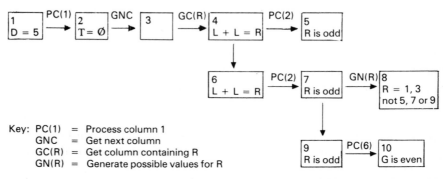

Fig. 2.14 Part of the Problem Behavior Graph (PBG) for S3. The boxes represent states of knowledge and the arrows represent operations that move the subject from state to state. Reproduced with permission from Newell, A. and Simon, H.A. (1972). *Human problem solving*, p. 174. Englewood Cliffs, N.J.: Prentice-Hall.

columns'. Their analysis is in terms of *'production rules'*. A production rule is of the form: 'If condition C applies, take action A'. A collection of such rules forms a production system. Computer programs can be written in the form of such systems and a number of researchers (e.g. Young, 1974; Baylor and Gascon, 1974; Anderson, 1983) have found production systems to offer a useful way of building models. Production rules are reminiscent of stimulus-response links, but are more flexible. The conditions may refer to memory contents, goals or observed states of the world; the actions may be overt or internal. Each action leads to a new state of affairs which in turn triggers a new rule and so on.

Newell and Simon were able to account for around 90 per cent of state-to-state transitions in the PBG with just 12 production rules. It should be noted, however, that the rules were not sufficient to form a complete running production system, and the analysis appears to have been carried out by hand rather than by computer.

Finally, Newell and Simon extended their analysis to other related problems and to new subjects. Broadly similar results were obtained, but some novel problem spaces were tried out by at least one of the subjects (S8). For instance, there was a 'typographical space' in which similarities in appearance between letters and digits were sought as a guide to the answer. There was also a 'cryptogram space' in which rules were sought to associate digits to letters on the basis of letter position in the alphabet. Solution is unlikely within these spaces. Evidently, the initial phase of developing an understanding of the task (i.e. a problem space) is crucial to later action. So, we now turn to some studies directed at task comprehension or problem space construction.

C. Understanding task instructions

In a typical laboratory study of puzzle solving the subject is presented with written or spoken instructions from which he must develop a representation of the task. Despite the evident importance of the task interpretation stage, relatively little work has been carried out on it.

Simon and Hayes have reported some studies that indicate how the topic can be tackled within the information processing framework. They propose that understanding instructions involves two sub-processes (Hayes and Simon, 1974), which they label the *language process* and the *construction process*. The language process deals with the basic interpretation of the sentences in the instructions and draws on the subject's knowledge of syntax and semantics. After every sentence or two, the construction process tries to build up an internal model of the task and the operators available to deal with the task. It is assumed that the internal model can be represented by list processing notions, i.e. the internal representation involves symbols, lists of symbols and operations that change symbols on lists or transfer symbols from list to list.

A computer model (called UNDERSTAND) incorporating these ideas was developed and compared (albeit loosely) with human protocol data obtained using the Tea Ceremony problem (Hayes and Simon, 1974). The Tea Ceremony (TC) problem is an isomorph of the Tower of Hanoi (TOH), i.e. it has the same abstract structure but differs in form. In the TC problem there are five tasks of varying 'nobility' and there are three participants. Initially, all tasks are the responsibility of one participant (host) and the goal is to transfer all the tasks to a specified other participant (the most senior guest). The major constraints are that only the least noble task that a person is performing can be transferred and it can only be transferred to someone who does not already have a less noble task. A TC task can be translated into a TOH task and vice versa by using the correspondences below.

Tea Ceremony	*Tower of Hanoi*
3 participants	3 pegs
5 tasks	5 discs
Nobility of tasks	Size of discs

The UNDERSTAND program incorporated sufficient methods to produce from the problem text a list processing representation of the task that could, in theory, serve as input to a GPS-like program for solving the problem. However, some differences emerged between the program and human protocol data. For instance, the program alternated between language and construction processes but never returned to earlier parts of the text to reanalyse them for possible misunderstandings. The human subjects, in contrast, went back, re-read and reinterpreted certain portions when they realized that their first interpretation of the task was leading to difficulties. Also, when the problem was attempted, subjects often went back to the instructions and modified earlier mistaken attempts at understanding. The program thus requires extra flexibility to make it a closer simulation.

Hayes and Simon's (1974) analysis suggests that list processing operations are used in the task representation that is finally constructed as a result of the understanding process. An interesting check on this idea was reported on in a study (Simon and Hayes, 1976) involving further isomorphs of the Tower of Hanoi. Subjects were presented with 'monster' problems, e.g. in which three monsters of different sizes each hold a different sized globe and have to transfer globes so that the monsters end up holding globes proportionate to their sizes. Variants of the problem required that the globes be shrunk or expanded to attain the desired consistency of monster-to-globe assignments. Despite differences in the surface descriptions, all problems could be represented by a common abstract structure. Simon and Hayes (1976) argued, however, that the UNDERSTAND program and human subjects would reach different representations for problems of *transferring* items as compared to problems of *changing* items. In list processing terms, if each monster is represented by a list of globe names (i.e. the globes he is holding) then a 'transfer' task requires symbols to be shifted from list to list while a 'change' problem involves replacing symbols on lists. In both cases the moves must be in accord with the task constraints. It happens that the "change" representation requires a more complex testing procedure to ensure that proposed moves are legal than does the "transfer" representation, and so it was predicted that change problems would take longer. Consistent with this analysis, Hayes and Simon (1977) found that the change tasks took almost twice as long (28.1 minutes) as the transfer tasks (16.9 minutes).

Human subjects' comments showed a tendency to modify the names or labels that they used with certain of the problems as they continued to work on them. This was the case where the monsters were referred to by variable names (e.g. the monster with the small name) that would not be directly appropriate later on (e.g. in a task that involved name swapping). Subjects would replace variable names by shorter permanent ones (e.g. 'the first monster', 'the leftmost monster'). These changes presumably helped to reduce demands on working memory.

To sum up, it appears that people are more flexible in constructing and revising problem representations than the UNDERSTAND program, but that like the program they interpret the instructions in terms of list structures and general purpose operators, presumably drawn from long-term memory.

D. Analogy in problem solving

A possible route to solving a problem is to try to solve it by analogy with some other problem for which a solution is known. A helpful analogous problem may be sought within the same domain as the current problem or in a quite different domain. Extremely difficult problems of theory development in science have sometimes been solved by means of such inter-domain analogies. Examples from the history of science include the model of the heart as a pump, the planetary model of the atom and the billiard ball model of gases. At a more modest level, Polya (1957) recommends seeking out analogous known problems when tackling new geometry problems, and Clement (1982) found that expert physicists spontaneously developed simpler analogue problems when searching for solutions to novel physics problems.

A series of studies by Gick and Holyoak (1980, 1983) have revealed some of the conditions under which analogies are detected and used in the case of solving ill-defined puzzles which draw on real-world non-technical knowledge. The main problem that Gick and Holyoak have used in their experiments is Duncker's (1945) radiation problem (which was introduced in Chapter 1). In this task, the subject has to find a way in which a doctor would destroy a tumour deep inside an imaginary patient's body, without surgically operating or damaging surrounding tissue. A source of radiation is provided. The solution involves a convergence of weak rays on the tumour. Gick and Holyoak (1980) examined the effects of making analogous problems and their solutions known to subjects faced with the radiation problem. In the first experiment, each subject read one of three military stories and then had the story available for reference while tackling the radiation problem. In one story a general captures a fortress by attacking it with groups of soldiers from a number of directions simultaneously (mines on all the approach roads prevent a direct concentrated attack). In the second story, one road to the fort is left unmined and a concentrated onslaught succeeds. In the third story, a tunnel is constructed to get inside the fort. Experimental subjects were told to try to use their story problem as a hint in solving the radiation problem. Control subjects did not receive the story problems or, of course, the hint. Subjects' solutions were classified as to whether they invoked convergence of rays, use of an already existing passage (e.g. the oesophagus) or use of an operation. The three story-problems led to the production of corresponding solutions for the radiation problem. (That is, the first story was associated with convergence solutions, the second with 'open passage' and the third with 'operation' solutions.) Thus, subjects could and did use analogous problems to solve the radiation task (at least when instructed to do so). Subsequent experiments, with hints to use the story analogies, also showed that the *closer* the analogy the better the 'transfer'; that is, memorized stories could also be used, with a hint, as well as currently present stories, and that timing of the story (before beginning the radiation task or after a period of work in the task) had no effect. Overall, *spontaneous* use of the analogies was low; however, the 'no hint' groups did somewhat better (roughly 30 per cent solving) than controls (roughly 10 per cent solving), who had had no analogous stories. Gick and Holyoak (1980) surmised that the level of encoding of the stories for memory may have been too specific to be very helpful in the problem-solving context, where more general similarities would be useful in mediating transfer.

This consideration led to the studies reported by Gick and Holyoak (1983) which concerned the development of problem schemata from analogous problems. A problem *schema* (plural: schemata) is a general solution concept which applies to a class of problems. Gick and Holyoak propose a schema for 'convergence' problems which can be summarized by the principle: "If you need a large force to accomplish some purpose but are prevented from applying such a force directly, many smaller forces applied simultaneously from different directions may work just as well." Gick and Holyoak report three individual experiments in which they attempted to bring about the induction of schemata by (a) presenting single analogous problems and having subjects summarize them, (b) by presenting an analogous problem plus a statement of the underlying principle of the solution, or (c) by using single analogue problems with or without diagrams. None of these manipulations using single analogue problems were effective in improving performance in subsequent target problems. A further three experiments involving two-story analogues proved more successful. Performance in the target radiation task was particularly good, even without a hint, when the story analogues were dissimilar to each other and subjects either extracted a principle from the stories or were told one. It seems then that extraction and use of a relevant ('convergence') problem schema was most facilitated by prior exposure to dissimilar analogues, for which the key principle was made explicit. Under such conditions roughly 60 per cent of subjects solved without any hint being given; this compares with a 10 per cent solution rate for control subjects receiving no story analogues.

More recent studies (Keane, 1988; Holyoak and Koh, in press) indicate that single analogues *can* be useful – especially when they are very closely analogous to the target problem. In one study, Keane used either a very close analogy involving a surgeon treating a brain tumour by radiation or the more remote analogy of the general taking a fort by a simultaneous attack on it with small groups of soldiers. Despite a week's delay between memorizing the analogue story problem and tackling the radiation problem subjects retrieved the literal analogue quite readily but only rarely the remote analogue. A similar result was obtained by Keane in a further study where analogous stories involving military applications of rays and lasers were retrieved readily on tests with the radiation problem, while the standard "general" analogue was rarely retrieved. Holyoak and Koh (in press) have examined the relative roles of structural and surface similarity between analogue and target problems. They used as their analogue task two versions of the 'lightbulb' problem. In one lightbulb problem, a broken filament has to be fused together without damaging the glass; converging low-intensity laser beams provide a solution. In the second version, the filament has fused and needs to be jarred apart, without breaking the glass bulb: converging ultra-sound waves are the solution. Each problem was also presented either as stated above or with the 'glass breaking' constraint removed and a statement that the instruments available were individually of insufficient power. In all four versions of the problem story a convergence solution was given. Relative to the target radiation problem, the degree of *structural* similarity was highest when the container-damage constraint applied and the degree of *surface* similarity was highest when the instrument was the laser (which is more like an X-ray than is ultra-sound). Prior study of the lightbulb problem produced greatest transfer (without hint) to the radiation problem when both structural and surface similarity were high. Both structural and surface similarity had comparable effects before a hint to use the story analogue. After a hint, structural similarity was more influential in reaching solution. Holyoak and Koh suggest that both structural and surface similarity play a role in the automatic retrieval of problem analogues, but that structural similarity is crucial if the analogue is to be applied successfully. It would be interesting to see replications of this result with a wider range of problems and varying levels of structural and surface similarities.

Overall, these studies suggest that successful spontaneous use of remote inter-domain analogies is hard to demonstrate even in favourable laboratory conditions. Indeed, as Perkins argues (1981, pp. 89–91), the use of novel remote analogies is probably also very rare outside the laboratory. However, equally it appears that close analogies are quite readily used in the laboratory and are probably often sought, or arise uninvited, through automatic retrieval processes outside the laboratory.

A good analogy often elicits a feeling of insight. In the next section I consider some recent research which focusses on the notion of insight in problem solving.

E. Insight revisited

1 The 9-dot task

The Gestalt approach to problem solving, which was outlined in Chapter 1, stresses the notion of 'insight' as against blind trial-and-error. One definition of 'insight' is to say that it is an understanding of how the solution is necessitated, given the nature of the problem. This 'accomplishment' definition is probably widely acceptable. A less widely acceptable view is of insight as a special process that leads to good solutions and which is distinguishable from ordinary processes of recognition, retrieval, goal-setting, and so on. The notion of insight as a special process is often associated with the Gestalt approach. However, the corpus of Gestalt writings is sufficiently large and vague that this association can be both supported and denied by suitably selective quotations (for example, see Ellen, 1982; Dominowski, 1981; Weisberg and Alba, 1981b). Setting aside the historical controversy, there has been a recent renewal of interest in the concept of insight.

As Sternberg (1987) puts it, one can distinguish the 'special process' approach from the alternative 'nothing special' approach to insight. Currently, the 'nothing special' approach is associated particularly with Weisberg (1986) and Perkins (1981). A particular test-bed for these opposing views has been the set of problems often referred to as 'insight' problems. Such problems have the characteristics that a misleading representation is usually formed initially, within which solution is impossible and so a less obvious representation must be found or developed, in which the solution is generally quickly found (and understood). Subjects are often described as 'fixated' on the initial inappropriate representation, and such 'fixation' may be classed as a major obstacle to 'insight' (e.g. Scheerer, 1963). Weisberg and Alba (1981a) sought to examine the role of one possible source of fixation in the 9-dot task, which is often classed as an 'insight' problem. In the 9-dot problem, the subject is faced with a 3 × 3 array of dots, arranged as follows:

● ● ●

● ● ●

● ● ●

The subject's task is to draw four straight lines through all the dots without lifting his or her pen from the paper. If you are not familiar with this problem you may find it instructive to try to solve it, before reading further. Naive subjects usually find the problem to be very difficult. Why? Until recently the generally accepted view was that subjects assumed that lines drawn had to remain in the square shape formed by the dots. Since the problem cannot be solved on that assumption, most subjects failed to solve it. If you have been trying to solve and have not succeeded, try again, in the light of this hint. (The solution is given in the Appendix at the end of this chapter.) However, Weisberg and Alba (1981a) found that that while none of their subjects solved without the hint, only 20 per cent solved when given the hint. Therefore, they concluded that a fixation on staying within the square array of dots was not the whole explanation for the difficulty of the 9-dot task. It may be noted that a similar result had also been reported by Burnham and Davis (1969). Weisberg and Alba carried out further studies using the 9-dot task and a simpler but analogous 4-dot problem They found that only quite specific hints, such as the experimenters' drawing in two lines of the solution, going outside the square, were helpful. Overall, Weisberg and Alba concluded that the concepts of 'insight' and 'fixation' were not helpful in discussing problem solving in the 9-dot task; instead, they emphasized the role of highly problem-specific knowledge.

Dominowski (1981) raised the point that although 'fixation' may not be a useful explanatory concept, there was still a need to explain persistence and change in problem representations and directions of attack on problems. Ellen (1982), also commenting on Weisberg and Alba, stressed the restructuring of problem representations as a source of insight (in the sense of a sudden understanding of how the goal is to be reached). Weisberg and Alba (1982) replied that such 'perceptual' accounts of problem solving had not been helpful despite a long history. In an empirical study, Lung and Dominowski (1985) found that practice with other dot-connecting problems which required extension of lines beyond the dot-pattern, facilitated subsequent performance in the 9-dot problem. They also found facilitations from strategy instructions that stressed the need to extend solution lines beyond the dots. These results counter Weisberg and Alba's (1981a, 1982) view that only very detailed specific solution information will facilitate in the 9-dot task. A more general solution schema can apparently be formed for a class of dot-connecting problems.

2 Other 'insight' tasks

The reader may well feel that the issue of 'insight' has become lost in the minutiae of the 9-dot and related tasks. Indeed, it appears that the 9-dot task is not an ideal test-bed for the study of insight. Sternberg (1987) reports findings from a broader range of tasks which, he argues, reflect different *forms of insight*. In particular, Sternberg distinguishes three types of insight. First, he proposes insights of *selective encoding*. These involve selecting relevant information from irrelevant information. Typically, real-life problems present a mass of information, only a fraction of which may be relevant to the solution. It may be that once the key pieces of information are selected, the solution is obvious. However, it might be the case that the problem requires a new way of combining or interrelating the key pieces of information. If so, Sternberg argues, an insight of *selective combination* is required. A third form of insight proposed by Sternberg is insight of *selective comparison*. This involves relating newly acquired information to information in long-term memory, for example, by analogy.

Sternberg and Davidson (1982) examined performance on insight problems, such as the following:

(1) If you have black socks and brown socks in your drawers mixed in the ratio of 4 to 5, how many socks will you have to take out to make sure of having a pair of socks of the same colour?

(2) Suppose you and I have the same amount of money. How much must I give you so that you have 10 dollars more than I?

(3) Water lilies double in area every 24 hours. At the beginning of the summer there is one water lily on a lake. It takes 60 days for the lake to become covered with water lilies. On what day is the lake half-covered?

The first problem is presumed to mainly require selective encoding, the second to require selective combination and the third to require both selective encoding and combination. (The answers are given in the Appendix at the end of this chapter.) On the basis of subjects' written protocols while they tackled 12 such problems, selective combination was the most common strategy. However, selective encoding was more successful and use of both selective encoding and combination was most successful. A further study of selective comparison, indicated that subjects would use related prior examples, especially if the fact of relevance was pointed out. This is very similar to the findings by Gick and Holyoak (1980) on the use of analogy in problem solving discussed in the previous section of this chapter.

Overall, Sternberg's analyses and results support the view that there are multiple routes to 'insight', in the sense of understanding a problem solution. However, the postulated processes of selection, combination and comparison are not in themselves 'special'. Rather, with certain types of problem these processes in various combinations can lead to a 'special' state of problem understanding or 'insight'.

IV. SUMMARY AND CONCLUDING COMMENTS

The following picture seems to emerge from the studies reviewed above of processes involved in solving small-scale, well-defined, non-adversary problems (puzzles). The person faced with a novel laboratory puzzle spends some time building up a symbolic model of the task materials, the available operations and the desired goal (Simon and Hayes, 1976). The person's model of the task determines the problem space within which he or she will work and explore consequences of possible actions. Two kinds of problem representation that could be used in modelling a problem were distinguished, viz. state-action and problem reduction. With a state-action representation, the solver explores the consequences of alternative actions forwards from the starting state while the problem reduction representation involves breaking the overall problem into more manageable sub- and sub-sub-problems. Models of the solving process that postulated state-action representations and heuristic searches of the resulting state-action space, gave reasonable fits to data from missionaries-and-cannibals and water jar problems (Polson and Jeffries, 1982). These models proposed only a small degree of mental look-ahead, involving two or three immediate successor states, thus reflecting working memory limitations as proposed by the "modal" model of thinking. Problem reduction approaches were implicated in cryptarithmetic (Newell and Simon, 1972) and Tower of Hanoi problems (Luger, 1976). In the case of the latter task, preliminary evidence (Anzai and Simon, 1979) suggests that degree of acquaintance with the problem may be influential in determining the adoption of one approach or the other. On initial exposure to a Tower of Hanoi task, Anzai and Simon's subject adopted a state-action representation but switched to a problem reduction representation when more experience of the task had been gained.

On the question of when and why in general people adopt state-action or problem reduction approaches, it does not seem possible to give definite answers at present, because few, if any, studies have been carried out with this question in mind. Intuitively, a problem reduction approach seems more likely in tasks that permit a large number of possible actions. After all, problem reduction offers a useful way of cutting down on the number of actions to be considered at each step. Within a given task area, it may well be that a problem reduction approach is more likely with subjects experienced in that area than with naive subjects. Some experience with the task area is probably required to enable subjects to learn which differences between starting states and goal states are relevant and in what order these differences are best dealt with. The results of Anzai and Simon are consistent with this view. Further studies are still needed, especially of problem formulation and interpretation as a function of task structures and subject experience, to help answer this question. This general topic of strategy and representational changes with increasing experience in a problem area will be taken up again in Chapter 4.

Analogies can play a role in suggesting useful formulations (Gick and Holyoak, 1980, 1983; Keane, 1988). However, remote, unprompted analogies appear to be rarely used (Perkins, 1981). Suitable formulations and reformulations may lead to a sudden understanding of how the solution is to be accomplished. It is controversial whether such states of insight should be regarded as 'special'. However, they appear to be achieved by means of non-special processes, such as selection, combination and comparison (Sternberg, 1987).

The tasks considered in this chapter have been unfamiliar puzzles and so solution processes could not draw on expertise stored in long-term memory. The unfamiliarity of the puzzles is useful from the point of view of controlling for level of prior experience among the subjects, but it also must be seen as a limitation on the problem-solving conditions being studied. It is quite possible that when working in more familiar domains, people can usefully structure a task more rapidly and look ahead further than they can with unfamiliar types of task. The next chapter concerns an area in which this possibility can be checked, viz. the area of board games, in which fresh problems can be readily generated within frameworks which vary greatly in familiarity between novices and expert players. Chapter 4 goes on to consider expertise in non-adversary problem solving.

V. FURTHER READING

Boden, M.A. (1987). *Artificial intelligence and natural man*, 2nd edition. Cambridge, Mass: MIT Press. Chapter 12 provides a very readable discussion of computer methods of problem solving.
Keane, M. (1988). *Analogical problem solving*. Chichester: Ellis Horwood/New York: John Wiley. This book clearly outlines the main theories of analogical problem solving and reports a number of original and informative experiments.

VI. APPENDIX: PROBLEM SOLVING

A. *9-Dot problem*:

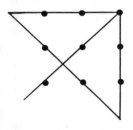

B. *'Insight' problems*:
(1) Three.
(2) 5 dollars.
(3) 59th day.

3

Expertise 1: Adversary problems

In tackling adversary problems solvers must consider not only their own possible sequences of actions but also those of an opponent. The games chess, GO, bridge and poker provide good examples of adversary problems and have been studied from psychological, AI and normative points of view. (The normative approach is concerned with how best to play the games concerned.) Psychologists have found it helpful to use some of the terminology and concepts that have been developed in the normative Theory of Games (e.g. Von Neumann and Morgenstern, 1944) and in studies of machine game playing. Accordingly, I will first outline the basic notions of 'game tree' and 'minimax' and then briefly describe AI developments in chess before going on to studies of human game playing.

I. GAME TREES AND THE MINIMAX PRINCIPLE

In board games the possible sequences of moves and counter-moves from a given position can be represented by state-action trees known as 'game trees'. If it is possible to look ahead from the start to all the possible endings of the game then the best starting move can be chosen by application of the 'minimax' principle. This principle was illustrated by Newell and Simon (1972) for the artificially simple two-move game shown in Fig. 3.1. The first player determines his or her best move by *looking ahead* to the possible endings and then works backwards, applying the *minimax* strategy to assess the worth of intermediate states. This strategy assumes that the opponent will do his or her worst to you and that you will always choose the best alternative available. Working backwards, minimaxing would label W3 as (–), W2 as (–) and W1 as (O), and recommend W1 as the best starting move, since it is bound to lead to a draw whereas the other moves must lead to losses.

The problem with a simple application of this approach to many games, including chess, is that in order to determine the value of a move the player must consider the opponent's possible replies and then his or her own replies to each of the opponent's replies to those, and so on. In theory, a 'brute

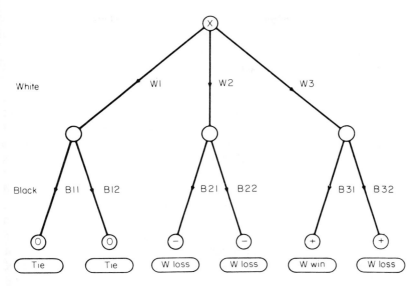

Fig. 3.1 Minimaxing in a game tree (see text for further explanation). Reproduced with permission from Newell, A. and Simon, H.A. (1972). *Human problem solving*, p. 669. Englewood Cliffs, N.J.: Prentice-Hall.

force' program could generate such information and select the best move on each trial. Unfortunately, the tree of possibilities is just too big – approximately 10^{120} possible sequences of moves in chess and only 10^{16} micro seconds per century to explore them all.

The cognitive effort required to explore all the possible chess games is just too much for any present or likely future machine, or for any human. Computers and humans can only investigate and keep track of the consequences of relatively few moves, and then only to a limited extent. So, in order for humans or computers to play reasonable chess, some strategies or heuristics must be available to restrict search to plausible moves and to evaluate lines of development in the absence of complete information about their remote consequences.

II. ARTIFICIAL INTELLIGENCE AND CHESS

Some of the early chess programs are worth a brief consideration. In 1956 and 1958 a computer called MANIAC at Los Alamos was programmed to play chess using the following methods. At each turn the machine looked ahead to a depth of four turns and considered *all* legal moves on each turn. In other words, given a starting position of the board, all of the average 30 moves were generated, then all the opponents replies, then all machine replies and finally all the opponent's replies to those replies. On average, $30^4 \simeq$ 800,000 continuations were generated. Each of the near 1 million possible states of the board after four moves was then *evaluated* by adding a measure of material advantage and piece mobility. A minimaxing procedure was then followed to work back up the tree of possibilities to find the best first move. This program is near the brute force end of a sophistication continuum and could not be regarded as a simulation. According to Newell and Simon (1972), the program played rather weak chess and was susceptible to serious blunders, even though close to 1 million possibilities were considered! Presumably, many of the possible moves were not really worth looking at and the evaluation of possibilities may have been too crude to select good moves.

Additional sophistication was introduced into a program devised by an IBM programmer named Bernstein in 1958. Instead of considering *all* legal moves at each step, Bernstein's program considered only seven, which cut the size of the tree at depth four, from near 1 million branches to around 2500 branches.

The program incorporated about eight so-called "plausible move generators", each of which was related to some feature of the game, such as King safety, development, defence, attack, etc. When the program had to select a move it generated seven alternatives by applying the generators in a priority order. For each of those seven alternative moves, seven opponent moves were generated and so on to a depth of four moves. So, this program searched the tree of possibilities very selectively. The end positions, four moves ahead, were evaluated by numerical measures of material strength, defence, area controlled and mobility of pieces. The program then minimaxed back up the tree to select its "best" move. The program's play is reported to have been rather uneven – sometimes it played well for a series of moves, and then displayed glaring blind spots. Although not a great deal of evidence is available about the program's performance, it appears to have been an improvement over the less selective MANIAC program in method and in end results. Further details on early chess programs can be found in Newell and Simon (1972) and Bell (1978).

The 1977 world champion computer chess program (CHESS 4.6) exploited the speed and storage space of modern machines and examined an average of 400,000 successor positions per move. It looked ahead about four or five moves and could beat 99.5 per cent of rated human players, although it was relatively weak in the end-game. CHESS 4.6 is clearly not human-like in its methods (Levy, 1978).

Although a number of advances have been made in computer chess playing since the late 1950s, almost all the programs seem to possess the same kind of structure. They all search ahead through a tree of possibilities with some heuristic restrictions on the search, evaluate positions at the end of the search, and minimax. (This general structure was anticipated by Shannon, one of the founders of information theory, in a 1950 paper.) Essentially all of the programs choose moves in given chess positions, rather than play a chess game with an overall plan, although the end-product may look quite planned.

The effort to develop chess playing programs helps underline the difficulties faced by any system that deals effectively with complex adversary problems. How do humans tackle such difficulties? This question is addressed in the following sections.

III. EXPERIMENTAL STUDIES OF HUMAN ADVERSARY PROBLEM SOLVING

A. Human chess play

1 Search in chess: early studies

Perhaps the most direct way to try to find out about thought processes during chess play is to present subjects with a chess problem and ask them to think aloud as they decide which move should be made next by one of the players (usually white). This method was followed by De Groot (1965), Wagner and Scurrah (1971), Newell and Simon (1972, Ch. 12) and Charness (1981b).

De Groot (1965) was particularly interested in possible differences between players of differing degrees of expertise. Five Grand Masters and five expert players were given the same position and thought aloud while choosing a move. The search trees that they developed could be abstracted from their protocols and De Groot reported the summary statistics shown in Table 3.1.

Table 3.1 Average protocol statistics for De Groot's position A

Variable	Grand Masters ($n = 5$)	Experts ($n = 5$)
Time to choose move	9.6 min	12.9 min
No. of different first moves considered	4.2	3.4
Max. depth of search (moves)	6.8	6.6
Total no. of moves considered	35.0	30.8
Rated value of move selected (max. = 9)	8.2	5.2

From De Groot (1965), *Thought and choice in chess*, Table 12, p. 319. Reprinted by permission of Mouton Publishers, The Hague.

A number of points emerge from these data. First, there was little or no difference in the quantitative aspects of the search patterns of the Grand Masters and the experts. The only major difference was in the quality of the move finally chosen. (Move quality was rated by independent experts.) Both groups looked ahead to similar maximum depths (about 6–7 moves), considered a similar number of possible first moves (about 4) and a similar total number of first moves and subsequent replies and counter-replies (30–55). Although, as Hearst (1977) suggested, the Grand Masters might be able to search deeper and broader if they were sufficiently motivated (e.g. in competition), it is still noteworthy that they consistently reached a better conclusion without any more search than the weaker players. Also, of course, the amount of sheer search is very small compared to that of the best computer chess programs. [According to Levy (1978), the program CHESS 4.6 sometimes examined around 3 *million* possible positions that could be reached from the current position before choosing a move, while De Groot's players were averaging around 35 possible positions.]

As well as being more selective in search than most chess programs, the way in which human chess searches developed was also different from the way program searches usually develop. De Groot's players and those of Wagner and Scurrah (1971) followed a *progressive deepening* method in which the same small number of alternative first moves were returned to repeatedly and generally followed up in greater depth on each occasion that they were re-examined. Re-examinations to greater depth were quite often immediate, but delayed re-examinations were also fairly frequent. Progressive deepening offers a way of gradually building up in long-term memory a representation of a long sequence of moves which would overload working memory. Also, the method permits repeated checks of apparently promising lines, in case some danger has been overlooked.

Finally, we note that human players do not search to a fixed depth but to a 'quiet' position where no immediate exchanges are possible. Such positions appear then to be evaluated on the basis of some salient feature or 'general impression' (e.g. 'awkward for black') rather than in terms of some explicit combinatorial weighting of many features (which is how the programs tend to make evaluations).

How is it that expert human chess players can be so selective to such good effect when they search for a next move? According to a much investigated hypothesis, the answer may lie in the extensive repertoire of chess patterns and schemata built up by experts over many years of study of the game. These patterns help the expert players structure their perceptions of the board appropriately and could be attached to recommendations for possible actions, in a production system organization. Evidence suggesting this possible explanation was obtained from a task that De Groot found was much easier for master players than for amateurs. This is the chess memory task described in the next section.

2 Chess memory and perception

De Groot (1965) put chess positions – taken from actual games – in front of subjects for 5 seconds; then he removed the positions and asked subjects to reconstruct them. Chess masters could reconstruct the positions without error (91 per cent correct), whereas poor players made many errors (41 per cent correct). (There were 20/24 pieces on the board in the positions concerned.)

A clue to the chess masters' performance is given by another of De Groot's findings. When good and poor players were shown boards with the 20 or so pieces *arranged at random*, both groups did equally poorly. This corroborates some early Russian results that showed chess masters not to have superior visual memory *in general*. Chase and Simon (1973a,b) argued that the chess memory data are consistent with the view that perceivers of the chess board store about seven familiar units or 'chunks' (Miller, 1956) in short-term memory during the inspection period irrespective of their skill level. However, the chess masters' seven chunks of information are much richer than the novices', i.e. they are larger units. Similarly, if you have learned to read in a given language, you could reproduce about seven words after brief exposure to a set of random words, whereas a non-reader of the language might only manage to reproduce about seven letters (especially if the words were difficult for the non-reader of the language to pronounce).

Chase and Simon (1973a,b) sought to demonstrate quite directly the proposed superiority of master player's chunks compared to those of weaker players. In their study, three players varying in skill were given chess perception and memory tasks. The perception task required the subjects to reconstruct on one board a chess position which remained in view on another board. The main variables of interest were the numbers of pieces placed following each glance at the stimulus board, the times between piece placements and the nature of the relationships between the pieces placed between one glance and the next. For all players the average number of pieces placed after a glance was similar (between two or three). However, the master's glances were significantly shorter, indicating more rapid encoding. The chess recall tasks were similar to those of De Groot and involved 5 seconds presentation followed by board reconstruction. Times between placements of pieces were recorded and intervals of 2 seconds or more were taken to correspond to boundaries between chunks in recall. On this basis, the number of pieces per chunk varied systematically (if not dramatically) with skill level from 2.5 to 1.9 pieces per chunk from strongest to weakest player. Pieces within a single chunk tended to have relations of defence and attack, be close together and be of common colour and type. Thus, Chase and Simon's studies indicated that, compared to weaker players, the stronger player encodes chess information more rapidly when perceiving the board and encodes a given position in larger chunks when recall is required.

Research on chess perception and memory is relevant to chess playing in that players seek to structure board positions in terms of familiar patterns before trying to choose a move. De Groot and others have found that when a chess position is given and the player must select a move, the first 15–30 seconds are occupied with gathering information about the situation in order to build up an internal representation of the position. Players do not begin to explore possible moves until an initial perceptual preparatory phase is complete. Indeed, it is sometimes suggested that the initial perception or structuring of a problem is the most important stage in problem solving in general. The early chess simulation programs did not take account of this perceptual phase (nor do most current AI programs). However, Simon and Barenfeld (1969) have reported a program labelled PERCEIVER which can simulate eye movements in the first 5 seconds of examining a chess board for the next move.

PERCEIVER begins with a central fixation point and follows lines of 'attack' or 'defence' as they are noticed and stores relationships of attack/defence between pairs of pieces. In this way it builds up a representation of the board position. Very little data on eye movements in chess are available, but PERCEIVER'S successive fixations on a particular board have been compared with Russian eye movement data for a single expert subject. Both program and subject tended to focus on the same squares, and the overall patterns look similar. Further data would be useful to refine the program – but Simon and Barenfeld were mainly concerned to demonstrate the *possibility* of simulating the initial perceptual phase and succeeded in that aim.

To sum up on the evidence so far, the expert chess player apparently detects and stores about as many 'chunks' as a poor player but the better player's 'chunks' or units are larger. Thus a good player 'structures' a given situation differently from a poor player and, in a sense, 'sees' the same problem quite differently from a poor player. The advanced coding scheme of the expert is, of course, bought with many years study. The extended study required is consistent with Simon's suggestion that a slow serial system with limited short-term memory, equipped with a discrimination learning program, could build up a sufficiently complex discrimination net to recognize many thousands of chess patterns over a lifetime's play.

3 The Memory-aided Pattern Perceiver (MAPP) model

Simon and Gilmartin (1973) converted the general notions sketched by Simon and Barenfeld (1969) into a working computer model for the chess memory task. This model, known as the Memory-aided Pattern Perceiver (MAPP), assumed that a position is encoded as a set of chunks (pattern labels) that occupy a limited capacity short-term memory. The pattern labels are then decoded during the position reconstruction phase. The chunks or pattern labels are produced by a pattern recognizer that seeks to match board configurations to known patterns permanently stored in a long-term memory. The pattern recognizing component consists of a discrimination net that is organized around salient pieces. It is assumed that the skilled player has a large discrimination net that incorporates a great many different patterns while the weaker player has fewer patterns available with which to describe any given position. The program can thus simulate different levels of expertise by varying the number of patterns in its long-term store.

Two versions of MAPP were explored. One had available 894 patterns and the other 1144 patterns. Given the same board positions, the more 'knowledgeable' version was able to encode the positions more efficiently into its short-term memory and thus scored better on position reconstruction than the less knowledgeable version. The 'knowledgeable' version's performance seems to be intermediate between that of a master player and a Class A (good amateur) player according to comparisons between the program and human data on positions used by Chase and Simon (1973a) (see Table 3.2).

Table 3.2 Percentage of pieces placed correctly by MAPP (with 1144 patterns in long-term memory) and Chase and Simon's (1973) Ss after 10 seconds exposure.

Position	Master (%)	MAPP (%)	Good amateur (%)
Set 1	62	43	34
Set 2	81	54	49

From Simon and Gilmartin (1973). A simulation of memory for chess positions. *Cognitive Psychology* **5**, 29–46. Reprinted by permission.

Simon and Gilmartin estimate that a MAPP-like system could replicate master level performance on the chess memory task with somewhere between 10,000 and 100,000 patterns in long-term memory. Assuming the model has some validity, similar estimates would apply to the store of patterns available to the human master. Acquisition of this order of patterns is certainly possible over many years study, since a well-educated person's vocabulary, for instance, has been estimated at around 75,000 words (Oldfield, 1966). Furthermore, the estimated number of patterns required may be reduced if, as Holding (1985, p. 109) points out, it is assumed that the patterns are not simply arrangements of particular pieces on particular squares. If the chunks remain recognizable when shifted a few squares, or if they are changed from black to white, then the estimated number of patterns needed for master level performance can be reduced to the more manageable levels of 500–5000 patterns.

Some of MAPP's assumptions have been tested independently by Frey and Adesman (1976) and Charness (1976). Frey and Adesman confirmed the importance of chunking by showing that recall of a position, the development of which had been shown from the start in a sequence of 2-second 'snapshots', was better than recall of the same position shown without its development. Presumably the chess patterns were more evident when their build-ups were known. The effect was present for three levels of players and tended to be stronger for the more expert players. Also, memory performance was better for positions that had been built up in a meaningful order than for positions that had been built up in a random order. Again, skill level was an important factor in performance in both order conditions. However, when Frey and Adesman examined the assumption that the chess chunks are stored in a limited capacity short-term memory the results were contrary to expectations based on MAPP. Subjects were presented with chess positions for 8 seconds and then required to count backwards from a three-digit number for either 3 or 30 seconds before attempting to reconstruct the position. The counting backward procedure is usually assumed to 'clear' short-term memory by preventing rehearsal and/or displacing the contents of short-term memory (Brown, 1958; Peterson and Peterson, 1959). This manipulation had only a very slight effect. Correct recall after 3-seconds interpolated activity was 13.1 pieces and after 30 seconds was 11.6 pieces. These data cast doubts on the assumption that chunks are held in short-term memory.

Further strong evidence against the 'short-term memory assumption' was reported by Charness (1976). He carried out a number of studies using 5-second presentation and Brown-Peterson interference paradigms. The 30-second interpolated tasks varied in complexity and modality (shadowing digits, summing digits, copying symbols, rotating and then copying symbols, studying other chess problems, naming pieces on a chess board). Recall of chess positions was only reduced by about 6–8 per cent by the most effective of these manipulations. (Control conditions indicated that recall of trigrams was affected by some of the interpolated tasks.) As usual, the skilled players performed better across all the memory task conditions than the weak players. One interesting effect was a marked increase in time to place the first piece as a function of interpolated processing. It appears that the interpolated tasks did have some effect on *ease* of retrieval but not such as to reduce *accuracy* of retrieval. The degree to which memory for briefly presented chess positions resists interference, strongly suggests that the information is stored in long-term memory rather than short-term memory. Charness and Frey and Adesman suggest a 'depth of processing' interpretation whereby the skilled player can encode to a deeper level, more rapidly than the less skilled player. However, even the least skilled groups used in the experiments discussed here appear to have encoded sufficiently deeply to be little affected by inter- polated processing tasks of the type found very effective by Brown and the Petersons in recall of verbal materials.

4 Age and skill in chess

The studies of chess perception, memory and play discussed so far, have focussed on individual differences in skill and have proposed that strong and weak players differ in the efficiency of their chess encoding schemes. Charness (1981a,b) investigated possible player-age effects additional to skill effects. Ageing is generally thought to affect memory operations, particularly those of retrieval, and so Charness hypothesized that players of equivalent skill, but widely differing ages, might differ in the underlying processes that yielded similar molar results (i.e. similar skill ratings).

Charness (1981a) assembled a sample of 34 chess players who varied independently in age (16–64 years) and skill level (skill ratings ranged from 1283 to 2004). The players were presented with four positions in which they had to choose a move while thinking aloud. Next, they were asked to rapidly evaluate end-game positions as being wins, draws or losses for white. After this task, the players were asked unexpectedly to recall the four initial positions by reconstructing them. Finally, a recognition task was admini- stered in which the subjects attempted to identify the first four problem conditions among a set of 26. Only skill level was predictive of performance in the move choosing task and in the end-game evaluation task. Skill level was positively, while age was negatively, related to chess recall scores. Measures of chunk size in recall were obtained using a procedure similar to that of Chase and Simon (1973a,b) described above. This indicated that chunk size was positively related to skill and negatively related to age. That is to say, the older subjects made use of more but smaller chunks in recall than did younger subjects of similar skill levels. These results then suggest that differences in encoding efficiency may not be sufficient to explain differences in skill levels. It should be noted, however, that Charness's (1981a) memory task involved delayed testing while the usual chess memory study has involved immediate memory. A follow-up study (Charness, 1981c), however, confirmed the result by showing age effects on immediate recall of chess positions, indepen- dent of skill levels.

Charness (1981b) followed up the question of possible differences in the processes underlying move selection between older and younger players by analysing thinking aloud records produced in his 1981a study. Analysis of these records indicated that the more skilled players searched more extensively and deeply than the less skilled. This result departs from De Groot's (1965) finding, based on fewer subjects (see Table 3.1), that skill level was independent of search depth or breadth. The discrepancy is probably due to the wider range of skills sampled by Charness. The average maximum depth reported by Charness (5.7) is of a similar order of magnitude to that reported by De Groot (6.7). Also, Charness found that the older players searched less extensively, though as deeply as younger players and did not differ in quality of move finally chosen.

So, given similar skill levels the older player searches less extensively than the younger player, yet reaches conclusions of similar value. Perhaps older players can evaluate possible positions more accurately and dispense with the prolonged checking and verifying more typical of the younger players. More sensitive 'evaluation functions' could compensate for the apparently poorer encoding of chess positions by older players indicated both by Charness's delayed memory study (1981a) and by his further results showing age effects on *immediate* recall of chess positions (Charness, 1981c).

5 Counter-evidence to the pattern recognition theory of chess skill

The results of Charness described in the previous section may have raised some doubts in the reader's mind about the analysis of chess skill in terms of pattern storage and recognition. In its strongest form, the pattern-recognition theory proposed by Chase and Simon, states that chess skill is explained by superior memory storage and recognition of familiar patterns. Holding (1985) points out that the reverse is in many ways more plausible, i.e. that superior storage and recognition of chess patterns is explained by greater skill. Charness's results show that the same skill level can be achieved even when chess memory performance varies. At the least, this implies that chess memory cannot be the sole determinant of chess skill.

Holding and Reynolds (1982) tested the further possibility that skill differences could be shown even when no memory differences were present. They did this by having high- and low-rated players attempt (a) to recall random positions after 8 seconds exposure and (b) to decide on the best move when they were shown the correctly reconstructed random positions. As usual, there was no skill effect on memory for the random positions. However, there was a marked linear increase in the quality of the moves chosen by the players as their skill ratings increased. Such a trend cannot be explained by the pattern recognition theory of chess skill.

These results have thus led to a re-evaluation of the pattern recognition theory and have made other difficulties with the theory appear more salient. For instance, the sizes of the chunks reported by Chase and Simon (1973a,b) are rather small (2–4 pieces) to represent important chess patterns and the exact mechanisms for linking pattern recognition to choice of moves is unclear. Indeed, Holding (1985) lists some 40 objections to the pattern recognition theory of chess skill. Rather than chess skill being determined by chess memory it seems that chess memory is an incidental side-effect of chess skill. Consistent with this view, Pfau and Murphy (in press) found that ratings of chess skill in 60 players were better predicted by a tactical skill test, a positional judgement test and a 75-item chess knowledge test ($r = 0.70$ with the criterion) than by memory scores following 5-second exposures of chess positions ($r = 0.44$ with criterion). General chess *knowledge*, rather than chess memory for specific patterns, appears to be critical to chess skill.

6 Re-examination of human search in chess

The results of De Groot (1965) which showed few differences between highly skilled and less skilled players in their search patterns helped motivate the concentration of research on the pattern-recognition hypothesis. In view of the difficulties with that hypothesis, research attention has begun to switch back to human search in chess; this is particularly evident in the work of Holding (1985) and Charness (1981b).

From analyses of thinking aloud records obtained from 34 players in a move choosing task, Charness found steady increases in the depth, breadth and speed of search as skill increased from ratings of 1283 to 2004; similar findings were also reported by Holding and Reynolds (1982). Thus, it appears that De Groot's early results were somewhat misleading and reflect the small sample sizes and the relatively small range of skill levels used in his study.

Accepting then that forward mental search increases in scope and speed with increasing skill, are any other changes in search patterns detectable with changes in skill? One important aspect of search is *evaluation*. If poor evaluations are made at the limits of search, then the choices made at the top level of the search tree are likely to be in error. Indeed, it has been shown in computer studies that when evaluation procedures are poor, deeper look-aheads can lead to worse decisions than shallower look-aheads (Pearl, 1983).

Holding (1979) investigated the relationship between overall skill level and quality of evaluation. He asked 50 players to assess the relative advantages of whichever side the players thought was winning. The assessments were made on a 10-point scale over 10 board positions. The results indicated clearly that judgements of which side was winning were much better in the more skilled players and that the different classes of player differed in the degree of discrimination they showed among the game positions. Thus, more skilled players used a wider range of the scale than the weaker players. Holding also compared the subjects' judgements with evaluations of the positions delivered by Slate and Atkin's (1977) highly rated program, Chess 4.5. This program assigns overall scores to positions on the basis of features such as king defence, pawn structure, rook connection, file control, and queen mobility and attack. The program's evaluations correlated very highly with those of the top half of Holding's players ($r = 0.91$). The correlation with the lower half of Holding's sample was lower, but still striking ($r = 0.80$). These results suggest a reasonable measure of analogy between the factors entering into human chess evaluation and those incorporated into the evaluation function used in the Chess 4.5 program.

B. Memory, perception and play in GO

A number of the basic findings reported by De Groot, Chase and Simon and others for chess have now been replicated in a range of games. In the case of GO, Reitman (1976) showed superior board reconstruction, after brief exposure, by a master level player as compared with a beginner. A typical GO board position is shown in Fig. 3.2. As with chess, the Master's recall superiority only held for positions that were meaningful and not for random positions. Reitman was also able to show that the way in which the Master structured meaningful positions was rather complex, and involved percep-

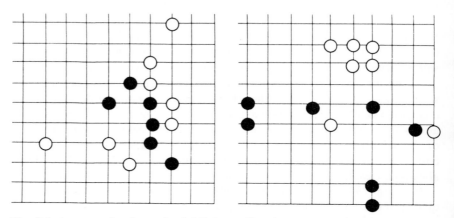

Fig. 3.2 An example of meaningful (left panel) and random (right panel) GO board patterns. Reproduced with permission from Reitman, J.S. (1976). Skill perception in GO: Deducing memory structures form inter-response times. *Cognitive Psychology* **8**, 336–356.

tion in terms of overlapping clusters of pieces rather than simply as independent chunks or as hierarchically nested chunks and subchunks.

Further aspects of internal representation and perceptual scanning in board games have been examined in the contexts of both GO and GO-moku. Both these games use the same board and the same black and white 'stones' or counters; but GO is the more complex game.

First, Eisenstadt and Kareev (1977) were able to show that subjects represented the same board configurations differently, depending on whether the configurations were presented as coming from a GO game or a GO-moku game. Subjects were shown positions and told either that the positions were from a GO game or a GO-moku and asked to decide what the best move would be for one of the players. After they had done this and an intervening task, they were unexpectedly asked to reconstruct the position that they had originally worked with. Different pieces were of critical importance for the GO and GO-moku interpretations and the accuracy of the reconstructions of the positions of the critical pieces varied in line with the interpretations. So, it can be concluded that people encode the board position in a manner relevant to the game they are playing.

This result suggests that people look for patterns typical of (or important to) the game in which they are engaged. Scanning the board may then be guided by expectations about types of patterns to be found. Indeed, Simon and Barenfeld's (1969) simulation of scanning in chess successfully assumed that scanning followed lines of attack and defence. Eisenstadt and Kareev suggest that Gestalt principles of similarity, proximity and continuity might also play a role – especially in GO-moku, since its basic game-specific patterns are straight lines.

In particular they examined the extent to which players detected an important type of configuration known as an 'open-three'. This pattern has two forms, continuous and non-continuous, as shown below:

X/X/X	/X/X /X/
continuous	non-continuous

If the player does not notice that his opponent has constructed an open-three and so *fails to block it*, he will lose the game. The winner is the first to establish a row of five pieces in his colour and an unblocked open-three is bound to lead to a winning line.

Additionally, open-threes can either be non-diagonal (high proximity) or diagonal (low proximity).

Subjects played against a computer program and the proportions of trials on which they failed to respond to open-threes were recorded. As would be predicted from the Gestalt principles, probability of responding was greater for open-threes on non-diagonals as against diagonals, and for continuous as against non-continuous patterns. These results indicate that Gestalt principles had a strong effect on scanning with this material.

C. Bridge

Expertise in a third game, bridge, has also been studied. Successful bridge play involves memory demands in that a bridge player benefits if he or she can remember the cards that have been played in the preceding rounds and what was the bid at the initial auction stage. So, in addition to a working memory load involved in planning which sequence of plays to attempt at a given point, a player also has to remember which cards have already been played and what happened during bidding. Thus, accurate memory is essential for good play. As with chess and GO, we might expect skilled players to demonstrate superior memory for bridge information, indicating a large repertoire of familiar patterns in long-term storage. Evidence reported by Engle and Bukstel (1978) and Charness (1979) bears out this expectation.

Engle and Bukstel (1978) gave four subjects (an expert, a life master, an average player and a novice) three tasks. First, the subjects played 10 hands of bridge and were then given an unexpected memory test for the cards in the 10 hands. An intentional memory task required subjects to reconstruct four bridge hands from one deal where the cards within each hand were either arranged systematically or at random. Finally, a perception task required subjects to reconstruct stimuli similar to those used in the memory task after brief glances at the stimulus. The higher the level of bridge expertise of the subject the better his or her performance on the structured tasks, but no effect of expertise on the unstructured tasks was found.

Charness (1979) confirmed these results in a study that had a firmer empirical basis, since it used 20 subjects of varying degrees of bridge ability. The subjects were given the following tasks: planning the play of a contract, rapid bidding, incidental learning and recall memory for structured or unstructured bridge hands. Performance on all tasks, except memory for randomly arranged hands, was strongly positively related to the level of bridge expertise.

A further result from this study was that memory performance declined with age of the player, independently of level of expertise (though it may be noted that age had no effect on recall of randomly arranged hands). This suggests that, as in chess, skill differences in bridge cannot be explained simply in terms of differences in pattern encoding.

D. Poker

Chess and GO are games of complete information in which the opponents' material strengths and weaknesses are available to inspection. In many real life cases of adversary problem solving such complete information is not available and partial information must be relied on, thus introducing probabilistic considerations. Bridge clearly involves some uncertainty about where particular cards lie, and poker even more so. Thus poker playing has been studied as a microcosm of problem solving in uncertain conditions.

Lopes (1976) reported experiments on how poker players' internal models of the game and of their opponents' styles of play influence decision making in a modified version of five-card stud poker. In stud poker, players initially receive one card face down and one card face up. Normally a round of betting follows in which some players might drop out. A further card is dealt face up to the remaining players and another round of betting ensues. This procedure continues until five cards have been dealt (or until only one player remains active). Final rounds of betting are then held between those players left in the game. Lopes used a simplified task in which subjects saw two hands (four cards face up, one face down) together with the amounts bet on those hands and had to make various judgements and side bets. They rated the likelihood that a pair of sevens could beat both opposing hands and then bet on the pair of sevens. The results supported the view that the subjective probability of beating both hands was a multiplicative function of the probabilities of beating each of the individual hands. The subjective probability estimates were generally accurate reflections of the objective probabilities. The more likely the players judged that they would win, the larger the bet they would make. Interestingly, when in further conditions, subjects were told that some hands and bets were from 'conservative' (low bluffing) players and others from 'average' players they varied their bets to take into account the different bluffing tendencies of their imaginary opponents. As Lopes concluded, this series of studies showed that performance was affected by the players' model of the probabilities of having the winning hand and by the player's model of the opponents' bluffing tendencies.

Findler (1978) explored computer models of processes underlying play in the related game of five-card draw poker. In draw poker all cards are hidden from the players except their own. Five cards are dealt initially and a first betting round is followed by the discarding of up to four or five cards and the drawing of replacements. All that a given player knows is his or her own cards, the number of cards drawn by the other players and the bets made. Thus, draw poker involves even more uncertainty than stud poker. Findler has developed a number of programs to play draw poker that incorporate both fixed static strategies and adaptive learning routines. The 'simplest' strategy is that of the *mathematically fair player* who decides when and what to bet in accord with the objective odds of winning, but taking no regard of the other players' styles of betting. This strategy serves well against unsophisticated opposition but is vulnerable to bluffers who bet enough to make the perceived risk of losing unacceptable to the mathematically fair player. A more useful static strategy uses the objective odds and incorporates an index of the desirability of staying in the game at a particular juncture. This index takes into account the number of other players left in the game, how long they have remained in and how much extra must be bet to stay in the game. Programs embodying this strategy do well in competition with the mathematically fair player. A number of learning programs have also been devised that attempt to take account of their opponents' playing styles as relevent evidence accumulates through a game session. Such programs that update models of their opponents were the most successful investigated, and it seems likely that good human players also use similar processes. Indeed, Findler reports that human players usually cannot tell whether they are competing with other humans or with an adaptive program when the game is played over computer terminals.

IV. SUMMARY AND CONCLUDING COMMENTS

In this chapter recent studies of processes involved in adversary problem solving have been reviewed. From the game theory literature on how best to tackle such problems, came the useful notions of game trees and minimaxing. These ideas have been taken up both in analysing human play of board games, and in developing AI programs capable of high-level performance in chess and other games. Board games provide a useful focus for studying thought because they permit the generation of an indefinite number of fresh problems within tight frameworks.

This is very useful from the AI point of view since the basic rules of such games can readily be programmed. From the point of view of studying human processes, an extra benefit of games as research tools is that people's experience of particular games varies widely, and so studies of the effects of varying familiarity with the task area can readily be carried out. In comparison with traditional studies of non-adversary problems then, a strong emphasis on effects of experience is found in the study of human game playing.

De Groot (1965) reported little difference between good and excellent chess players in depth of look-ahead or breadth of search or other easily quantified aspects of mental search, and yet the excellent (master level) players almost always chose a better move. It may be noted in passing, that the depth of look-ahead (5–6) reported by De Groot and by Charness (1981b), is markedly larger than that assumed by the successful models for the water jar and missionary-and-cannibal problems discussed in the previous chapter. This difference may be due to the complete unfamiliarity of those non-adversary problems as against the relative familiarity of the chess task to the subjects concerned. One would expect to obtain quantifiable differences in search patterns between novices and good chess players [and the results of Charness (1981b) and Holding and Reynolds (1982) support this expectation].

However, since De Groot's results appeared to rule out a search-based explanation for the superior move choices made by his master level players compared to his good amateurs, other explanations were sought. A possible explanation for skill differences in chess was suggested by data on memory for chess positions after brief exposures. Master level players could reconstruct complete board positions much better than weaker players. This difference only held up if the board position made 'chess sense'. The level of playing skill made no difference to recall of positions constructed by arranging pieces at random on the board. Similar results have been reported for GO (Reitman, 1976) and bridge (Charness, 1979; Engle and Bukstel, 1978).

Simon and Gilmartin (1973) put forward an explanation for the chess memory results in terms of 'chunking' (Miller, 1956) in working (or short-term) memory. The master level player was assumed to have a larger store of patterns in long-term memory with which to label board configurations and thus could find pattern labels that encoded the position more economically than the weaker player. Support for this view came from the successful simulation program, MAPP. The notion that the 'chunks' are held in short-term memory until recall, is no longer plausible following Charness's (1976) and Frey and Adesman's (1976) reports of little or no effects from interpolated tasks on chess memory. These results suggest, rather, rapid encoding in long-term memory. They do not, however, damage directly the major assumption of the pattern recognition model for chess skill, viz. that master level players have a more advanced coding scheme than weaker players.

More direct evidence against the pattern recognition model for chess skill comes from studies by Charness (1981a,b,c) and Holding and Reynolds (1982). Charness found that when older and younger players were equated for skill level, the older players had poorer immediate and delayed memory for chess positions, i.e. a difference in memory not reflected in a skill difference. Conversely, Holding and Reynolds found that when players chose moves in random positions, clear skill differences emerged but there were no memory differences for the positions, i.e. a difference in skill not reflected in a memory difference. These results jointly and separately make the simple pattern recognition model of chess skill untenable.

Both the artificial intelligence (Findler, 1978) and the human experimental studies (Lopes, 1976) of poker playing underline the need to consider players' internal models of their adversaries as well as of the task materials.

Overall, then, the implications of the studies of adversary problem solving are quite consistent with those of investigations of non-adversary problem solving. Both lines of research indicate the role of internal models in problem solving and are consistent with the view that the human subject searches trees of possibilities in a serial fashion.

There is no sign of parallel searches of different branches of the game tree in chess, for instance. A small capacity working memory appears to be implicated in view of the limitations on look ahead depth within a single exploratory sequence; although these limits seem to be overcome by building up long-term memory representations of longer sequences by use of progressive deepening strategies. A more general use of long-term memory is indicated by the role of general chess knowledge, indicated by the results of Pfau and Murphy (in press), for example, which show chess skill ratings to be closely related to scores on chess knowledge tests.

V. FURTHER READING

Holding, D.H. (1985). *The psychology of chess skill.* Hillsdale, N.J.: Lawrence Erlbaum Associates. This is a very thorough and readable exposition of research on all aspects of chess skill.

4

Expertise 2: Non-adversary problems

This chapter deals with solving semantically rich non-adversary problems. First, I will consider research in the domains of physics, mathematics, computer programming, political science and medicine. The findings in these studies mainly bear on the quantitative and qualitative differences in performance between experts and novices. In Section II, I will go on to discuss recent findings and models regarding the acquisition of expertise.

I. EXPERT – NOVICE COMPARISONS

A. Physics

At the textbook level, at least, physics is a formal domain that includes a set of principles logically sufficient to solve physics problems. The problems posed to physics students are essentially well-defined. The major difficulty in solving physics problems lies in selecting which principles to apply, rather than in applying the principles to generate equations. How then do skilled physicists select useful principles to apply to problems? Perhaps expert subjects have developed a repertoire of familiar problem categories and have associated each category with relevant principles? (This is a similar hypothesis to the pattern-recognition model of chess skill discussed in Chapter 3).

One technique that has been used to investigate this hypothesis involves asking subjects to sort or categorize problems according to their similarity. Chi *et al.* (1982) asked advanced Ph.D. and undergraduate students to sort physics problems on the basis of similarities in how they would solve them, but without actually solving them. The results showed no evidence of *quantitative* differences between the two skill groups, such as number of categories used, or time to categorize. However, *qualitative* differences were apparent in the categories into which novices and experts sorted the problems. Novices grouped together problems which were similar in "*surface structure*", that is, they were similar in terms of the objects and key words referred to in the problem.

In contrast, experts did not sort on the basis of similar surface structures. Instead, their categories reflected sortings on the basis of "*deep structure*", that is, in terms of major principles involved in solution, such as "conservation of energy". This result suggests that in the case of the expert, knowledge useful for tackling a particular problem is accessed when the problem is first perceived.

Part of the skill of expert physicists then lies in their ability to categorize a problem appropriately. An appropriate categorization may then help the subject to access large-scale units for solving problems (i.e. 'groups' or 'chunks' of related principles). Larkin (1978) set out to examine this by having two experts and one novice think aloud while solving textbook physics problems. If principles useful for solving particular types of problems are stored as groups or chunks, this might be reflected in the solver's generation of "bursts" of related equations. If no such chunks exist, then equations should be generated at random intervals through time. Also, if chunking develops with experience, novices should show less pronounced evidence for chunking than experts. Hypothesized chunks were constructed by Larkin and physicist colleagues such that each chunk contained one fundamental principle together with those subsidiary principles commonly applied with the fundamental principle. Consistent with the hypothesis, Larkin found that the pairs of equations generated by experts with intervening times of 10 seconds or less were typically "same chunk" pairs. Those with intervening times of 15 seconds or more tended to be "different chunk" pairs. In contrast, the novices' temporal data fitted a random distribution curve well, suggesting that, for novices, principles were accessed individually rather than as part of a large-scale method.

However, these findings were not replicated by Chi *et al.* (1982), who used the same method of analysis. If anything, their results contradicted the hypothesis, as their novices seemed to have generated a greater number of related principles in close succession. Unless the discrepancy can be resolved, it cannot be concluded that storage of equations in long-term memory differs for experts and novices. It may be that Chi *et al.*'s novices generated clusters of equations as a result of a problem-solving strategy rather than because of structure in long-term memory. (A problem-solving strategy that might produce such results is to generate all principles known, in the hope that some are recognized as useful.)

The sorting experiments of Chi *et al.* indicated marked differences in problem representation between experts and novices. Are there differences in the way experts and novices build up representations of specific problems before attempting solutions?

Larkin (1978) addressed this question through the analysis of think aloud protocols produced by expert physicists as they solved a problem. She found that her experts engaged in an extensive *qualitative* analysis of the problem prior to generating equations. By "qualitative analysis" is meant a phase in which the subject makes inferences essential to solve the problem. It seems that this phase lays the foundation for the successful selection of principles appropriate to solution. Chi *et al.* (1982) found that novices also carry out a qualitative analysis of a problem. However, the difference between experts and novices lies in the *quality* of inferences made, because novices often fail to draw necessary inferences and so work with less useful representations of the problems.

Differences between experts and novices in their long-term knowledge bases have now been discussed but we have not yet examined differences in *strategies* employed by solvers differing in levels of expertise. Larkin *et al.* (1980) found that novices used a "working backwards" strategy whereas experts used a "working forwards" strategy when solving physics problems. In more detail, novices solved a problem using a "naive" representation, which provided little guidance in selecting principles for application. Thus, novices fell back on a means–end analysis which involves working backward from the unknown to the given, gradually eliminating differences between the written equations and an equation that would provide the desired answer. Experts, however, worked forward from the given to the goal, suggesting that they have the solution procedure available as one "large functional unit", as Larkin (1979) described it. Thus, it seems that problem solving is primarily *search driven* for the novice and *schema driven* for the expert.

B. Mathematical problem solving and problem perception

The research in physics discussed above suggests that the ability to categorize a problem correctly in terms of relevant principles facilitates the problem-solving process. The correct perception of a problem seems to cue a "problem schema" which suggests a straightforward, sterotypical solution method. At the other extreme an incorrect perception can send the solver up a blind alley. Problem perception, then, is clearly an important component of problem-solving performance. What changes occur in problem perception with skill acquisition? If researchers could identify the critical changes, then training might capitalize on this and enhance problem-solving performance. This issue was addressed in an experiment by Schoenfeld and Hermann (1982) in the domain of mathematical problem solving.

Schoenfeld and Hermann's study replicated previous findings that novices sort problems on the basis of surface structure whereas experts sort on the basis of deep structure. Their results also showed that after a 1-month long course in mathematical problem solving, an experimental group of subjects subsequently sorted problems significantly more often on the basis of their deep structure than did a control group who had received training in computer programming. As would be expected, the course, which focussed on general mathematical problem-solving heuristics, enhanced performance of the experimental group in solving mathematics problems.

C. Computer programming

A number of studies have examined problem-solving skill in the context of computer programming. Adelson (1981) addressed the question of how novice and expert programmers represent and use programming concepts. In each trial of Adelson's study, novice and expert programmers were shown 16 randomly ordered lines of Polymorphic Programming Language (PPL) code drawn from three short programs. Subjects were then asked to free-recall as many items as possible at the end of each of nine trials. Experts recalled more lines of code than novices. In addition, average chunk size for experts (i.e. lines of code recalled with inter-response times of 10 seconds or less) was larger than that of the novices. Novices clustered terms from the same syntactic category (e.g. all 'FOR' statements together), whereas experts clustered items belonging to the same program function (e.g. a sorting routine). These results suggest that both experts and novices have categories for elements of a programming language, the novices' being syntactically and the experts' being semantically based. The results do not, however, indicate whether the programmers' memory performance was due to encoding or retrieval.

A similar study was carried out by McKeithen et al. (1981). Subjects of three skill levels were shown a 31-line Algol W program in either normal or scrambled version for five 2-minute study trials. Skill level was found to predict recall performance for the normal version but not the scrambled version, replicating Chase and Simon's (1973a,b) results for random chess patterns. Differences in the way subjects organized their recall were also examined and connections were found between high expertise and a particular organization of concepts in Algol W. While the data do not prove that this organization *produces* expertise, they do show that experts know more or less the same things, and know them in the same way, as indicated by the fact that several chunks were common to the experts.

The studies just outlined by Adelson and McKeithen et al. appear somewhat contradictory. Adelson reported an expert–novice difference on memory for scrambled programs, while McKeithen et al. report no such difference in their scrambled program condition. Also, Adelson's finding seems to contradict the well-established result in a number of fields, that experts and novices do not differ in recall of randomized, unstructured material. On this latter point, Adelson argued that the scrambled programs were potentially meaningful when re-organized by experts, while a scrambled chess pattern could not be reconstructed into a meaningful form. The former point is a little harder to deal with. Why should two apparently similar studies produce discrepant results? However, examining the details of the experimental procedures in the two studies gives some clues. Adelson used a line-by-line presentation, allowed 20 seconds per line, the material consisted of three small programs, extended free recall was allowed (8 minutes per trial) and, finally, the recall score was simply the number of lines correct irrespective of order. McKeithen *et al.* differed in every one of the experimental parameters just listed. They presented the whole of a 31-line program to be learned at once, allowed 2 minutes study (i.e. just under 4 seconds per line) per trial, the recall period was 3 minutes only, and recall was scored in terms of lines in correct order. Overall, it would seem that McKeithen *et al.*'s version of the scrambled program memory task was considerably more difficult than Adelson's. (Adelson's experts averaged scores of about 75 per cent correct whereas McKeithen *et al.*'s appear to have averaged about 20 per cent correct in the scrambled conditions.) This difficulty factor may have suppressed any possible expert advantage in imposing structure on the randomized program. There would appear to be a need for further parametric research to clarify the conditions under which expertise advantages will or will not show in memory for scrambled programs.

A study by Erlich and Soloway (1984) examined the use of "tacit" plan knowledge by expert programmers. Erlich and Soloway argue that expert programmers use higher-level knowledge to code programs for ease of recall, and that this higher-level knowledge is in the form of script-like plans which represent certain stereotypical actions in a program. Since experts may be unaware of using a structure such as the "running total loop plan", the focus of the study is on "procedural" as opposed to "declarative" knowledge. The technique involved was a "fill-in-blank" task, and used the programming language PASCAL. Problems concerned the initialization of variables and context effects. Results were consistent with the hypothesis that experts use tacit knowledge, enabling them to react appropriately to constraints operating on the initialization and updating of variables, and to contextual constraints implicit in a program. Skilled programmers seem to engage in a process of selecting from memory an appropriate plan and adapting this to meet the needs of the current situation.

D. Political science problem solving

Political science problems differ from physics, mathematics and programming problems in that they are typically ill-defined. That is to say, the
goal is often vaguely stated, candidate operators may not be defined and
often there is not a generally agreed-upon solution. Given these additional
considerations, how do individuals solve such ill-defined problems and to
what extent does the political science expert resemble the expert in better
defined domains?

These questions were tackled in a study carried out by Voss *et al.* (1983),
who employed think aloud protocols obtained from expert and novice
solvers. The problem for the subjects was to suggest how to increase crop
production in the Soviet Union. One interesting feature of this study was that
the researchers also collected protocols from two kinds of non-expert
"experts", viz. individuals expert in political science but not in the domain-
area of the Soviet Union, and subjects expert in a totally different domain
(chemistry). This design helps to "unconfound" some expert–novice differences by attempting to distinguish general world knowledge and general
problem-solving strategies from domain-related strategies.

The results showed that experts tended to review the problem initially and
then build a representation of the task. This seems to correspond to the qualitative analysis carried out by physics experts. Their approach was to find one
general solution to the problem, such as "greater capital investment in agri-
culture", which would also solve a number of subordinate problems. The
proposal of a general solution was followed by extensive exploration of the
ramifications of the solution and by supportive argumentation. Social scientists unfamiliar with the field of the Soviet Union tended to fall back on
general knowledge of the political science area, but did utilize domain-related
strategies. The chemists, however, lacked *both* the knowledge base and
domain-related strategies and thus performed at the same level as novices.
Thus, experience within the domain provides for the acquisition of knowledge and strategies, which may be content-independent, such as problem
conversion, or content dependent, such as historical analysis.

Voss *et al.* (1983) conclude, first, that learning within the domain involves
the development of networks providing information about relations among
concepts and facts. Secondly, the individual acquires knowledge of the inter-
dependencies that exist within a domain, and this knowledge facilitates the
development of arguments in support of solutions. Thirdly, the knowledge
base becomes hierarchically organized so that some problems, such as "lack
of fertilizer", become subordinate to a more abstract problem, such as "lack
of capital investment". In general terms, Voss *et al.* conclude that the
political science expert is like the chess master, in whom experience brings

about the development of a large repertoire of recognizable "patterns". Unlike physics, where "exposing learners to selected, special cases" (Larkin 1979, p. 112) may be crucial, it is suggested that exposure to a wide *variety* of problem types is important in developing skill in political science problem solving.

E. Medicine: diagnostic problem solving

Medical diagnosis frequently presents problems that are difficult even for experts to solve. Thus the typical 'working forward' pattern seen in other areas of expertise may not hold so fully in this area. As Gick (1986) and Bhaskar and Simon (1977) noted, when problems are unfamiliar then even experts have to engage in some working (or reasoning) backwards. Medical diagnosis has been quite extensively studied and a number of contrasts have been established between expert and novice diagnosticians.

In general terms, medical diagnosis, in cases of any difficulty, proceeds by a process of *hypothetico-deductive reasoning*. That is to say, one or more initial hypotheses regarding the disease are elicited by the presented symptoms of the patient (i.e. reasoning forward). These hypotheses are then tested, by deducing what further symptoms should be present for each disease and then checking for the presence or absence of these symptoms (i.e. reasoning backward). It appears that both experts and novices follow a hypo-thetico-deductive approach and show few quantitative differences in terms of number of hypotheses generated or number of symptoms examined before forming a hypothesis (Elstein *et al.*, 1978; Johnson *et al.*, 1981). However, the experts develop better sets of initial hypotheses and derive more specific hypotheses earlier. According to Clancey (1984), the expert's set of hypo-theses tends to consist of mid-level disease categories, e.g. 'meningitis' rather than 'infection' (a more general category) or 'tb-menigitis' (a more specific category).

It appears then that the expert's advantage lies mainly in the structure of knowledge brought to bear on the diagnostic task rather than in greater effi-ciency in executing the hypothetico-deductive process. Johnson *et al.* (1981) obtained more specific data on knowledge differences between different levels of expertise in a study comparing diagnostic performance of experts, trainees and students (novices). Subjects thought aloud as they worked on information in a patient file. The experts quickly developed a candidate set of hypotheses, consisting of closely related diseases and could use the available data to distinguish correctly among those hypotheses. The less skilled subjects tended to work with more distinct 'textbook' cases of diseases as their hypotheses, and were not so successful at using the data to distinguish among their hypotheses.

Perceptual factors play a role in medical diagnosis and Lesgold (1984) and his colleagues have studied closely the skill of interpreting X-ray plates. In terms of expert–novice comparisons, it is notable that novices give more weight to perceptually salient features than experts and this often leads to novices considering too few hypotheses, leading to mistaken interpretations. A plausible analysis of this result is that novices first developed links between salient features and underlying causes and only later develop links from more subtle features to causes.

F. Interim summary and conclusions

In the areas reviewed (physics, mathematics, computer programming, political science and medical diagnosis) expert–novice comparisons indicate that experts form better representations of problems in their field and generally reason forward from the givens to a solution. However, this 'working forward' pattern tends to break down with problems that are unfamiliar for the expert. Particularly in the case of medical diagnosis, a mixed pattern of working forward and backward appears in the hypothetico-deductive approach of both experts and novices. As in other domains, the expert's initial formulation of the diagnostic problem is better; the alternative hypotheses considered by experts in diagnosis are more similar to each other than those considered by the novices, and experts have better tuned knowledge of what evidence is or is not consistent with alternative diagnoses.

Thus far, our focus has been on cross-sectional contrasts of the knowledge possessed by experts but not by novices. But how does the transition from expert to novice take place? Studies and theories bearing on this question will be discussed in the following sections.

II. DEVELOPMENT OF EXPERTISE

Both empirical studies and theoretical developments will be considered under this heading.

A. Empirical studies

Real expertise takes a very long time to develop. The figure of 10 year's study and practice is generally accepted as a rough minimum for high-level performance in a wide range of areas (see Holding, 1985, p. 33 for relevant results on the time between starting play and the first major successes in chess play). Because of the long time periods involved, it is difficult to obtain longitudinal data on the course of development of expertise. The full process is clearly beyond the methods of laboratory-based cognitive research. One approach is to concentrate on relatively small-scale or narrow skills and try to obtain information on factors relating to particular well-established changes on the route from novice to expert. This approach has been adopted by Sweller and his colleagues in their studies of the shift from working backwards to working forwards. Another line of attack is to carry out more fine-grained cross-sectional analysis. This is exemplified by the work of Lesgold (1984) on the development of skill in the interpretation of X-ray plates. Lesgold and his colleagues have not simply compared 'experts' at one end of the scale with 'novices' at the other, but have examined performance at a number of points along the skill continuum. These two lines of research on expertise development will now be discussed.

1 Strategy changes

Sweller *et al.* (1983) reported a series of experiments concerning the shift in strategy from working backwards to working forwards that characterizes the change from novice to expert in many fields. To make the research problem tractable, they focussed on a very narrow cognitive skill, consisting of the ability to solve certain problems in kinematics. The domain of kinematics problems was restricted to those that could be solved using one or two of a set of three equations ($V = at, s = vt$ and $v = 0.5V$). In the first experiment, subjects tackled 25 different problems of which the middle 13 were repeated five times. Thus, subjects experienced a total of 77 problems. The subjects' problem-solving steps could readily be classed as either showing a working backwards or a working forwards approach, and Sweller *et al.* (1983) found a significant tendency for working forwards to occur more often with increased practice. This result is of interest because it demonstrates differences within individuals over time as against the more usual demonstration of cross-sectional differences in strategy use.

Previous research (Sweller and Levine, 1982; Mawer and Sweller, 1982) had indicated that use of a means–ends or working backward strategy might hinder the acquisition of knowledge about a problem area. However, the previous studies had concerned maze-learning and some simple symbolic-rule learning tasks and so might not generalize to the more complex area of cognitive skills. Sweller *et al.* (1983) examined the effects of reducing the use of means–ends strategies on expertise development. They did this using kinematics problems, as in the study of practice effects. One group of subjects worked through 12 problems each with a specific goal set (e.g. 'given v and t, find the distance travelled'); a second group worked through problems each of which had a *non-specific goal* (e.g. 'given v and t, calculate the value of as many variables as you can'). Both groups received four specific goal problems at the start and a different set of four specific goal problems at the end.

The subjects who had worked with specific goal problems showed little use of forward working on either the initial or final four problems (around 12 per cent on both sets). However, the subjects who had worked with the non-specific goals showed a marked increase (from 12 to 75 per cent) in use of working forward between the initial and final problems. Thus, use of non-specific goals in training promotes use of a working forward strategy in subsequent specific goal tasks. A subsequent study showed that (a) use of non-specific goals in training also positively affected moves to solution and (b) showed that similar results held in geometry tasks as well as kinematics. An interesting effect of the greater expertise acquired through the non-specific goal procedure is that the more effective, working-forward subjects were more susceptible to 'set' effects than the less effective, working-backward comparison subjects. As in the water jars studies of Luchins (1942) discussed in Chapter 1, subjects displayed 'set' by adopting a longer solution path when a shorter one was available (e.g. in the kinematics problems, by ignoring possible use of $V = at$ and instead using $s = vt$ followed by $v = 0.5V$). This is taken as evidence of the development of problem schemata in the non-specific goal conditions.

Overall, then, Sweller *et al.*'s (1983) results suggest that expertise is acquired more rapidly if the training problems have non-specific goals. The proposed explanation is that specific goals induce in the novice a means–ends approach in which attention is focussed on reducing the differences between the current state and the overall goal. This reduces the likelihood of learning connections between problem-*givens* and actions. Reduced goal-specificity shifts control of moves from the goal to the problem-givens. (In the case of the kinematics problems, knowledge of the givens was in fact sufficient to categorize the three main types of problems since the same givens always had the same goal.) The results obtained by Sweller *et al.* are undoubtedly intriguing and suggestive of links with "exploration learning". However, a question mark must hang over the generality of these results, given that they have been established in very narrow skill areas compared to the full-blown forms of expertise addressed in the more typical cross-sectional study.

2 Performance changes in radiology

While practice may indeed make perfect, it may not do so in a smooth and regular way, especially when complex skills with many components have to be acquired. The work of Lesgold and his colleagues [see Lesgold (1984) for an accessible account], addresses the development of skill in the domain of radiological diagnosis and has produced some striking results.

First, the domain should be explained. In radiology the physician has to know the relationships between variations in anatomical structure and the black and white patterns seen in X-ray plates. Given a plate the task is to infer the underlying pathology (if any). Lesgold (1984) reported finding a non-linear, U-shaped curve of performance over beginning, intermediate and expert radiologists. That is, beginners and experts were better at X-ray plate interpretation than subjects of intermediate levels of experience.

Apparently, beginners rely on a few clear surface features of the plates that will sometimes lead to correct diagnoses, but because the complete context must be taken into account, cannot permit high-level performance. The expert can take the context into account and so performs well. However, the intermediate level subject attempts to take context into account, but often fails to do so correctly. This leads to his or her higher error rate. However, these short-term losses in efficiency are a necessary step on the way to expert performance.

Lesgold et al. (1988) point out that the acquisition of expertise may be similar to long-term developmental processes, in which U-shaped growth curves are not uncommon. For example, initially, young children usually handle irregular plurals and past tenses correctly, learning each as a separate item; but then, as they learn the regular rules, performance on the irregular words deteriorates because the rules are applied to the irregular words as well as to the regular words. Later, the regular and irregular words come to be dis-associated and performance improves once more (Brown, 1973).

B. Theories of the acquisition of expertise

Despite the paucity of hard data on the acquisition of cognitive skills, a number of theories of varying scope have been put forward. In the following sections, two theories of broad applicability will be discussed; these are Anderson's (1983) ACT* theory and Holland et al.'s (1986) Framework for Induction theory.

1 Anderson's ACT* theory

Anderson's *Adaptive Control of Thought* (ACT) approach has evolved through a number of versions into its current form, ACT* (Anderson, 1983). ACT* is intended as a general framework for understanding cognition, but it particularly addresses the acquisition of cognitive skills. Anderson stresses the time-honoured distinction between 'knowing that' and 'knowing how'. The latter knowledge is said to be 'procedural' and the former 'declarative' in his system. Declarative knowledge takes the form of propositions and is only slowly converted into action by means of general interpretative procedures (e.g. recipe-following). Procedural knowledge takes the form of production rules, discussed earlier in Chapter 2, which permit rapid and appropriate action. Skill acquisition involves, first, the conversion of declarative into procedural knowledge and, secondly, refinements of procedural knowledge. The initial conversion is labelled *knowledge compilation*. In computing, a 'compiled' program is one which has already been translated from a high-level language into machine code and, in this form, is ready to be run. Initially in skill acquisition then, declarative knowledge is used, possibly from textbooks or from instructors' verbal guidance. Declarative knowledge is only slowly converted into procedural form. Anderson argues plausibly that rapid knowledge compilation would be maladaptive. Since compiled knowledge controls behaviour quite directly, it is important that such knowledge be 'tried and tested'.

Knowledge compilation is seen as involving two sets of processes, *proceduralization* and *composition*. Proceduralization creates highly specific rules that eliminate any need to search long-term memory during skilled activity. For example, through repeatedly using a new acquaintance's telephone number, the need to consult directories or to search long-term memory for the number reduces as a new production is formed, the conditional part of which is the goal of dialling the acquaintance's number and the action of which is simply to dial the appropriate sequence. The other process, composition, smooths performance by collapsing a repeated sequence of actions into a single sequence (a 'macro-operation').

The refinement or tuning stage of skill acquisition involves sub-processes of *generalization, discrimination* and *strengthening*. Generalization creates general rules from more specific ones, where the action parts of the rules are the same.

Anderson (1983, p. 242) gives an example from the game of bridge. Suppose the following two rules are known:

Rule 1: IF I am playing no trump *and* my dummy has a long suit,
THEN
try to establish that suit *and* then run that suit.
Rule 2: IF I am playing spades and my dummy has a long suit,
THEN
try to establish that suit *and* then run that suit.

ACT* would form a generalized rule from these two rules:

Rule 3: IF my dummy has a long suit,
THEN
try to establish that suit *and* then run that suit.

Discrimination works in the reverse direction, by adding necessary extra conditions to rules when they prove to be too general. All rules in the system have their own current strength level and the strength of a rule is adjusted up whenever it is applied and adjusted down if punishment results. The conditions of rules with a greater strength index are matched more rapidly and thus come to dominate rules of lesser strength.

Overall, Anderson's system copes well with many of the standard observations regarding skill acquisition. For example, repeated composition would collapse sequences of operations into a macro-operation that could be applied as soon as a familiar problem was detected; this would produce a working-forward pattern of activity, typical of expert performance. Again, proceduralization and strengthening produce the typical speed-ups, automatization and susceptibility to set that result from repeated exposure to familiar types of problems. Some difficulties are that composition has been shown to be formally inadequate to explain the development of expert skill in solving algebraic equations (Lewis, 1981); also, the theory makes no provision for the development of *new rules*, as against the refinement and modification of old ones. This last point is taken up by Holland *et al.*'s (1986) theory, to which we now turn.

2 *Holland* et al.*'s Framework for Induction*

The framework proposed by Holland *et al.* (1986) takes production rules as the basic building blocks of knowledge. They distinguish three types of rule. These are (1) empirical rules, (2) inferential rules which modify existing empirical rules, and (3) system-operating rules which serve performance functions, such as resolving conflict among competing rules or automatically adjusting strengths assigned to rules.

Unlike earlier production system models which have generally envisaged serial processing, Holland *et al.* allow a degree of parallel processing, in that a number of rules can 'fire' at once. One result of a rule firing is that a 'message' is posted on a 'message list'; the messages on the message list can then trigger other rules which place new messages on the message list . . . and so on. At any one time all the rules in the system are eligible for firing, but only those rules whose conditions are matched completely get a chance to post messages. All the rules with completely matched conditions enter a strength competition and only the rules above a threshold strength actually fire and post messages.

How does this framework apply to the acquisition of cognitive skills? The speed up of performance typical of the expert may be accounted for by rule strengthening. Holland *et al.* note that rule strengthening following success raises the question of 'apportionment of credit'. If only the last rule in a long sequence is strengthened, then earlier rules that set the scene for later success will not be strengthened. The solution offered takes the form of the picturesquely named 'bucket brigade' algorithm. In this scheme, strength increments are passed back along the sequence of linked rules that led to success. Rules which may have fired in parallel but did not form part of the successful sequence are not strengthened. The strength increments are larger at the end of the sequence than at the beginning. This feature accounts for the usual result that behavioural chains are best established in reverse order (Millenson, 1967).

New rules are produced by modifications of old rules. Two main types of rule modification are *specialization* and *generalization*. Specialization is invoked when an overgeneral rule leads to error. In such a case, any unusual condition that held when the rule fired is added to the rule's old conditions to produce a new, more specialized rule. If a number of different rules are formed such that they all lead to the same action but have different conditions, then generalization seeks to produce a single rule to cover all the conditions of the separate rules. Novel rules (rather than modified or strengthened rules) are formed by a genetic-like process, whereby rules are broken up into component conditions and actions and recombined to form new rules.

An interesting point stressed by Holland *et al.* is that new rules do not replace old rules, but rather co-exist with earlier learning. Thus, physics graduates, for example, will have both the rules of Newtonian mechanics and those of pre-Newtonian mechanics (acquired before formal physics instruction, in their 'naive physics' stage of life). This explains why a person who can readily solve textbook physics problems will exhibit more developmentally primitive rules when faced with a real-life physics problem. For example, most college students in a study by McCloskey (1983) believed that if they walked along carrying a ball and then dropped it, that the ball would land directly under the point where it was released. Similarly, in the First World War, hand-held bombs dropped from aeroplanes, very frequently overshot their targets (McCloskey and Kaiser, 1984). 'Dissociations' of textbook knowledge from everyday beliefs are consistent with Holland *et al.*'s framework.

Holland *et al.*'s approach is ambitious and seems a potentially useful one in which to examine skill acquisition. Further specification of the framework into models for particular cases of skill acquisition would be useful in order to assess the approach more fully.

III. SUMMARY AND CONCLUDING COMMENTS

This chapter has reviewed research concerned with characterizing differences in knowledge and strategy between more and less skilled solvers of problems in a range of semantically-rich domains. Most of this research has been cross-sectional with relatively few studies yielding data on the transition from novice to expert. Nevertheless, some quite detailed theories of cognitive skill acquisition have been proposed and two approaches based on production-system notions were discussed (Anderson, 1983; Holland et al., 1986).

From the studies of expert–novice differences in physics, mathematics, computer programming, political science and medical diagnosis it seems that experts spend relatively more time in representing problems and then usually work forward from the givens to the solution. Novices spend less time on initial representation and usually attempt to work backwards. However, when problems are difficult even for experts (e.g. medical diagnosis), then a mixed working-forward and -backward pattern has been observed. With very difficult problems, it is surmised that experts too will show a fairly pure means–ends analysis working-backward approach (Gick, 1986). While it is generally agreed that experts have acquired extensive-problem schemata that support richer representations of problems and facilitate working forward, the processes of schemata acquisition are difficult to observe, in that expertise in most areas requires several years of practice (10 years is often cited). In many ways, explaining the acquisition of expertise is a problem on a developmental scale, and is not easily tackled in the typical laboratory study. Sweller et al. (1983) have focussed on very narrow skills, e.g. using three equations in kinematics. While this research is suggestive it is not clear how well it relates to full-scale acquisition of expertise in broader domains, such as physics. Sweller et al.'s experimentally based recommendations of using non-specific goals during training are plausible and should be testable in real-life studies of physics teaching.

The work of Lesgold et al. (1988) is valuable, notably in its use of a number of levels of experience in the subjects. Using just two levels (expert and novice) could easily hide important trends such as the U-shaped curve of performance against experience in radiology.

The theoretical approaches of Anderson and of Holland et al. are somewhat similar in that both are based on production systems. Anderson's is at present better developed and more tightly specified. However, Holland *et al.*'s framework seems promising and incorporates useful notions of parallel processing and of evolution of new productions, lacking in Anderson's ACT*.

Future research may profitably focus on (a) performance of experts with problems at the limits of their expertise, and (b) use of more fine-grained cross-sectional studies, with more than two levels of skill being compared within single studies.

IV. FURTHER READING

Lesgold, A.M. (1984). Acquiring expertise. In J.R. Anderson (Ed.), *Tutorials in learning and memory*, pp. 31–60. San Francisco: W.H. Freeman. Lesgold gives a clear discussion of the problem area, illustrated with details from his team's work on expertise in radiological interpretation.

Gick, M. (1986). Problem solving strategies. *Educational Psychologist* 21, 99–120. Gick provides a useful overview of expert–novice differences over a range of areas.

5
Deductive reasoning

This chapter and the next deal with reasoning and continue the theme of considering how people "go beyond the information given". The preceding three chapters concerned studies of how people tackle problems that involve extensive mental searches and, in the case of experts, an extensive long-term memory of relevant problem schemata. By contrast, the reasoning tasks to be considered here would not appear to require extensive mental searches or extensive prior knowledge structures. Nevertheless, the tasks to be dealt with are frequently found to be very difficult despite their apparent simplicity.

The reasoning problems discussed in this chapter and in the next may conveniently be labelled "deductive" and "inductive" respectively. In deductive tasks, people are required to determine what conclusion, if any, necessarily follows when certain statements are assumed to be true. In the case of inductive reasoning, people are required to determine the implications, if any, of some particular observation(s) for the truth of possible generalizations (hypotheses). The topics of deductive and inductive reasoning are very closely related and both have been studied extensively in recent years. To keep the text to a manageable length, I will largely deal with selected "prototypical" instances of the two types of inference.

I. SYLLOGISTIC REASONING

A fairly common type of deductive problem in everyday thinking, is to determine what conclusion, if any, must follow from certain assumptions about category membership.

Because the classical argument form of the *syllogism* provides small-scale instances of such deductive problems, it has been widely used in laboratory studies of reasoning. The main features of syllogistic arguments may be conveyed by a few examples. Consider the following:

All mammals have backbones.
All dogs are mammals.
Therefore, all dogs have backbones.

Since the third statement (the conclusion) follows necessarily from the first two (the premises) this is a *valid* syllogistic argument and may be compared with:

    All cats are mammals.
    All dogs are mammals.
    Therefore, all dogs are cats.

In this case the conclusion plainly does not follow from the premises and the argument is *invalid*. It should be noted that the validity of an argument is independent of the truth of the premises. So, for example, the following is a deductively valid argument:

    All cats have nine lives.
    All dogs are cats.
    Therefore, all dogs have nine lives.

A valid argument is simply one in which, if the premises are true, then the conclusion is also, necessarily, true.

In addition to validity, syllogisms can be varied in many other ways for experimental purposes. For example, they may be varied by changing the *quantifiers* ('some', 'all') used in the argument; the *terms* may be abstract or concrete; the premises and conclusion may be *negative* or *affirmative*; the *propositions* in the argument may be empirically true or false, . . . and so on. Clearly, many features of the task can be readily manipulated. A number of variations are also possible in the response requirements. Subjects can be asked to *produce* valid inferences from given premises, to *judge* a possible conclusion as valid or not, or to *select* a valid conclusion from a set of possibilities.

Early studies (e.g. Wilkins, 1928) established some of the main factors associated with the difficulty of syllogisms, such as concreteness. Intuitively, the invalidity of an argument seems less clear when the terms are abstract, e.g.

    All P's are M's.
    All S's are M's.
    Therefore, all S's are P's.

This abstract argument may well be accepted, even although it exhibits the same invalid pattern as a previous concrete example that led from true premises to the conclusion that 'all dogs are cats'.

The role of concreteness in facilitating syllogistic reasoning was experimentally established by Wilkins. She found that syllogisms which employed concrete terms resulted in more correct deductions than syllogisms in abstract form. A total of 81 subjects were given a series of problems like the following:

All good ballet dancers have many years of training.
Some of the dancers in this musical comedy have many years of training.
Therefore:

(1) Some of the dancers in this musical comedy are good ballet dancers.
(2) All good ballet dancers are in this musical comedy.
(3) Some of the dancers in this musical comedy are not good ballet dancers.

Or, the same thing in symbols:

All A's are B's.
Some C's are B's.

Therefore:

(1) Some C's are A's.
(2) All A's are C's.
(3) Some C's are not A's.

The instructions were 'to put a plus sign before every conclusion which you are sure follows necessarily from the given statements . . . a minus sign before every conclusion that does not necessarily follow from the given statements . . .'. The average score was 76 per cent correct for the letter terms and 84 per cent for the syllogisms expressed in familiar words.

Why, even in the case of concrete syllogisms, did the subjects accept so many invalid conclusions? Misunderstanding of the use of the term 'some' could have caused errors. In logic, 'some' means 'at least one and possibly all' whereas in normal usage it means 'not all but at least one'. Thus, in logic, it is *not* valid to infer from 'some X are Y' that 'some X are not Y'.

An additional proposal has been that there is an 'atmosphere effect' which leads subjects to accept invalid conclusions. This proposal has generated a long-lasting controversy which will now be surveyed.

A. The 'atmosphere effect' controversy

1 Basic Results

All C's are M's.
All D's are M's.
Therefore, all L's are C's.

The above argument is invalid. (In logic it is known as the 'fallacy of the undistributed middle'.) To account for this common form of error, Woodworth and Sells (1935) hypothesized an 'atmosphere' effect which predicted that the form of the premises would influence people's expectations about the form of the conclusion. They proposed that if both premises involve the universal ('all'), people are disposed to accept an 'all' conclusion. Similarly, if both premises are particular ('some'), people will be disposed to a 'particular' conclusion. Similar predictions apply if both premises are negatively particular or universal; in such cases, the preferred conclusion is predicted to be negatively particular or universal, respectively. With mixed premises it is proposed that (1) a negative premise creates a negative atmosphere even when the other premise is affirmative, and (2) a particular premise creates a particular atmosphere, even when the other premise is universal.

To test the atmosphere hypothesis, Sells (1935) presented 65 subjects with 180 syllogisms, using abstract material, e.g.

> If all Z's are Y's
> And all X's are Y's
> Are all X's then Z's?
> True, probably true, false or indeterminate? (Correct answer – indeterminate.)

The meaning of 'some' in logic was explained in advance.

Of the 180 syllogisms 52 were valid and 128 invalid. With the invalid syllogisms, the conclusions that accorded to the atmosphere of the premises were predominantly accepted as true/valid conclusions, in accord with the hypothesis.

Sells and Koob (1937) report a similar result in a study that required subjects to draw their own conclusions from premises rather than merely judging already set out conclusions. This study required subjects to 'work quickly' which would probably favour an atmosphere effect.

How might atmosphere operate? The suggestion is that one becomes quickly set or adjusted to the total impression of the presented situation and respond accordingly. This would lead to fast responses – some of which would be correct. Accurate reasoning, on the other hand, surely requires analysis of the situation, and noting of relations – presumably a slower, more deliberate process than is suggested by the atmosphere hypothesis.

As a model, the atmosphere hypothesis proposes very superficial processing with minimal understanding – and it may be correct, when abstract problems are given to untrained subjects working under time pressures.

2 Conversion errors and probabilistic inference

More than 20 years after Woodworth and Sells proposed the atmosphere hypothesis, an alternative was put forward by Chapman and Chapman

(1959). First, they collected some fresh data by giving subjects 42 syllogisms that had no valid conclusions, e.g.

Some L's are K's.
Some K's are M's.

Therefore:

(1) No M's are L's.
(2) Some M's are L's.
(3) Some M's are not L's.
(4) None of these.
(5) All M's are L's.

The correct conclusion is (4), 'None of these'. Subjects tended to be wrong on these items and the kind of error made depended on the form of syllogism. The study involved 14 main types of syllogism and the atmosphere effect predicted the preferred errors on many of these. But it failed on syllogisms that involved premises of the following type

	Some X are Y			Some X are not Y
(A)		and	(B)	
	No Y are Z			No Y are Z

The predicted error (on atmosphere) is 'Some Z are not X', but in fact subjects tended to choose 'No Z are X', especially on (A) but split fairly evenly between the universal and the particular conclusions on (B).

Chapman and Chapman proposed that their results could be better explained by the operation of two reasoning errors that they called 'conversion' and 'probabilistic inference'. There are two conversion errors. These are to assume (1) from 'all X are Y' that 'all Y are X' and (2) that 'some A's are not B's' implies 'some B's are not A's'. That these are errors is shown clearly by concrete material. 'All women are human' does *not* imply that 'all humans are women'. Again, 'some humans are not politicians' does *not* imply that 'some politicians are not human'.

However, Chapman and Chapman argued that conversions often happen to be correct with real material (e.g. 'all 3-sided figures are triangles') and they suggest that subjects tend to make conversions unless they have information to the contrary (which they do not have with abstract material).

Probabilistic inference involved 'plausible reasoning' that is not strictly valid, *deductively* speaking, e.g. 'Some cloudy days are wet', 'Some wet days are unpleasant', therefore 'Some cloudy days are unpleasant.' Chapman and Chapman report that the joint operation of illicit conversion and probabilistic inference accounts better for their obtained error patterns than does the atmosphere hypothesis. This is largely on the strength of improved predictions for the types of syllogism mentioned before. On other syllogisms the alternative hypotheses make the same predictions. It is notable that Chapman and Chapman's results differ from those of Sells on the 'crucial' syllogisms. (Sells's results favoured the atmosphere prediction). To sum up, Chapman and Chapman have presented a plausible alternative to the atmosphere hypothesis, an alternative that is congenial to a cognitive approach; however, their data do not represent a complete demolition of the atmosphere hypothesis.

In 1969 Begg and Denny re-examined the atmosphere v. illicit conversion etc. controversy and provided a brief reformulation of the atmosphere hypothesis, that covers most of the obtained effects. They proposed two principles:

(1) Whenever at least one premise is negative, the conclusion is negative and otherwise it is positive.
(2) Whenever at least one premise is particular (some), the conclusion will be particular, otherwise it is universal.

These two principles can be combined for any pairs of premises to predict the preferred conclusion.

For most syllogisms these assumptions predict the same results as the conversion and probabilistic inference hypothesis. Begg and Denny analysed error patterns on 45 syllogisms, representing the main types and found that, again, atmosphere predicted the majority choices very well. They also re-analysed the data of Sells (1936) and Chapman and Chapman (1959). There was great consistency among the three sets of data and, on the average of the three studies, the atmosphere predictions were more often upheld than the conversion and probabilistic inference predictions.

Begg and Denny emphasize that their study is not informative about the processes that lead subjects to error; but their results do support the use of the atmosphere 'formula' as a convenient predictor of error patterns, even if the underlying processes may not be as described by the atmosphere hypothesis.

Wason and Johnson-Laird (1972) bring out some other points which suggest that, at the least, the atmosphere hypothesis is inadequate as a *complete* explanation, e.g. from Sell's own data:

When subjects are given
All B are A
All C are B

they accept the correct conclusion 'All C are A' twice as often as the incorrect conclusion 'All A are C'. Both are equally predicted by the atmosphere hypothesis. Again, Wilkins's (1928) data show that the atmosphere effect is weaker with familiar as opposed to abstract or unfamiliar material and the atmosphere hypothesis does not explain this difference. Wason and Johnson-Laird ran a further informative study. This differed from most of the previous experiments in that the subjects were simply given the premises and asked to draw a conclusion. They were not asked to evaluate given conclusions or to select one from a multiple choice list. Also, the premises they were given permitted *valid* inferences to be drawn [c.f. Sells (1936) and Chapman and Chapman (1959)].

Wason and Johnson-Laird found that there were reliably more errors *incompatible* with atmosphere (average of 3.9 per problem) than compatible with atmosphere (1.8 per problem). Further, the tendency to conform to atmosphere varied from one sort of problem to another. They concluded that the atmosphere explanation left something to be desired and, in view of the 'anti-atmosphere' evidence, go so far as to suggest that "Perhaps there is no atmosphere effect in syllogistic reasoning at all, but merely an amassed set of data which, when casually viewed, gives rise to the illusion of such a phenomenon" (1972, p. 139).

Another attack on the atmosphere hypothesis that has led to some interesting work was developed by Henle (1962) and this will be discussed next.

3 Henle's defence of 'rationality'

The atmosphere notion portrays people as non-logical and under the influence of non-rational sets; on the other hand, Chapman and Chapman's hypothesis suggests that people are somewhat rational – but may misinterpret premises (leading to illicit conversion) and may draw plausible but not strictly warranted conclusions from premises (probabilistic inference). This second kind of approach is consistent with the views put forward by Mary Henle (1962) in a paper that argued for the essential logicality of everyday thinking.

Henle argues that many apparent instances of illogical thinking may involve the implicit introduction of additional premises, the ignoring of some of the given premises and the misinterpretation of still other premises – *but* she claims the *inferences* are generally rational, given the subject's real premises. Henle here harks back to the old view that logic and thinking are closely related – as against the more recent view that thinking is not intrinsically logical and only conforms to logical paths under special circumstances. She illustrates her points with typical responses given by a sample of graduate students to syllogisms that one might come across in everyday life, e.g.

It's important to talk about things that are in our minds.
We spend so much of our time in the kitchen that household problems are in our
   minds.
Therefore, it's important to talk about household problems.

Subjects were asked to assess the validity of the argument, and give their
reasons. Some subjects failed to accept the task at all, and did not distinguish
logical validity from factual truth, e.g. 'No it's not important to talk about
things in our minds unless they worry us.' In a number of cases, subjects
tacitly re-stated premises or the conclusion so that the intended meaning was
changed. [Since Henle's syllogisms omitted quantifiers they were very open
to changes of this sort. Indeed – to digress slightly – omission of quantifiers
is a prime source of crooked and confused thinking according to Thouless
(1953, p. 24).] Other examples showed that subjects sometimes omitted
entire premises and sometimes introduced premises that had not been given.
   Henle (1962) concludes:

> that when subjects arrive at apparently invalid conclusions, or when they fail to
> spot a fallacy, they often do so because they have worked with materials diff-
> erent from those intended or because they have undertaken a task different
> from the one intended. In such cases, if we consider the materials and task as
> they were actually understood by individual subjects, we fail to find evidence of
> faulty reasoning. It must be concluded that the presence of error does not
> constitute evidence that the laws of logic are irrelevant to actual thinking. The
> data tend, rather, to support the older conception that these laws are widely
> discernible in the thinking process.

Although Henle's final conclusion from her informal study of a small,
highly educated sample may be regarded as debatable, she made a very sound
point in stressing the need to consider subjects' *interpretations* of the task
materials and goals. It is easy to assume that subjects interpret a task exactly
as the experimenter intends and then go on to make extraordinary blunders,
that the experimenter is perplexed to explain. Consideration of possible interpretations may well make subjects' behaviour more intelligible.

4 Misinterpretation of premises: further evidence

The question of premise interpretation was again taken up by Ceraso and
Provitera (1971) who examined the ambiguity of the traditional statements
used in syllogistic tasks. There are four basic statements, obtained by
combining universal or particular quantifiers, positively or negatively. These
statements are as follows:

   (A) All A are B,

(I) Some A are B,
(E) All A are not B,
(O) Some A are not B,

and are traditionally labelled A, I, E and O. These labels come from the initial vowels of the Latin words 'affirmo' and 'nego', meaning 'I assert' and 'I deny' respectively. An A statement can refer to two different situations, an I statement to four situations and an O statement to three, while an E statement is unambiguous and refers to only one state of affairs. These points should become clearer by reference to Euler circles (see Fig. 5.1). If, as seems likely, many subjects misinterpret the traditional, ambiguous premises, then apparently mistaken conclusions (e.g. those attributed to atmosphere effects) may be *valid* inferences based on misconstrued premises.

Ceraso and Provitera gave subjects syllogisms in which the premises were given a definite interpretation, e.g. instead of 'Some A's are B's', subjects were told "Some of the A's (but not all) are B's, but all of the B's are A's". Another group of subjects were given the traditional syllogism statements. The subjects with the clarified premises performed much better (averaging 2.5 errors/13 syllogisms) compared to the traditional group (who averaged 5.5 errors/13 syllogisms). Also, the responses of the traditional syllogism subjects could largely be explained by proposing that they tended to interpret their premises in a more restricted way than was intended by logic.

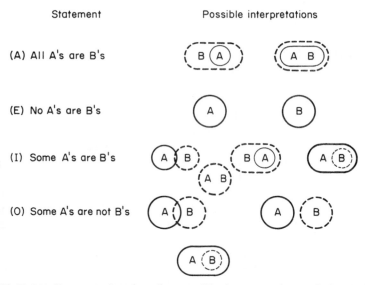

Fig. 5.1 Euler diagrams showing the possible interpretations of the traditional premises of syllogistic logic.

Even with the modified premises, some difficulties still arose, which seem to be related to the multiple possibilities that could follow from certain premise combinations. Subjects do not seem to completely analyse all the possible consequences of such premise combinations. Rather, they develop one *possible* consequence and adopt it as the conclusion. This leads to an over-restricted conclusion which is *consistent* with the premises but *not necessarily* true, e.g. from

All B are A,
All B are C

subjects tended to conclude 'All A are C' rather than the more general and correct deduction 'Some A are C'.

Ceraso and Provitera dub this an example of 'could be' reasoning. Wason and Johnson-Laird (1972) report other evidence supporting the notion of premise misinterpretation and incomplete analysis of consequences. They also suggest that when subjects have drawn a plausible, consistent conclusion they are reluctant to try to *falsify* it by, for example, checking whether the negative of the initial conclusion is also consistent with the premises.

B. Approaches based on set-theory

1 Erickson's Model

Erickson (1974, 1978) has also considered the problems of premise interpretation and inadequate analysis of proposed conclusions. He found consistent patterns of interpretations that held over large student samples drawn from four different universities. When subjects were asked to draw Euler diagrams corresponding to the statement 'All A are B', approximately 40 per cent of responses were in terms of a set identity interpretation while 60 per cent were in terms of a set inclusion interpretation (see Fig. 5.2).

These different interpretations would logically lead to different conclusions if they were used in syllogistic reasoning. Erickson (1978) focussed his research on 'AA' syllogisms, in which both premises are 'A' statements, i.e. affirmative universals. Since subjects were quite self-consistent and would tend to interpret all universal statements in the same way, he could then consider only identity–identity interpretations and inclusion–inclusion interpretations of the premises in AA syllogisms.

At this point we must consider an aspect of the structure of syllogisms that has been possible to ignore up to now. This aspect relates to the terms and their arrangement within the syllogism. A syllogism involves three terms

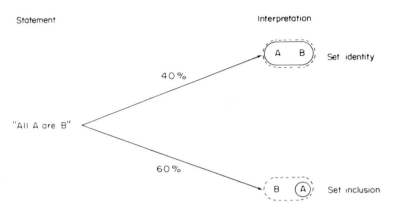

Statement   Interpretation

40%   Set identity

"All A are B"

60%   Set inclusion

Fig. 5.2 Distribution of interpretations given to the universal affirmative premise by Erickson's (1974) subjects.

(category or individual names). The premises state the relationships of one term (the middle term, M) to a predicate term (P) and to a subject term (S). A valid conclusion states the relationship that must hold between the S and the P terms. So, a typical example reads 'All M are P. All S are M. Therefore, all S are P' in accord with the tradition that the first statement relates M and P and the second relates S and M. Clearly, the order of the terms within each premise can be varied in two ways. Putting together the combinatorial possibilities for two premises yields four syllogistic patterns known as the four *figures* (see Table 5.1).

Erickson (1978) pointed out that the possible conclusions consistent with the premise interpretations of AA syllogisms differed over the four figures. Figure 5.3 illustrates the conclusions consistent with the figures. Note that only one conclusion follows from the identity–identity interpretation over all figures. When subjects were given Euler circles representing the different AA premise interpretations, their drawn Euler circles conclusions were generally consistent with the premises and showed reliable (and different) distributions over the possible conclusions for the four argument figures.

Table 5.1 Possible syllogistic figures

figure I	figure II	figure III	figure IV
M–P	P–M	M–P	P–M
S–M	S–M	M–S	M–S
S–P	S–P	S–P	S–P

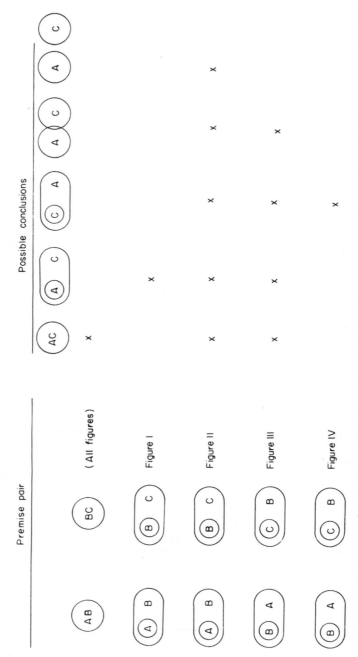

Fig. 5.3 Conclusions consistent with set identity and set inclusion interpretations of two universal affirmative premises. The consistent conclusions are marked 'X' for each syllogistic figure. Reproduced with permission from Erickson, J.R. (1978). Models of formal reasoning. In R. Revlin and R. Mayer (Eds), *Human reasoning*, p. 43. Washington, D.C.: V.H. Winston.

On the basis of (a) the estimated proportions of subjects making identity–identity and inclusion–inclusion interpretations, and (b) of the estimated proportions who would produce each alternative conclusion from each premise–premise interpretation, Erickson was able to predict very accurately the proportions of subjects who would draw each of the possible conclusions (A, E, I, O) to AA syllogisms in the four figures. The data from five independent studies were fitted very well by predictions based on the above analyses. Thus, there is a good measure of support for Erickson's model which proposes a three-stage process of (1) premise interpretation, (2) combination of interpreted premises to yield a conclusion, and (3) response formation depending on the conclusion and on the task demands (e.g. draw a diagram, give a verbal statement, select one from a list of alternatives, etc.). This analysis is quite consistent with Ceraso and Provitera's (1971) results which showed that disambiguated premises improved performance. Erickson's three-stage model would explain Ceraso and Provitera's results by assuming that correct interpretations at stage 1 were made more likely by the clarified premises.

2 The transitive-chain model

Guyote and Sternberg (1981) have proposed a rather complex model which, like Erickson's, assumes that subjects represent premises in set-theoretic terms. They draw a distinction between a "competence model" and a "performance model" of syllogistic reasoning. This is akin to the competence/performance distinction in psycholinguistic theory. In psycholinguistics, "competence" is the ability possessed by an idealized speaker of a language which, for example, permits that speaker to class sentences as grammatically acceptable or not; a performance model details why actual performance falls short of ideal performance, e.g. why spoken language is not always grammatically correct. Usually, constraints on processing, such as limited working memory, are invoked to explain departures from ideal competence. Similarly, Guyote and Sternberg first present an idealized competence model which would allow perfect performance on syllogistic tasks and then detail constraints on performance.

According to the competence model, subjects carry out two main steps when presented with premises and a list of alternative conclusions from which one must be selected. The two main steps are (a) encoding the premises, and (b) combining information in the premises.

In the encoding stage the category relationships between the terms in each premise are represented symbolically. Each possible interpretation of the two premises are made and given corresponding symbolic representations. Thus, unlike Erickson or Ceraso and Provitera, it is assumed that *all* possible interpretations are made. *All* combinations of the possible interpretations of the two premises are then considered, to determine what conclusions may follow. Note that since two premises of form "I" each have four possible interpretations, 16 combinations would have to be considered in such a case. The combination rules attempt to form "transitive chains" linking the "end" terms (subject and predicate) *via* the middle term of the syllogism.

The performance model involves stages of (a) encoding the premises, (b) combining information from the premises, (c) selecting a label to describe the combined representations (where the label is one of the four traditional statements, A,I,E,O or "no valid conclusion"), and (d) making a response on the basis of a match between the label and the conclusions offered for evaluation. The performance model assumes that the encoding stage is carried out completely and without error. In the combination stage it is assumed that errors can creep in because subjects are limited in the number of pairs of representations that they encode. It is assumed that the subject always combines at least one pair of representations but never combines more than four pairs (due to working memory limitations). The subject's choice of pairs to combine is based on simplicity. Simpler pairs are dealt with in preference to pairs involving more complex representation. In choosing a label for the combined representations, which represent possible inferences, subjects are assumed to be biased to 'strong' labels and to labels that match the 'atmosphere' of the premises (as defined by Begg and Denny, 1969). The 'stronger' a label, the less ambiguous is its interpretation in set-inclusion terms. Thus, the labels in order of strength are E,A,O and I.

In order to test their complex performance model, Guyote and Sternberg first expressed the model in mathematical terms and then assessed its fit to data from five studies. These studies involved a wide range of syllogistic problems varying in both form and content. The mathematical model required five parameters to be estimated from the data, but once these were obtained, it yielded a good fit to percentage correct scores and latencies over the problems used in the five studies. Indeed, their model gave better fits to the data than did mathematical versions of Erickson's model, although these had more parameters than Guyote and Sternberg's.

Despite good overall fits to data, the model suffers from the inherent implausibility of its assumptions regarding complete encoding (which are countered empirically by Ceraso and Provitera, 1971). Furthermore, as Johnson-Laird (1983) has pointed out, the model makes it impossible for subjects to reason, with understanding, when more than four premise combinations need to be considered before a correct conclusion can be drawn. Also, as we shall explain in the next section, there are certain effects ('figural effects') that this, and other set-theory based models, cannot explain.

Finally, it is worth noting an incidental observation of Guyote and Sternberg that subjects' scores on a test of spatial ability correlated considerably better with syllogistic reasoning performance than did scores on verbal ability. This suggests that some form of spatial representation is used in syllogistic reasoning (but, as the next section will indicate, it may not be in the form of 'mental Euler circles').

C. Mental-model approaches

1 Figural bias

A series of studies by Johnson-Laird and his colleagues (Johnson-Laird, 1975; Johnson-Laird and Steedman, 1978) has revealed an interesting effect due to the figure of the syllogism and this effect can be accounted for by models of syllogistic inference developed by Johnson-Laird. In the experiments in question, subjects had to draw conclusions from syllogistic premises dealing with concrete but uncontroversial matters, e.g. 'Some of the parents are scientists; all of the scientists are drivers; therefore . . .?' This particular form of syllogism (figure IV) tended to elicit the conclusion 'Some of the parents are drivers' rather than the equally valid 'Some of the drivers are parents.'

On the other hand, the premises 'Some of the scientists are parents; all of the drivers are scientists' (figure I) would tend to elicit the conclusion 'Some of the drivers are parents' rather than the also valid 'Some of the parents are drivers.' Indeed, throughout their experiments, premises of the form 'A–B; B–C' (i.e. figure IV) produced a bias towards conclusions of the form 'A–C' ('C–A' conclusions being also valid). This strong 'figural' effect had not been noticed hitherto, perhaps because of the widespread use of forced choice testing formats that would not include the unorthodox (from the classical point of view) conclusion 'A–C' to the 'A–B; B–C' syllogism. This conclusion, it should be explained, is unorthodox because it has taken the first premise as relating subject to middle term, while, traditionally, the first premise has related predicate to middle term. Johnson-Laird points out that traditionally 64 'moods' of syllogism were recognized, since the two premises and the conclusion have to be chosen from the four sentence moods (A, E, I, O) giving $4^3 = 64$ possibilities. Combining the 64 moods with the 4 figures (explained in a previous section) yields $64 \times 4 = 256$ different syllogistic structures. While this number had been taken for granted by psychologists, Johnson-Laird observed that one could in fact generate twice as many. Logicians had decided to arrange their syllogisms so that the subject of the conclusion always appeared in the second premise, but the logic of the argument is not really affected if the subject term (S) happens to appear in the first premise, as in:

S–M
M–P
———
S–P
c.f. traditional figure I,
M–P
S–M
———
S–P

It seems that the failure to consider all 512 possible syllogisms led to the figural bias effect remaining undiscovered until recently.

It is noteworthy that the figural bias effect is not predicted by previous approaches. The atmosphere hypothesis, the conversion and probabilistic inference hypothesis and Erickson's or Guyote and Sternberg's set-theoretic approaches are alike in failing to predict any effect of the order of occurrence of the major premise (relating middle term and predicate) and the minor premise (relating middle term and subject). In view of this and of other problems with the earlier approaches, Johnson-Laird and Steedman (1978) put forward a theory for syllogistic reasoning, initially known as the *analogical* theory. [A preliminary version was reported by Johnson-Laird (1975).]

2 The analogical model

The broad stages proposed by the theory are mostly similar to those suggested by other recent analyses (e.g. Erickson, 1978). They are (1) interpretation of premises, (2) an initial *heuristic* combination of the representations of the two premises, (3) the formulation of a conclusion corresponding to the combination of premises, and (4) a *logical test* (or series of tests) of the initial heuristic combination which may lead to the conclusion being modified or abandoned. In terms of broad stages, the main novelty is the provision of a final testing stage that can lead back to a changed combination of premises which in turn may be tested again. In terms of detail, an explicit information processing model has been developed that incorporates a number of distinctive ideas.

First, the premise representations are assumed to take the form of list structures. A clue to the possible use of list structure representations in this task came from one of the subjects' retrospections on how he had tackled the syllogisms. In connection with the premise "All the artists are beekeepers", he reported, ''I thought of all the little artists in the room and imagined that they all had beekeeper's hats on.'' This remark suggested the hypothesis that a class is represented by thinking of an arbitrary number of examples. So, to represent the above premise, the reasoner imagines an arbitrary number of artists and tags each of them as a beekeeper. Since the sets are not identical he should add an arbitrary number of beekeepers to the representation. The elements in the representation may be images, or verbal or abstract items; the important feature is the relationship between the elements, rather than the exact nature of the elements. The structure of the representation of the current example may be taken to have the form:

artist	artist	artist		
↓	↓	↓		
beekeeper	beekeeper	beekeeper	(beekeeper)	(beekeeper)

(The arrows represent the relationship 'is a'.) It is asserted that this representation is structurally analogous to what the reasoner thinks when he understands the sentence 'All artists are beekeepers.' The proposed representation is a list-structure and this has the advantage of being readily encodable in computer programming. In list-structure terms, each entry on the artist list has stored with it the address of a corresponding beekeeper on the beekeeper list and there are entries on the beekeeper list who are not connected to entries on the artist list. It is notable that such list-structure notions were also found useful by Simon and Hayes (1976) in their analyses of problem comprehension, discussed in Chapter 3.

Having fixed on a representation of the individual premises, the next step is to combine them in some way. Johnson-Laird proposes that there is a heuristic bias towards forming connections that link up all the classes if possible. So, given

All A are B	a		a		
	↓		↓		
	b		b		(b)
and					
Some B are C		b			(b)
		↓			
		c			(c)

these would be combined to yield the structure:

a	a	
↓	↓	
b	b	(b)
↓		
c	(c)	

This structure readily suggests the invalid conclusion 'Some a's are c's' (and this conclusion is often erroneously made).

To draw a conclusion the paths between end-terms must be considered. Taking the structure resulting from the initial combination of 'All A are B' and 'Some B are C' the paths would be labelled:

+	?	
a	a	
↓	↓	
b	b	(b)
↓		
c	(c)	

One path is positive and one indeterminate. (Negative paths can arise if the negative operators 'no' and 'not' occur in the premises. For the sake of simplicity negatives will not be considered here.) The path labelling of the above structure would lead to the (erroneous) conclusion 'some a are c', in accordance with the principle that "where there is at least one positive path the conclusion is of the form 'Some X are Y', unless there are only positive paths in which case it is of the form 'All X are Y'; in any other case no valid conclusion can be drawn".To avoid invalid conclusions, it is proposed that logical tests are applied to the combined representation in an attempt to remove links between end-items without damaging the correctness of the individual premise interpretations. In the example, "All the artists are beekeepers: Some of the beekeepers are chemists", the initial combined representation has an artist tagged as a beekeeper who in turn is tagged as a chemist. This particular beekeeper–chemist linkage can be broken without losing the initial meaning. The modified representation would not include any artist positively linked to any chemist. No conclusion could be drawn and the final overt answer would correctly so indicate.

The analogical theory, then, proposes a heuristic combination of premises to yield a tentative conclusion, followed by a logical testing process. Differences in persistence of testing preliminary conclusions could well lead to differences in the conclusions finally drawn by different individuals to the same premises.

The theory was expressed in the form of a computer program and its performance compared to that of human subjects on a set of 64 problems. With some syllogisms the process of testing does not lead to any modifications (hence thoroughness of testing does not matter). Such syllogisms were predicted to be easier than those to which the model would produce a modified conclusion after testing. This prediction was upheld (80.4 per cent correct on predicted 'easy' problems v. 46.5 per cent correct on others). Also, the model predicts the figural bias effect because the directionality of the linkages in the figures in question leads naturally to the particular ordering of terms most often observed in subjects' conclusions. Further support for the theory comes from responses to those premises that do not permit a valid conclusion to be drawn. Invalid syllogisms in figures I and IV, in which it is easy to form paths in the initial representation, are predicted to be more difficult than invalid syllogisms in the other figures. The predicted difference was upheld by 18 out of 20 subjects.

Although the original analogical model was more successful than previous analyses in coping with a wide range of results in syllogistic reasoning, certain new data, reported in the next section, have caused the analogical model to be considerably revised.

3 Figural bias: a process explanation?

Johnson-Laird and Steedman's (1978) analogical model explained figural bias as arising from biases in scanning the structures representing the combined premises. Another possibility, which was mentioned in passing in the 1978 paper, is that the figural effect arises from the process of combining the premise representations in working memory. That is, with the A–B, B–C premises, subjects can encode the first premise and then add on to it a representation of the second premise (A–B, B–C) with a resulting bias toward a conclusion of the form A–C. In the case of B–A, C–B premises, since the middle terms are not adjacent, it would be necessary to store the second premise in working memory first, then recall the first premise to make the combination (C–B, B–A), giving a bias toward C–A conclusions.

Johnson-Laird and Bara (1984) obtained relevant data from an experiment concerning conclusions given to syllogisms that were presented for brief exposures (10 seconds). Even with this short exposure there were clear figural effects; more significantly, however, there were unpredicted effects, due to the frequency of responses indicating 'no valid conclusion'. The A–B, B–C figure yielded the fewest such responses and the B–A, B–C figure produced the most. This result cannot be explained by Johnson-Laird and Steedman's (1978) analogical model, and so Johnson-Laird and Bara propose that the figural effect reflects the process of integrating premises within working memory. With short presentations subjects experience difficulty in effecting combinations of premises in certain figures and thus have a high rate of (incorrect) conclusions that 'no conclusion can be known'.

It has also been pointed out (Johnson-Laird, 1983; Johnson-Laird and Bara, 1984) that for certain syllogisms, two or three combined models of the premises are possible and that all the possible models must be considered before a correct conclusion can be drawn. Johnson-Laird (1983, p. 104) reports data from studies which find that the rate of drawing correct conclusions declined sharply as the number of possible combined models increased from one to three. These results are attributed to the load on working memory that is occasioned when more than one model must be constructed and evaluated.

II. SUMMARY AND CONCLUDING COMMENTS

From the evidence reviewed in this chapter, what answer can be given to the often raised question, "Do people think logically?" If the criterion of logical thinking is reaching conclusions consistent with those of formal logic then one must answer that people are not always logical reasoners. They do make errors. Indeed, according to one authority (Erickson, 1978, p. 41), 'in fact, for *most* syllogisms the modal response is incorrect'. However, the errors do not appear to be random and various suggestions have been made regarding the processes underlying both errors and correct responses.

A proposal of completely non-logical processing is embodied in the atmosphere hypothesis. This hypothesis is consistent with many typical responses to syllogistic tasks; however, it is 'over-inclusive' and is thus consistent with many possibilities that tend not to happen. Furthermore, it does not cope well with fine-grain effects, such as the figural bias effect or the often correct choice of 'no conclusion' by subjects. The atmosphere hypothesis always predicts that some conclusion can be drawn but, at least some of the time, people can appreciate that certain syllogisms are inconclusive. An alternative proposal is that various 'illogical' processes which have some plausibility may jointly produce many errors. In particular, illicit conversion of premises and probabilistic inference have been proposed by Chapman and Chapman (1959). However, the empirical evidence distinguishing this suggestion from the atmosphere hypothesis is not strong (Begg and Denny, 1969). Again, the figural bias effect and many fine-grain features of reasoning data are not dealt with by this hypothesis.

Henle (1962) put forward the very influential view that people *do* reason logically, but frequently misinterpret the premises or the task demands, thus producing overt errors. Indeed, Henle (1978, p. xviii) has gone so far as to say, "I have never found errors which could unambiguously be attributed to faulty reasoning." Unfortunately, this may reflect the difficulty, in principle, of obtaining falsifying evidence for the Henle position. No matter what response is given, a suitable interpretation of the premises (or task) can be inferred to make the response seem 'logical'. Clearly, some independent check on premise and task interpretation is required when considering individual examples. However, most research has involved the more indirect methods of group analysis. For example, Ceraso and Provitera (1971) showed that clarified, unambiguous premises led to many fewer errors than traditional ambiguous premises. This is consistent with Henle's position. Erickson (1974, 1978) proposed a specific form of 'Henle' model in which premise interpretation was assumed to take the form of mental Euler circles. Using the proportions of people in one group who interpreted universal affirmative (A) statements as set identity and as set inclusion, he was able to predict the obtained proportions of alternative conclusions to AA syllogisms, in the four different figures, for independent groups of subjects. Again, this result is consistent with the Henle approach. A stronger test would have been to compare the inferences of subjects classed as 'set-identity interpreters' with those of subjects classed as 'set-inclusion interpreters' of AA premises.

Guyote and Sternberg (1981) presented a more wide-ranging theory than Erickson's but which was also based on the notion of mental Euler diagrams. Complete and error-free premise interpretation was assumed. However, subjects were assumed to be constrained by working memory limits when combining premise interpretations; these limits were taken to underlie the relative difficulty of syllogisms. Although Guyote and Sternbergs "transitive chain theory" predicted performance well over a wide range of syllogisms, its assumptions of complete and perfect premise interpretation are implausible; furthermore, the theory cannot explain figural bias effects.

An alternative proposal is contained in Johnson-Laird's (1975, 1983; Johnson-Laird and Steedman, 1978; Johnson-Laird and Bara, 1984) analysis of reasoning in terms of mental models. In the 1984 model most of the individual variability in reasoning behaviour is not attributed to differences in the premise interpretation stage but to different degrees of thoroughness in constructing possible models of premise combinations. Differences in syllogism difficulty are explained in terms of the number of models required to represent the premise combinations. Figural bias effects are explained in terms of preferred ways of combining premise representations.

Overall, Johnson-Laird's mental model is the best specified, most broad-ranging and promising current approach. Furthermore, it readily relates to other studies of comprehension processes (e.g. Simon and Hayes, 1976; Johnson-Laird, 1983). By contrast, the other models tend to be purely focussed on syllogisms and lack obvious ways of connecting with other topics in the thinking area.

How might syllogistic reasoning relate to the processes of problem solving discussed in earlier chapters? On the surface, syllogistic tasks are well-defined and appear to require but one 'move' from a given starting state (the premises) to a goal state (a valid conclusion). However, from the review in this chapter, a variety of processes seem to be involved. First, as in all problems, the starting state has to be defined by the subject. In dealing with syllogisms, this is the process of premise interpretation. Since premises are frequently ambiguous, alternative interpretations are often possible, though it would appear that only one interpretation is considered at a time, i.e. a serial search among interpretation possibilities is undertaken. Indeed, it often seems that only one interpretation is derived (Erickson, 1974). Once an interpretation of the premises has been made, by using general procedures presumably stored in long-term memory, more than one conclusion might often be drawn (e.g. 'strong' or 'weak' conclusions). According to Johnson-Laird's (1983) analysis, it seems that rather lax 'evaluation functions' are often used to determine whether a possible conclusion is valid or not. There seems to be a tendency to accept conclusions that are *consistent* with the premises, but which are not required by them. To the extent that there is a search among alternative conclusions, it seems to be a serial search. Frequently, however, it seems that if the first conclusion drawn is acceptable to the subject, then alternatives are not generated.

There is nothing in the syllogistic reasoning data to counter the view that, when problem solving, we work as limited-capacity, slow, serial processors of information. Indeed, recent analyses (Guyote and Sternberg, 1981; Johnson-Laird, 1983) have particularly stressed the role of working memory limitations in syllogistic reasoning.

III. FURTHER READING

Henle, M. (1962). On the relation between logic and thinking. *Psychological Review* **69**, 366–378. This very readable paper contains Mary Henle's classic statement in defence of human rationality. Much later research can be seen as amplifying or reacting against her position.

Johnson-Laird, P.N. (1983). *Mental models*. Cambridge: Cambridge University Press. This is a very full and thorough exposition of Johnson-Laird's mental models approach to reasoning and language processing.

6
Inductive reasoning

In the last chapter we considered studies of deductive inference from statements (premises) that were to be taken as true. Somewhat different but related tasks arise when one has to test statements (hypotheses) for truth against external data. Detectives and scientists, for instance, constantly face the inductive problem of deciding whether certain hypotheses are true or false. A possible general approach is to follow the 'hypothetico-deductive' method. In this technique, implications are deduced from the hypothesis and are then checked empirically for truth or falsity. If the implications of the hypothesis turn out to be true, then the hypothesis is supported, otherwise it can be rejected – on the grounds that if validly drawn inferences from the hypothesis lead to empirically false conclusions then the hypothesis must be false. Whether the apparently simple prescription embodied in the hypothetico-deductive method is descriptive of behaviour in the face of inductive problems has been the topic of numerous studies, a selection of which will be considered in this chapter. Our review will start with tasks in which people are *given* both some particular hypothesis to test and sources of potentially relevant data. Next, we will discuss a range of more complicated tasks in which people are required to both *generate* and *test* their own hypotheses. The hypothesis testing behaviour of scientists in real life will be considered in the final section.

I. THE FOUR-CARD SELECTION PROBLEM

Wason (1966, 1968) devised the following deceptively simple paradigm in which to explore hypothetico-deductive reasoning. Suppose you are given four cards showing:

E	K	4	7

Each card has a letter on one side and a number on the other. Your task is to name the cards which *need* to be turned over to test the following statement:

"If a card has a vowel on one side, then it has an even number on the other side." You may find it instructive to pause here and decide on your answer before reading on.

By far the most common answers are wrong. Why they are wrong, and what the correct answer is, should become clearer with the aid of a more concrete example. Take the statement 'Paper ignites at 481°F.' If we had a furnace set at 481°F we could test this proposed rule by inserting samples of paper and noting whether they ignite or not. A difficulty arises, however, in that no matter how many different samples of paper conform to the rule there could always be as yet untried papers that would not. Thus, no matter how many 'positives' are recorded, the rule can never be absolutely verified; but, it would be *falsified* if just one sample failed to ignite at 481°F. This is a general characteristic of such universal hypotheses and the example should alert us to the need to consider *potentially falsifying* data as well as potentially supporting data in testing proposed rules. Suppose now that a study was conducted on what sorts of things ignite at 481°F and that four cards are available representing four individual experiments. On one side of each card is listed the type of material put into the furnace and on the other side, whether it burned or not. Which of the four cards below would have to be turned over to test the hypothesis 'If it is paper, it will ignite at 481°F'.

| Paper | Plastic | Burned | Did not burn |

Clearly we must look at the 'Paper' card to see if it burned or not. The 'Plastic' card can be ignored as irrelevant. Surprisingly, perhaps, the 'Burned' card need not be turned over. Once we know that the material burned, whether the material was paper or not does not affect the status of the hypothesis. No information regarding the hypothesis could be gained by turning over the 'Burned' card and so it should be left untouched. The 'Did not burn' card should definitely be turned over, since it would be falsifying if 'Paper' were on the other side.

Similarly, in the abstract version, i.e. 'If vowel on one side, then even number on the other side', the cards showing 'E' and '7' should be examined because they are potentially falsifying. The '4' and the 'K' cards may be left unturned since the truth of the hypothesis would not be affected no matter what is on their other sides.

The kind of rule involved in the four-card task has been used extensively in studies of hypothesis testing. Before reviewing the empirical research, we should briefly examine the logic of such rules in a little more detail. The rules are of the abstract form, 'If p, then q', and are known as 'conditionals' or 'implication' rules. In propositional logic there are two main valid inference patterns involving such rules and two main fallacies. These are shown in

Table 6.1 Valid and fallacious inferences based on implication

Valid inferences			Fallacious inferences		
1.	(Modus ponens)	if p, then q p $\overline{}$ ∴ q	1.	(Denying the antecedent)	if p, then q p̄ $\overline{}$ ∴ q̄
2.	(Modus tollens)	if p, then q q̄ $\overline{}$ ∴ p̄	2.	(Affirming the consequent)	if p, then q q $\overline{}$ ∴ p
					(p̄ = not p)

Table 6.1. Note that a bar over a letter means 'not', so that q̄ is to be read as 'not q'.

Another way of thinking about the implication rule is to consider how its truth or falsity varies as a function of the truth of the component terms. The two terms in the rule can be independently true or false, yielding four combinations. The rule's status given these combinations is represented in Table 6.2, which shows the 'truth table' for implication.

A. Basic results

In testing a rule of the form 'if p then q', there are four possible cases that might arise, viz. pq, pq̄, p̄q and p̄q̄. (Remember q̄ is to be read as 'not q'). In logic, only the second case (pq̄) is inconsistent with the rule while the remainder are consistent (see Table 6.2).

When subjects are given a conditional rule to test and the opportunity to observe what is paired with cases of p, q, p̄, q̄ in the four-card task, they almost always select the cards showing p and q, rather than the logically correct p and q̄ cards. The results of four typical studies by Wason and colleagues are given in Table 6.3. One way to describe these results is to say

Table 6.2 Truth table for implication

p	→	q
T	T	T
T	F	F
F	T	T
F	T	F

T = True; F = false; → = 'implies', or 'if . . . then'.

Table 6.3 Results from four experiments on the four-card selection task[a]

Selection	Frequency
pq	59
p	42
ppq̄	9
pq̄	5
Others	13
	N = 128

[a] From Johnson-Laird and Wason (1970). A theoretical analysis of insight into a reasoning task. *Cognitive Psychology* **1**, 134–148. Reprinted by permission.

that subjects are 'set' for verification and so choose the potentially verifying cards (p, q) and ignore the potentially falsifying card (q̄). (Note: p is potentially falsifying as well as verifying.)

Subjects generally recognize the q̄ card falsifies the rule if the q̄ card is turned over to reveal p – but they rarely examine it spontaneously.

B. Procedural variations

Wason and others examined a number of procedural variables in an attempt to locate the sources of difficulty in this task. For example, in one study (Wason, 1969), the task materials were made strictly binary – with only two possible letters and numbers – but this had no effect. Thus the source of the difficulty was not confusion induced by the sheer number of possibilities in the 'vowel–even number' cards.

It was suggested that subjects might have been confused by the expression 'the other side of the card' and might have misinterpreted this to mean 'the side face downward'. Wason and Johnson-Laird (1970), therefore, presented subjects with cards that had all the information on one side and used masks to hide the appropriate part of the card. Again, no facilitation occurred. Goodwin and Wason (1972) made a duplicate set of fully revealed cards available to subjects while they performed the task with equivalent partially masked cards. The fully revealed cards could serve as aids to memory or imagery in solving the problem. This had a slight but non-significant beneficial effect on choice of the q̄ card. But most subjects still chose the q card.

Perhaps the apparent 'set' for verification could be broken by instructions which emphasize falsification? However, Wason (1968) found that instructions to pick cards which 'could break the rule' did not enhance performance.

Perhaps more familiarity is required with the rule? Wason and Shapiro (1971) trained subjects to construct or evaluate instances of the four types of cards (pq, pq̄, p̄q, p̄q̄) for 24 trials in relation to a given rule. They were then given the selection task with four more partially concealed cards in relation to the same rule. The 'construction' group did a little better than normal, while the 'evaluation' group showed averagely poor performance. However, the difference between the groups was not significant.

A more successful method of rule familiarization was devised by Legrenzi (1971). He first gave subjects instances of four types of cards. The cards had a triangle or a circle on their left and right half. The cards were clearly marked as ' + ' or ' – ' and the subjects had to express a rule in their own words to describe the assignment of cards to the ' + ' and ' – ' categories. They were given partially covered cards and asked which ones should be uncovered to test the rule. The 'rule discovery' subjects were compared with 'yoked' subjects presented with the discovered rules and the selection task. The 'rule discovery' subjects performed very significantly better than the controls.

Interestingly, the rules 'induced' by the experimental subjects were rarely in the form of *conditional* sentences – but were more usually in terms of 'either . . . or', e.g. 'circle on right or two triangles together' instead of 'if circle on left, then circle on right'. In a second study subjects were required to find a rule of the form 'if . . . then' that fitted the figures. Again, rule discovery subjects did very much better on a selection task than control subjects simply given the rule.

Performance on reasoning tasks is often improved by concrete material. The task of testing conditional rules does not seem to be an exception. Wason and Shapiro (1971) found considerable improvement when the task was presented in terms of four journeys. The four cards were said to represent journeys, with names of towns (destinations) on one side and modes of transport on the other. Subjects were given cards marked, face up, as follows:

| Manchester | Car | Train | Leeds |

and were told that the cards represented journeys made by the experimenter. The proposed rule to be tested was 'Every time I go to Manchester, I go by train.' (*Answer*: turn over 'Manchester' and 'Car' cards.)

Subsequent analyses of this thematic effect by Gilhooly and Falconer (1974) and by Bracewell and Hidi (1974), indicated that the concreteness of the terms and the presence or absence of a concrete relationship contributed separately to improving performance on the task. [Despite this early accumulation of data in favour of the thematic effect, it should be noted that Manktelow and Evans (1979) failed to replicate many of the relevant results and thus cast some doubt on the strength of the effect.]

Further facilitation of performance was reported when the task was made very lifelike and concrete by Johnson-Laird *et al*. (1972). Subjects were asked to imagine that they worked in the Post Office, sorting letters. Their task was to discover whether the following rule had been violated.

'If a letter is sealed, then it has a 5d. stamp on it.' Envelopes were provided either sealed or not and bearing either a 4d. stamp or a 5d. stamp on their side that was showing. A parallel abstract condition had the following rule: 'If an envelope has a D on one side, then it has a 5 on the other side.' Again, suitable envelopes were provided to test the rule. A total of 24 subjects were given both tasks in a balanced order. Of these, 22 were correct in the concrete condition, and only 2 were correct in the abstract condition. Surprisingly, perhaps, there was no transfer from the concrete to the abstract form of the task.

In the context of rules using realistic material, Van Duyne (1974) found a high success rate when the rule was known to be false (e.g. 'If a student studies philosophy, then he is at Cambridge'). Further, in a later study (Van Duyne, 1976), more logical reasoning was obtained with rules that the subjects believed to be 'sometimes true' as against 'always true' (an example of the latter case is, 'If it is glucose then it is sweet'). Pollard and Evans (1981) extended this to include rules thought to be 'usually false' and 'always false' and found that perceived falsity had a significant effect on response frequencies in the direction of better (i.e. falsifying) performance.

In sum, it appeared from these early studies that the main facilitating effects on selection task performance were those of (a) using realistic material, (b) allowing rule familiarization through discovery learning, and (c) using rules of dubious truth value.

C. 'Insight' model

Wason tried to induce 'insight' into the task by means of post-task discussions or 'confrontations'. When subjects made a wrong selection they were asked to consider the q̄ card. Could it be relevant? Could it falsify? It was pointed out that it might have p on the other side. What then? Subjects were shown the reverse of the q̄ card (p) and asked if the rule still held.

On the basis of such 'dialogues', Johnson-Laird and Wason (1970) proposed a model for insight into the task. They proposed three levels of insight. First, there is the level of no insight, in which the person is fixated on verification and chooses p or p and q (depending on whether he thinks the rule is reversible or not). The second level, partial insight, is obtained when it is realized that potentially falsifying cards should be examined as well as potentially verifying cards. This leads to a choice of p, q and q̄. The third level, complete insight, consists in realizing that only cards which could falsify should be selected, i.e. p and q̄.

Some evidence in support of the 'insight' model was obtained from studies in which subjects wrote down their reasons for selecting or not selecting each card (Goodwin and Wason, 1972). These results were claimed to provide independent support for the model in that the choices were justified by reasons consistent with the insight model.

The 'insight' model explains errors partly in terms of misinterpretation of the rule as reversible, but mainly in terms of failure to appreciate the importance of potentially falsifying information in rule testing. Two main types of alternative explanations have subsequently been put forward. The first type focusses on the ambiguities of the task and essentially follows a similar line to that taken by Henle *et al*. in connection with syllogistic reasoning. The second type proposes an 'atmosphere-like' explanation known as the 'matching bias' hypothesis. This supposes that people have a tendency to simply select cards that match the terms mentioned in the rule. These alternatives will be discussed in the following sections.

D. Interpretation factors

A number of investigators have pointed to ambiguities in the standard four-card task. Typical patterns of performance on the task might be explained in terms of people making interpretations different from that intended, but reasoning correctly on their interpretations.

Smalley (1974) distinguished three sources of ambiguity.

(1) Is the rule 'reversible' or not? That is, does $p \rightarrow q$ also mean $q \rightarrow p$ or not?
(2) Does the rule refer to both sides of the card or just to the showing side?
(3) Is the task one of verification, falsification or both? Putting together these ambiguities leads to $(2 \times 2 \times 3) = 12$ possible interpretations of the task. These 12 interpretations logically require certain patterns of card selection. Smalley showed that such interpretations occurred and that his subjects' choices were consistent with their interpretations.

Bracewell (1974) gave some subjects a 'clarified' statement of the task (cf. Ceraso and Provitera's syllogism experiment discussed in Chapter 4). The rule was given as follows:

If either the showing face or the underside face of the card has a J on it then 2 is on the remaining face. This hypothesis should not be interpreted to mean that 2 only occurs with J.

Please indicate the card or cards it is necessary to examine in order to see if the above hypothesis is false.

The success rate with clarified instructions (7/12) was much higher than that obtained with standard instructions (1/12).

The beneficial effects of realistic material would be attributed, on the 'interpretation' view, to reductions in ambiguity with such material. A rule, such as "If I go to London, I go by car', is unlikely to be interpreted as reversible (i.e. as implying 'If I go by car, I go to London') because the reversed version is implausible. No such plausibility checks would prevent reversal of an abstract rule. In the 'Post Office' variant, the nature of the task – to seek potentially falsifying information – fits the thematic structure and so makes the task less ambiguous.

The interpretation approach was strongly criticized by Evans and his colleagues, and they put forward a collection of interesting, if somewhat loosely linked, ideas that constituted a radical alternative to previous approaches. This work will be discussed in the following section.

E. 'Matching bias'

Evans (1984; Evans and Lynch, 1973; Wason and Evans, 1975) has put forward the view that, in the abstract version of the selection task, most people simply select the cards showing the symbols mentioned in the rule, i.e. the responses match the input and no 'deeper' processing is involved. One main source of evidence for this view is the finding that with a negative form of the rule ('If B on one side, there will not be 3 on the other') the success rate is very high. Most subjects choose the 'B' card and the '3' card. Wason and Johnson-Laird's "insight" model would predict selection of 'B' and the 'not 3' card by naive subjects working under a verification set.

Interestingly, when subjects are given both the negative form of rule and the affirmative form of rule in succession, they tend to be correct on the negative and wrong on the affirmative. Furthermore, they give 'verification' reasons in the negative case. Evans argues that the reasons given are often *post hoc* rationalizations and that behaviour in this task is actually determined by an unconscious matching bias. The 'matching bias' proposal is clearly reminiscent of the 'atmosphere' hypothesis in syllogistic reasoning.

Evans (1980a; Evans and Wason, 1976) argues that the data on card selection and justification of selections may be explained in terms of two modes of thought labelled "Type I" and "Type II". Type I processes are conceived to be non-verbal and non-introspectible (and it seems to be suggested, non-logical), whereas Type II processes are verbal and apparently 'rational'.

If responses are made on the basis of a Type I process, and the subjects are asked 'why did you do that', it is proposed that they will generate rationalizations, using Type II processes to do so. As Evans (1980a, p. 235) points out, "The 'rationalization' itself is a form of reasoning: the subject asks, in effect, 'Given the structure of the problem and the instructions, what reason could I have had for the response I made?' " Consistent with this approach, Evans and Wason (1976) found that when subjects were asked to justify various answers presented to them as being "correct solutions" to the selection task, they confidently gave reasons for accepting all the answers, including wrong answers. Thus, it is possible in the normal selection task that responses are made on a basis unknown to the subjects, but that they can construct reasons (rationalizations) for their responses if asked. This demonstration by Evans and Wason seriously undermines Goodwin and Wason's (1972) arguments, in favour of the 'insight' model, which were based on subjects' justifications of their choices. The Goodwin and Wason analysis assumed that 'reasons' preceded and produced responses, while Evans' analysis and data suggest the reverse order.

More recently, Evans (1984) has extended the notion of Type I and II processes and has developed the concepts of "heuristic" and "analytic" processes in reasoning. By "heuristic" processes are meant pre-attentive processes that select items from the problem presentation for attention; "analytic" processes can then operate to draw inferences (not necessarily by means of logical rules). In this approach, typical selection task performance is explained by "heuristic" processes that select the matching cards as relevant. "Analytic" processes do not normally come into play in this task, unless justifications are required.

F. Memory-cueing accounts

The rule that Johnson-Laird et al. (1972) used in their 'postal' study was a rule current in real life and so was well-known to their subjects at the time of the experiment. However, the rule ceased to be operative some years ago and more recent studies, using young adult subjects, have failed to find facilitating effects of the postal rule condition compared to the abstract condition (Griggs and Cox, 1982). Thus, it is possible that prior experience of specific counter-examples facilitates performance. Subjects for whom the rule was a real everyday rule would, because of their prior experience, be more likely to think of possible counter-examples than would be subjects to whom the rule was an arbitrary laboratory invention.

Griggs and Cox (1982) found a similar effect to that of Johnson-Laird et al.'s 'postal study' in an experiment involving the rule governing the legal drinking age in Florida (where the experiment was conducted). Subjects were to imagine they were police officers and they were to ensure that the regulation "If a person is drinking beer, then the person must be over 19" was being followed. Four cards contained information about four people: on one side of each card was the person's age, and on the other side what they were drinking. Face-up the subjects saw the cards showing '16 years of age', '22 years of age', 'Drinking beer', 'Drinking coke'. The task was to turn over the cards that definitely needed to be turned over to determine whether the rule was being violated. Correct selections were made by 74.1 per cent of subjects. As with the postal task, a memory-cueing explanation was suggested.

A slightly different explanation seems to be called for for the task variant devised by D'Andrade (see Rumelhart, 1980). In this version, subjects imagine that they are managers in a store (Sears) and are responsible for checking sales receipts to determine whether the rule "If a purchase exceeds $30, then the receipt must be approved by the department manager" has been followed. If approved, the receipt is signed on the back. Four receipts are shown: one for $15, one for $45, one signed and one not signed. D'Andrade found approximately 70 per cent correct choices in this task. These results have been replicated by Griggs and Cox (1983). However, since none of the subjects had been Sears store managers, performance facilitation could not be due to specific memory-cueing but may reflect experience with analogous materials, e.g. perhaps as customers having receipts authorized or not.

G. Pragmatic reasoning schemata

It is a reasonable conclusion from the low levels of performance typical with abstract versions of the conditional rule testing task, that subjects do not bring to bear formal 'syntactic' rules of logical implication in these tasks. Data outlined in the preceding section raise the possibility of specific memory cueing. A third possibility has been developed recently by Cheng and Holyoak's (1985) work on the notion of *pragmatic reasoning schemata*. Such schemata are quite abstract rule systems, in that they apply to a wide range of contents, but are not so wide and abstract as syntactic, logical rules. A relevant schema in the context of the four-card problem is the 'permission schema'. The core content of the permission schema is, "If one is to do X, then one must satisfy precondition Y."

Cheng and Holyoak examined the possible role of the permission schema in the following study. Subjects in Hong Kong and Michigan were instructed in a problem about checking passengers' forms at an airport. The rule to be checked was "If the form says 'ENTERING' on one side, then the other side includes Cholera among the list of diseases." Four cases corresponding to p, q, not −p, and not −q were available for examination. Half the subjects were given a rationale for the 'cholera' rule by being told that the form listed diseases for which the passenger had been inoculated and that a cholera inoculation was needed to protect the entering passengers from the disease. It was expected that this explanation would invoke the 'permission schema' (which matches closely the logic of the conditional). The expectation was justified in that both the Hong Kong and Michigan subjects showed a marked increase in correct performance when given the rationale. This result is not consistent with the memory-cueing explanation since subjects did not have relevant memories; nor is it consistent with the syntactic rule view, since the logical structure of the task is not affected by the rationale. The result is, however, consistent with the pragmatic reasoning schema approach.

Cheng and Holyoak (1985) found further facilitating results of permission schemata when subjects were given an abstract version of the selection task in which the rule to be tested was based on the permission schema ("If one is to take action A, then one must satisfy precondition P"). The abstract description was apparently sufficient to evoke the permission schema and so facilitate solution.

II. GENERATING AND TESTING HYPOTHESES

In studies of conditional rule testing, such as those discussed above, subjects are *given* a rule and possible evidence which may or may not support or disconfirm the rule. Usually, in real-life research, one is not given a rule but must generate possible rules (hypotheses) which can then be tested.

The processes of generating and testing self-produced hypotheses have been subject to laboratory investigation in a number of ways. The three main approaches have involved the study of (1) concept learning tasks, (2) Wason's 'reversed 20 questions' task, and (3) most realistically, performance in simulated research environments. As we shall see, somewhat similar points seem to emerge from these different lines of research.

A. Concept identification

In a concept identification task, a collection of stimuli have been classified by the experimenter into two or more categories on the basis of some rule. It is the subject's task to induce the rule on the basis of information about the category membership of individual stimuli. Normally, the stimuli are constructed by combining values on a small number of dimensions (e.g.

colour: red/blue; *shape*: square/triangle; *size*: large/small). Information can be made available to the subject in two main ways. Either the stimuli and their classifications are presented to the subject in an order determined by the experimenter (reception paradigm) or the whole stimulus array is available and the subject chooses the stimuli to be informed about (selection paradigm).

As Bruner *et al.* (1956) put it, in their classic study, in the reception paradigm the subject is like a researcher on the effects of human brain damage on language. He must wait for accident cases to turn up and these may not arrive in the 'best' sequence. In the selection paradigm, the subject is more in the position of a researcher on brain areas underlying pattern vision in monkeys. Such a researcher can choose which areas to remove in each study and can devise an optimum sequence of tests. Similarly, the selection paradigm subject can choose an optimum sequence of stimuli about which to receive classification information.

Bruner *et al.* had their subjects write down their hypotheses after each trial (stimulus followed by feedback on the correct answer) in reception paradigm studies. They found that people had difficulty in handling correctly information that falsified their current hypotheses. This was true whether their initial hypotheses were complex (based on all attributes) or simple (based on one or two attributes). In the selection paradigm, two main types of strategy were identified, viz. focussing or scanning. Focussers took a particular instance which was a positive example of the experimenter's rule and sought out stimuli that differed in just one attribute from the 'focus'. If the new stimulus was still 'positive', then the changed attribute was irrelevant and could be ignored; if the new stimulus was 'negative', then the changed attribute was at least part of the answer and should be held constant when choosing a further stimulus to test. The focusser could thus narrow down to the correct set of attributes with little strain on memory or inference. The scanning approach was less efficient and produced information relevant to the question of verification bias. Scanners essentially picked on a particular hypothesis (e.g. '2 squares') and sought to test it against instances until it was falsified, whereupon another hypothesis would be selected. It was noticeable that subjects tended to pick stimuli that could verify their hypothesis rather than stimuli that could falsify it. For example, if the subject's hypothesis was 'red squares', he or she tended to enquire about red square stimuli – rather than checking green squares or red circles. (All red squares may be + , but the rule could be 'red' alone or 'square' alone or 'red *or* square', rather than 'red *and* square'.) Further evidence of 'verification bias' will be discussed below.

It should be mentioned that Bruner *et al.*'s (1956) pioneering work on the concept identification paradigm led to a flood of experiments over the following 20 years or so, particularly on the effects of varying parameters of the reception task. This work (e.g. Bourne, 1966) tended to focus on the overall effects of task variations on learning speeds rather than on particular theories of inference.

Recently, there has been considerable interest in more 'naturalistic' forms of concept learning, using less stylized stimuli. Such work tends to implicate unconscious learning and generalization processes (e.g. McClelland and Rumelhart, 1985) rather than the deliberate forms of inductive reasoning that are the focus of this chapter. Thus, the topic of concept learning has rather dropped out from the study of reasoning in current cognitive psychology.

B. Wason's reversed 20 questions task

Wason devised a special task in which subjects tend to generate over-restrictive hypotheses of the sort that would lead astray a scanner with verifying tendencies. Subjects were given three numbers (2, 4, 6) and told that these conformed to a rule which they had to discover. The means of discovery was to be by generating other three-number series that might match the rule or not. The experimenter gave feedback on each triple produced by a subject. Subjects were asked to announce their rule when they were highly confident that it was the correct answer. The correct rule was 'numbers in increasing order of magnitude'. As you might expect, subjects stuck to more restrictive hypotheses, e.g. 'intervals of 2 between increasing numbers', 'arithmetic series'. However, the main interest lay in *how* subjects tested their hypotheses. The overwhelming tendency (Wason, 1960) was for subjects simply to generate series *consistent* with their particular hypothesis and to keep on doing so until they felt sufficiently confident to announce their hypothesis as correct. Few subjects either tried out series that ran counter to their own hypotheses or spontaneously varied their hypotheses. About 20 per cent of subjects discovered the rule without any incorrect announcements, and these people had tended to vary their hypotheses spontaneously. Very little evidence was found for a falsification strategy.

A number of task variations were attempted – with little effect. The material was varied from 'numbers' to a task in which the subject is given an instance of some very general class (e.g. 'microphone' as an instance of the class 'inanimate objects') and is instructed to find the class by trying out other possible instances.

This modification was ineffective in changing the prevalent 'verifying' strategy. Instructions to discover all the rules which *could* be correct had no effect. Also, imposing a charge of 12.5 pence for each incorrect rule announcement made subjects more cautious about claiming to know the answer but did not affect the bias toward verification.

Gorman *et al.* (1984) found that training on a disconfirmatory strategy markedly improved performance (15/16 solved), relative to training on a confirmatory strategy (6/16 solved). Tukey (1986) argues that subjects in this task, without special instructions in 'ideal' methodologies, nevertheless behave in ways that are rational in terms of various alternative philosophies of science. The stress on falsification in many studies of inductive reasoning is derived from Popper's (1959) analysis of scientific method. Tukey points to alternative accounts of scientific inquiry by, for example, Mill (1875/1967), Lakatos (1970), Kuhn (1970) and Bayesian theorists (Hesse, 1975). Subjects were asked during the task to describe their procedures, to select from a list of terms those that best characterized their methods and to state their preferred hypotheses and their judgements of how likely their hypotheses were to be correct. Subjects had difficulty describing their methods of approach, but they could use the methodology terms in ways that were consistent with their performance. It emerged that subjects were not always testing particular hypotheses on each trial, but would quite often be examining instances 'at random' or just because they were 'different'. Certainly, subjects rarely reported attempting to 'disconfirm' their hypotheses. Attempts to confirm and to simply explore accounted for over half the trials according to the labels given the trials by the subjects. Overall, Tukey's study indicates that a rather narrow view based on the Popperian philosophy of science, was possibly applied to this task hitherto. When alternative philosophies are considered, much of the subjects' behaviour seems more rational and intelligible.

C. Simulated research environments

Although philosophers of science tend to stress the importance of falsification (Popper, 1959) and of considering more than one hypothesis at a time (Platt, 1964), the results of Wason and of Bruner *et al.* (1956) discussed above, suggest that naive subjects tend neither to consider alternative hypotheses nor to seek out potentially falsifying data. Studies by Mynatt *et al.* (1977, 1978) sought to investigate such tendencies in complex environments that are intended to simulate real-life research.

In the study, subjects saw computer-generated displays on a screen (see Fig. 6.1) showing various shapes (circles, squares, triangles) of varying degrees of brightness (dim or bright). A "particle" could be fired across the screen (from a fixed position) in any direction, and it would be stopped when it approached some objects but not others. The subjects' overall task was to produce a hypothesis that would account for the behaviour of the particle. The correct answer was that the particle stopped on approaching dim shapes.

Input particle direction ?

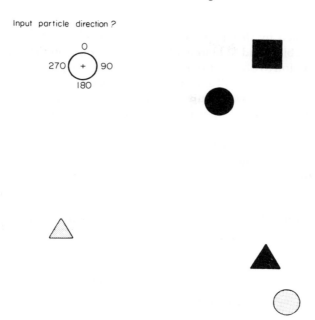

Fig. 6.1 Type of display used in study of confirmation bias. Textured features had 0.5 brightness levels. 'Particles' were fired from the grid in the upper-left of the screen. The subject controlled the direction of the particle's motion. Reproduced with permission from Mynatt, C.R., Doherty, M.E. and Tweney, R.D. (1977). Confirmation bias in a simulated research environment: An experimental study of scientific inference. *Quarterly Journal of Experimental Psychology* **29**, 85–95.

At first, subjects were allowed to formulate an initial hypothesis on the basis of the particle's behaviour with one particular configuration of objects (a configuration that favoured adoption of a wrong hypothesis in terms of object shape). They then chose between pairs of environments, in one of which they could make observations which would probably confirm the typical wrong hypothesis and in the other of which they would test alternative hypotheses. Evidence for a confirmation bias, involving failure to choose environments allowing tests of alternative hypotheses, was found. However, if subjects did obtain explicit falsifying information, they generally used this information to reject incorrect hypotheses. Behaviour in this task was not affected by instructions stressing confirmation or disconfirmation.

In Mynatt *et al.*'s (1978) study, subjects were allowed 10 hours to explore a very complex environment of 27 objects, varying in shape, size and brightness, in which particles were deflected on approaching objects. The angles of deflection were governed by a formula involving parameters whose values were determined by the shape, size and brightness of the objects. No one solved the problem and Mynatt *et al.* inferred a 'confirmation bias' from the subjects' reaction to observations that falsified their hypotheses but the interpretation of these results (Table 6.4) is debatable.

Mynatt *et al.* had two groups of subjects. One group was instructed in Platt's 'strong inference' approach to scientific methodology (this emphasizes developing and testing alternative hypotheses, especially with a view to falsification), and a control group received no special instructions about scientific research strategy. No major differences emerged between the two groups' patterns of results and, therefore, I have merged the data from the two groups in Table 6.4.

Table 6.4 Summary of reactions to hypothesis disconfirmation.

	Results of hypothesis tests	Cases	
		N	%
Responses	Permanently abandoned hypothesis	26	(30)
following	Temporarily abandoned hypothesis	11	(13)
disconfirmation	Revised hypothesis and retested	33	(37)
(*N* = 88)	Retested hypotheses without revision	18	(20)
		88	(100)

From Mynatt *et al.* (1978). Consequences of confirmation and disconfirmation in a simulated research environment. *Quarterly Journal of Experimental Psychology* **30**, 395–406. Reprinted by permission.

When falsifying data were obtained the subjects either abandoned or revised their hypotheses 67 per cent of the time. On 33 per cent of occasions the falsifying data do seem to have been discounted either immediately or after a delay during which forgetting could have intervened. So, if we allow hypothesis *revision* (as well as abandonment) to be a reasonable reaction to data that disconfirm a particular hypothesis, then subjects reacted in some appropriate way to 67 per cent of falsifications. It seems unfair, on these data, to class the majority of subjects as showing 'a strong tendency to discount or disregard falsification' (Mynatt *et al.*, 1978, p. 400). However, it was clear from the subjects' thinking aloud records that deliberate attempts to falsify their own hypotheses almost never occurred. There was an overwhelming tendency to seek confirming data, but the subjects in the 1978 study do seem to have reacted appropriately, on the whole, to the occurrence of disconfirming evidence. Perhaps because the environment was much more complex in the 1978 study there was less tendency to reject disconfirmed hypotheses totally and more of a tendency to modify than was evident in the 1977 results.

D. Real research environments

Studies of real-life hypothesis testing in the sciences (Chalmers, 1978; Mitroff, 1974) are consistent with laboratory studies in that scientists do not seem overly disposed to seek falsifying data or to accept that favoured theories require revision or abandonment in the face of apparently falsifying results.

For example, Galileo ignored much data that was apparently inconsistent with Copernican theory and protagonists of Newton's theory did not abandon it in view of the 'misbehaviour' of certain planets, such as Uranus. The typical reaction to observations inconsistent with a favoured theory is to seek an explanation that preserves the theory. In the case of Uranus's orbit a new undiscovered planet was postulated and in due course the theory received spectacular support from the discovery of Neptune in the predicted place. Other anomalies in Newtonian theory were never resolved, but the theory was not abandoned. In more recent times, Mitroff (1974) closely surveyed the attitudes and beliefs about scientific practice of a group of 43 geologists engaged in the study of lunar geology under the auspices of the Apollo space research programme. These well-established scientists saw their aim as (mainly) confirming rather than falsifying hypotheses. The only hypotheses that they were interested in falsifying were the hypotheses of rival scientists! As Mitroff puts it, these scientists differed markedly from the 'story book scientist' who is supposed to be completely disinterested and uncommitted to any particular hypothesis. The real scientists tended to be strongly committed to particular points of view and would only reluctantly abandon their views in the face of contrary evidence – rather than immediately, as a naive falsificationist position would suppose. Perhaps, then, the laboratory subjects of Mynatt *et al.* are not atypical in seeking confirmation rather than falsification. Indeed, the relatively high rate of appropriate reactions to falsifying data in Mynatt *et al.* (1977, 1978) may reflect the artificiality of the environment, e.g. subjects could not doubt their 'instruments' in the way that real scientists might. [Gorman (1986) has shown in a laboratory task that the possibility of error in feedback 'insulates' hypotheses from rejection.] Mitroff's moon scientists pointed out that 'commitment' was valuable from the point of view of motivating individual scientists. Also, since there would always be scientists with opposing commitments, the 'scientific community' would not be biased as a whole and the rivalry of competing factions would ensure that opposing views would be thoroughly tested by the opposition. Even a few cases of extreme commitment or outright bias could be useful to have around, because those biased individuals would keep alive ideas that might prove useful again at a later date, after having been abandoned by most researchers in a given area. These analyses of actual scientific practice suggest that the 'simulated research environments' of Mynatt *et al.* have, so far, lacked the social psychological dimension that appears to be crucial in real-life environments.

III. SUMMARY AND CONCLUDING COMMENTS

What conclusions, if any, can be drawn from the review of research in inductive reasoning presented above? A few themes seem to emerge consistently. These are (1) a tendency to ignore potentially falsifying information, (2) a preference for 'direct tests' of hypotheses using potentially confirming data, but also (3) a generally saving ability to take some appropriate action (abandonment or revision) when clear falsifying data are obtained. Let us now consider these points in more detail.

Available potentially falsifying information was not generally used in either the abstract version of Wason's four-card task or in the more realistic settings of Mynatt *et al.*'s simulated research environments. Preference for direct tests of hypotheses emerged in Wason's (1960) reversed 20 questions task, in Mynatt *et al.*'s (1977, 1978) studies and in Bruner *et al.*'s (1956) studies of concept learning. Appropriate reactions to falsification were often (if not always) observed in both Bruner *et al.*'s and Mynatt *et al.*'s studies. The preference for direct tests of hypotheses is the best established of the three conclusions and a plausible explanation was suggested by Bruner *et al.* (1956, p. 86) in terms of minimizing cognitive strain. The hypotheses being tested by the subjects in the relevant studies could be phrased as 'equivalences', e.g. 'if and only if the figure is red, is it a positive example of the rule' or 'if and only if the series is arithmetic, is it an instance of the experimenter's category' or 'if and only if the particle approaches a triangle will it stop'. The general form is 'if and only if p then q'. To make a direct test one only has to seek or generate instances of p and check if they are also q's. To make an indirect test, on the other hand, one would have to decide which out of the possible vast range of instances of not p to examine to check whether it was also not q. Thus, it appears to be simpler to rely on direct tests. Such tests also have the benefit that they will usually succeed eventually and will only be seriously misleading if the hypothesis being tested directly is included completely in the correct hypothesis, e.g. in concept learning, if the hypothesis 'red' was tried when the correct answer was 'red or square', or in the reversed 20 questions task if 'arithmetic series' is tried when the correct answer is simply 'increasing magnitude'. Direct testing, which involves not deliberately seeking falsifying data, would thus usually be a reasonable cognitive strategy that would often succeed with low cognitive strain in real life. Ignoring available but potentially falsifying data may also arise from customary habits of hypothesis testing. In the case of the four-card task, Wetherick (1970, 1971; see also Shapiro, 1971) has pointed out that it is 'unrepresentative' of real-life hypothesis testing. Wetherick argued that outside the thinking and problem-solving laboratory a hypothesis of the 'If p then q' variety would be formulated in order to facilitate *prediction* of 'q' from 'p' (e.g. predicting success at a particular job from a test score). Thus, the normal procedure would be to seek 'p's' and then check to see if they did *later* display 'q' or not. The suggestion is that if subjects treat the four-card task as representative of real-life hypothesis testing they will tend to focus on the 'p' card to see if 'p' predicts 'q' and will ignore the 'q' and 'q̄' cards as irrelevant to prediction.

Rule content emerged as an important factor in the four-card task. Currently, the most likely explanation for such 'content' effects seems to lie in the evocation of reasoning schemata (e.g. 'permission schemata') as described by Cheng and Holyoak (1985).

Overall, the general run of results and ideas outlined in our review are consistent with the usual information processing assumptions made in previous chapters, of small working memory, vast long-term memory and serial processing. Finally, it may be noted here that Evans, in the course of developing the notions of Type I and II thinking, has criticized the use of subjects' reports as a source of evidence about information processing (since the reports may be misleading rationalizations, rather than accurate accounts). This point raises important questions concerning the meaning and utility of subjects' reports (whether 'thinking aloud' or retrospectively justifying behaviour), which will be discussed further in the last chapter, when we have a broader range of background information on which to draw.

IV. FURTHER READING

Mitroff, I.I. (1974). *The subjective side of science*. Amsterdam: Elsevier. An intriguing empirical account of real-life 'inductive reasoning' among lunar research scientists.

Wason, P.C. (1983). Realism and rationality in the selection task. In J. St. B.T. Evans (Ed.), *Thinking and reasoning*, pp. 44–75. London: Routledge and Kegan Paul. A useful overview and a unique historical account of the origins of the selection task by its deviser.

7
Decision making

Decision making and problem solving are closely intertwined activities. Problem solving always involves some decision making, such as deciding whether a possible solution is acceptable or which alternative line of search or of problem reduction should be developed first. Decision tasks can be seen as a special form of problem in which the goal is to make a good selection from the available options. It may be necessary to think ahead to possible consequences of the alternative choices given different states of the world. Thus, deciding may require extensive mental exploration of tree-like mazes of possible sequences of events. Although decision making and problem solving are closely interrelated, the main foci of the two activities are different.

In problem solving the focus is on *generating* possible actions, whereas in decision making the focus is on *selecting* among possible actions. Indeed, in typical laboratory studies of decision making the options are presented and subjects choose among them without the load of option-generation.

Decision problems can be characterized on a number of dimensions. One important distinction is between *risky* and *riskless* decisions. In a risky decision there is some element of uncertainty about the outcome of the choices available. Choosing between gambles is a classic case of risky decision making. In a riskless decision there is no such uncertainty. (An example of a riskless decision might be choosing between two pairs of socks or similar reliable consumer goods. Unfortunately, in real life, even this choice may involve a perceived gamble. How likely are the socks to last a certain period of time? How likely are the socks to remain acceptably fashionable?

Furthermore, decisions may involve *single-attribute* or *multi-attribute* alternatives. Choosing between single- attribute objects is simple enough, but most choices are between multi-attribute objects (e.g. between cars varying in cost, maximum speeds, reliability, economy, servicing intervals, colours, etc.). Such choices require weighting of the attributes and an integration of information over the attributes to reach a decision.

Another useful distinction is between *single-stage* and *multi-stage* decisions. In multi-stage decisions, a sequence of decisions is involved, such that each choice leads to one of a number of alternative choices. Such multi-stage

decision making is probably more typical of real life than the 'one-off', isolated single-stage decisions most often studied in the laboratory.

Decision making has long been studied in a *normative* way. That is, with
the aim of recommending to decision makers what they should rationally do.
This approach leads to descriptions of how an idealized rational decision
maker would make choices. Although no one individual is likely to be per-
fectly rational at all times, normative decision theory has provided a basis for
economic theory in its attempt to understand and predict aggregate
behaviour (e.g. of stock markets). From the psychological point of view, normative models can provide a starting point for empirical research and for
empirically oriented theory. To what extent do people approximate to normative models? Can normative models be modified from empirical models
that will fit individual decision-making behaviour? More recently, psychological efforts have begun to focus on developing *process* models that try to
capture the cognitive processes underlying decision making.

I. NORMATIVE MODELS FOR RISKY DECISION MAKING

A. Values, utilities and probabilities

In real life one often has to choose between alternative courses of action without being completely certain what consequences the alternatives will have.
Choosing between gambles provides simplified risky decisions and the basic
ideas of the normative approach to risky choices can be best explained by
using gambling examples.

Suppose two horses, called Alpha and Beta, are racing each other. Alpha
will win with a probability of 0.8 and Beta with a probability of 0.2. (Assume
that probabilities may have been established over hundreds of races and can
be taken to be accurate.) You have a choice of betting 50 units of money on
Alpha to win or 10 units of money on Beta. If Alpha wins, you will gain 100
units. If Beta wins, you will gain 400 units. Which should you choose?

The basic notion of the normative approach to decision making is that the
decision maker should choose in such a way as to maximize a measure of
expected return. The main variations hinge on the degree to which the
measure to be maximized is derived from objective or subjective elements. In
the present simple example, the objectively expected value in money terms of
each course of action can readily be obtained. The *expected value* (EV) of
betting 50 units on Alpha, given it has a 0.8 probability of winning you 100
units, is determined as follows

$$EV(\text{Betting on Alpha}) = 0.8 \times 100 - 0.2 \times 50 = +70$$

While the EV of betting 10 units on Beta, given it has a 0.2 probability of winning you 400 units, is:

$$\text{EV (Betting on Beta)} = 0.2 \times 400 - 0.8 \times 10 = +72$$

Therefore, EV maximization would lead to Beta being chosen. Note that EV maximization implies that choice of either bet would be preferable to not taking one of the gambles at all. The EV of not accepting either gamble is simply zero, neither a gain nor a loss. The EV of a course of action is essentially the *average* value which would be obtained if that course of action was always chosen on a large number of repeated occasions. Thus, while the EV of betting 10 units on Beta is a gain of 72 units, on any one occasion you would either win 400 or lose 10 units. However, if this gamble were offered and accepted over many trials, your average gain per trial would be + 72 units.

To make use of EV analysis in decision making you must (a) know the objective probabilities involved and (b) assume that the worth of money to you is equatable with objective value (or is at least a *linear* function of objective value). In practice, objective probabilities (e.g. derived from frequency counts over many trials) are not always known. In such cases, a modified version of EV can be followed, in which objective probabilities are replaced by *subjective* probabilities representing an individual's degree of belief in the possible outcomes of each choice. Substituting subjective probabilities in the EV model leads to the *subjectively expected value* (SEV) model. Clearly, the subjective assessment of probabilities is very relevant to decision making and will be the focus of a later section in this chapter.

It is not immediately clear whether the subjective values (utilities) of money amounts do equate with objective amounts or even with linear functions of money amounts. However, a number of considerations strongly indicate that the utility of money is *not* a linear function of cash value. For example, it is generally accepted that the worth of an extra dollar or pound is greater for a pauper than for a billionaire. We would be confident that the pauper would cross a busy road to pick up a dollar bill or pound coin lying on the opposite side; a billionaire seems less likely to exert him or herself in that way for the same sum of money. Thus, it seems from this example that the utility of a unit of money for any individual is dependent on how much that person already has. Also, if money value was the criterion, it would be irrational to take out insurance (e.g. against loss of property), since to survive, the insurance company must pay out less than it takes in and, therefore, most subscribers must lose and the expected value of insurance must be negative for the insured. Similarly, if money value is the criterion, it is irrational to buy lottery tickets. The lottery has to arrange the 'odds' offered so that the average customer is a loser.

On the basis of similar considerations it was argued over 200 years ago by Bernoulli 1954; see also Savage, 1954) that a fixed increment of cash wealth results in an ever smaller increment in utility as the basic cash wealth to which the increment applies is increased, i.e. the Law of Diminishing Marginal Utility. Other features of the utility function for money gains and losses may be inferred from peoples' choices among gambles and certainties. For example, Kahneman and Tversky (1984) have found that most respondents in a sample of undergraduate students refused to wager $10 on the toss of a coin unless they stood to win at least $30 (expected value = + $10). Only a far from even bet was acceptable to these subjects. This is interpreted as reflecting *loss aversion*, i.e. that a loss of $x is more aversive than a gain of $x is attractive. Further, Kahneman and Tversky found that most subjects would prefer an alternative of $800 for certain, as against a 0.85 chance to win $1000 (with a 0.15 chance to win nothing). This preference holds despite the fact that the expected value of the sure thing ($800) is less than the expected value of the gamble (+ $850). Kahneman and Tversky class preferences for sure outcomes over gambles with higher expected values, as cases of *risk aversion*.

These various intuitions and empirical results regarding risky choices lead Kahneman and Tversky (1984) to a plausible function relating utility (or *value*, in their terminology) to gains and losses of money amounts.

They assume that decisions are basically about possible gains or losses relative to the individual's status quo and propose a function which is concave in the area of gains (diminishing marginal utility), but convex in the area of losses, and steeper for losses than gains (see Fig. 7.1). This last feature explains loss aversion (e.g. avoidance of fair gambles).

Kahneman and Tversky point out that although the notion of risk aversion in the area of gains has long been recognized in normative decision theory (i.e. preference for a sure thing over a gamble with a higher EV), the opposite

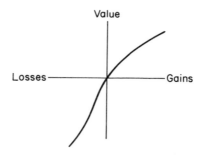

Fig. 7.1 A hypothetical value function. Reproduced with permission from Kahneman, D. and Tversky, A. (1984). Choices, values, and frames. *American Psychologist* **39**, 341–350.

phenomenon of *risk seeking* in the area of losses has been less discussed. An example of such risk seeking would be a preference for a 0.85 chance of losing $1000 (with a 0.15 chance of losing nothing) over a sure loss of $800. Most people, it seems, would prefer the gamble to the sure loss. This example is the mirror image of a problem already described in the domain of gains; when the problem is in the area of gains, subjects nearly always prefer the sure choice and avoid the gamble (risk aversion). The phenomenon of risk seeking in the area of losses has been upheld in a number of studies (e.g. Slovic *et al.*, 1982; Tversky and Kahneman, 1981). Risk seeking in losses and risk aversion in gains follow from the S-shaped value (utility) function shown in Fig. 7.1.

B. Normative theory and framing effects

Given a utility or value function and some means of estimating subjective probabilities, it may be argued that people would (or should) act so as to maximize their *subjectively expected utility* (SEU). If such rational behaviour is to be forthcoming, then certain principles, which seem intuitively clear, must hold. Two such principles or axioms of rational choice are *dominance* and *invariance*. The dominance principle states that if option A is at least as good as option B in all respects and better than B in at least one respect, then A should be preferred to B. Invariance requires that an individual's preference between two options should not be affected in the way in which the options are described.

Tversky and Kahneman (1981) examined the degree to which subjects respected the invariance principle when given the following pair of problems:

Problem 1: Imagine that the US is preparing for the outbreak of an unusual Asian disease, which is expected to kill 600 people. Two alternative programs to combat the disease have been proposed. Assume that the exact scientific estimates of the consequences of the programs are as follows:

If Program A is adopted, 200 people will be saved. If Program B is adopted, there is a one-third probability that 600 people will be saved and a two-thirds probability that no people will be saved. Which of the two programs would you favour?

The reader may care to decide which program he or she would favour.

Now consider Problem 2. The same introduction is followed by a choice between two programs, C and D:

Problem 2: If Program C is adopted, 400 people will die. If Program D is adopted, there is a one-third probability that nobody will die and a two-thirds probability that 600 people will die. Which of Programs C and D would you choose?

Tversky and Kahneman found that there was a strong preference in a large group of subjects ($N = 152$) for Program A over Program B (72 *v.* 28 per cent). In a similarly large group of subjects there was a strong preference for Program D over Program C (78 *v.* 22 per cent). The intriguing point of these results is that Program A is completely equivalent to Program C (in both, 200 live and 400 die) and Programs B and D are also completely equivalent to each other (in both, there is a one-third chance that 600 will live and a two-thirds chance that 600 will die). Tversky and Kahneman explain these results by saying that subjects 'frame' or construe the problems in different terms. In Problem 1, subjects are working in a 'gains' frame, i.e. in terms of lives *saved.* The majority choice of the sure option is typical of *risk aversion* in the domain of gains. On the other hand, in Problem 2, subjects are working in a 'losses' frame, i.e. in terms of lives *lost.* The choices here of the gamble reflect typical *risk seeking* behaviour in the domain of losses.

Thus, Tversky and Kahneman have induced subjects to show a striking departure from one of the major axioms of normative decision theory. Subjects have violated the invariance principle and are clearly affected by the way the problem is described. (The result has been demonstrated within individuals as well as between individuals.) As in many areas of problem solving, then, the way a decision problem is presented and, consequently, internally represented, is extremely important.

What of the dominance principle? It appears that the tendency to risk aversion in the domain of gains and risk seeking in the domain of losses can lead to violations of the dominance principle. Kahneman and Tversky (1984) demonstrated such violations in the following tasks. A total of 150 subjects were tested. Percentages choosing each option are indicated in brackets.

Imagine that you face the following pair of concurrent decisions. First examine both decisions, then indicate the options you prefer.

Decision (i) Choose between:
A. A sure gain of $240 (84%)
B. 25% chance to gain $1000 and
  75% chance to gain nothing (16%)

Decision (ii) Choose between:
C. A sure loss of $750 (13%)
D. 75% chance to lose $1000 and
  25% chance to lose nothing. (87%)

Clearly, then, A is preferred to B, and D is preferred to C. In fact, 73 per cent chose A *and* D and only 3 per cent chose B *and* C.

However, the preferred choice (A *and* D) is actually *dominated* by the rejected choice (B *and* C). Adding the sure gain of $240 (option A) to option D gives a 25 per cent chance to gain $240 and a 75 per cent chance to lose $760. While adding the sure loss of $750 (Option C) to option B gives a 25 per cent chance to gain $250 and 75 per cent chance of losing $750. In choosing the (B *and* C) combination, one has the same chances of winning and losing as in the (A *and* D) combination, but one stands to win more and lose less from the (B *and* C) combination. Thus, (B *and* C) dominate (A *and* D) and, rationally, should be chosen. Indeed, when the combined options were shown to subjects ($N = 86$), they unanimously chose in accord with the dominance principle. The failure to conform to dominance in the 'distributed' version of the task is attributed by Kahneman and Tversky (1984) to risk aversion and risk seeking in the domains of gains and losses respectively.

C. Interim conclusions on framing effects and rationality

Kahneman and Tversky's demonstrations of framing effects and consequent violations of basic principles of rational decision making, such as invariance and dominance, seem to have 'bleak implications' for human rationality. In that regard, these results are in line with the findings from studies of human deductive and inductive reasoning. However, as Kahneman and Tversky point out, being aware of likely sources of non-rational decision making may help us to avoid such behaviour and make us more thorough in examining our decisions for consistency and rationality.

II. RISKLESS DECISION MAKING

A. Framing, mental accounting and riskless choices

Consider the following problem:

> Imagine that you are about to purchase a jacket for $125 and a calculator for $15. The calculator salesman informs you that the calculator you wish to buy is on sale for $10 at the other branch of the store, located 20 minutes drive away. Would you make a trip to the other store?

Note there is no element of risk in this problem. The choice is between paying $15 for the calculator and not driving 20 minutes or paying $10 for the calculator and having a 20-minute drive.

Kahneman and Tversky (1984) argue that this problem can be framed in terms of a *minimal, topical* or *comprehensive* account. In a minimal account only the straight financial difference is considered; so, driving to the other store is framed as a gain of $5. On a topical account the value of the trip is the saving made relative to the initial price, i.e. a saving of $5 on a $15 item. The price of the jacket is irrelevant in the topical and in the minimal account.

A comprehensive account, however, also takes in the individual's total expenses, including the jacket and other costs, over a period.

Together with the usual assumptions about the shape of the utility function for money, topical accounting would predict that as the cost of the calculator rises, so the willingness to travel 20 minutes to save $5 would diminish. Topical accounting also predicts that the cost of the jacket is irrelevant in this problem. In line with these predictions, Kahneman and Tversky (1984) reported that in the version of the problem with a $15 calculator (and a $125 jacket) 68 per cent of respondents ($N = 88$) were willing to drive 20 minutes to save $5; but, when the calculator was priced at $125 (and the jacket at $15) only 29 per cent ($N = 93$) were willing to make the 20-minute trip to save $5 on the calculator. Since both minimal and comprehensive accounts would predict no difference between these two versions, the topical account hypothesis is upheld.

Similar support for the notion of topical accounts comes from a set of 'ticket' problems, which are as follows:

> Imagine that you have decided to see a play and paid the admission price of $10 per ticket. As you enter the theatre, you discover that you have lost the ticket. The seat was not marked, and the ticket cannot be recovered. Would you pay $10 for another ticket?

Out of 200 subjects, 46 per cent replied 'yes' and 54 per cent replied 'no' to this question. Consider now this second 'ticket' problem:

> Imagine that you have decided to see a play where admission is $10 per ticket. As you enter the theatre, you discover that you have lost a $10 bill. Would you still pay $10 for a ticket for the play?

To this problem 88 per cent of a sample of 183 answered 'yes' and 12 per cent answered 'no'.

In both 'ticket' problems the impact of buying a $10 ticket (after losing $10 or after losing a $10 ticket) is identical on the individuals total wealth. The main difference appears to lie in the topical account to which the loss is assigned.

B. Multi-attribute choices

1 Multi-attribute utility theory

Even when no risk is involved, making a choice among items that differ on many attributes can be demanding. A normative approach, known as *multi-attribute utility theory* (MAUT), suggests that the decision maker should (1) identify the relevant dimensions or attributes, (2) decide on weights to be assigned to the attributes, (3) obtain a total utility for each object by summing the weighted attribute values, and (4) choose the object with the highest weighted total (Wright, 1984). For example, if the decision maker has to choose between a number of houses, he or she might identify buying price, and distance from work, number of rooms, garden size, privacy, distance from services (shops, schools, etc.) as relevant attributes. Then the relative importance of the attributes would have to be considered. Is price a more important consideration than distance from services? Each alternative must then be scored on the attribute dimensions. The same scale length should be used for all attributes (e.g. from 0 to 100). So a given house may be assessed at '50' in terms of cost and '90' in terms of garden space, but '10' on distance from work. Clearly all the scales have to be used in such a way that a higher score is "more desirable" than a lower score. Having obtained the scores on each house for each attribute, overall utilities for each house can be obtained and the 'best' chosen. Needless to say, there are difficulties with this approach in practice. The decision maker may not be certain what the relevant dimensions are, and the attribute weightings and scorings may suffer from unreliability over time. Humphreys and Humphreys (1975) and Edwards (1977) discuss some of the practical aspects of using MAUT.

MAUT is a normative model and so may or may not be descriptive of unaided decision making. Given the limited capacity of working memory, it would seem unlikely that MAUT could be followed except in fairly simple cases with just a few attributes being considered. Before discussing some relevant data, two alternative, more empirically oriented models will be discussed.

2 Elimination by aspects

A less demanding procedure than MAUT was described by Tversky (1972) as a possible strategy that individuals might use in order to reduce processing load. This procedure is known as *elimination by aspects* (EBA). In an EBA process, the chooser would first select an attribute and eliminate all options that did not meet some criterion level on that attribute. In the example of house purchasing, for instance, 'price' is usually a critical attribute. The chooser will often have determined a ceiling price and so all houses over that ceiling price would be eliminated from consideration (irrespective of their other desirable qualities). Then, 'distance from work' might be taken as the next important consideration and all houses more than a certain journey time from work could be eliminated. If the chooser continues in this way to eliminate alternatives, sooner or later only one option will be left, and so the decision will effectively be made. EBA is clearly a less demanding procedure than that proposed by MAUT. Very different choices can arise depending on the order in which aspects are used to eliminate alternatives. Tversky suggests that the importance or weighting of attributes will influence the order of elimination.

3 Satisficing

A further simplifying technique which might be used in decision making, known as 'satisficing', has been described by Simon (1978). The fundamental idea is that rather than expend time and effort in a bid to maximize utility, people are generally content to set a minimum acceptable level which will satisfy them but be short of the maximum. This may apply especially in the case of sequential decisions. For example, in buying a house, houses come onto the market continually and it would be difficult to establish that a given house was actually the optimum choice, since a better one might appear the next day. Thus buyers may set acceptable levels, either for a total utility or on key aspects of the properties, and choose the first property that meets all their minimum requirements. Should the initial minimum requirements prove too ambitious, Simon (1978) suggests that the satisficing level is gradually adjusted in the light of the average values present in the market, so that the decision maker may become more realistic about his or her criteria in the light of experience.

C. Testing multi-attribute choice models

In order to determine which (if any) of the main models for multi-attribute choice are reasonably descriptive of behaviour one needs to be able to infer how subjects process information during decision making. Payne (1976) pioneered a technique which has proven useful in the study of choice processes. In Payne's study, subjects were presented with information on cards about aspects of a number of apartments. Each card was presented face down and gave information about one aspect of one apartment (e.g. Apartment A has two rooms). The cards were arranged in an Apartment x Attribute array so that subjects could easily *either* obtain information apartment by apartment *or* obtain information attribute by attribute (e.g. check all apartments for 'number of rooms', then for 'cost', etc.). Subjects were free to examine the cards in any order they wished. Payne distinguished two classes of strategies. One class was labelled 'compensatory' and the other 'non-compensatory'. The MAUT approach described above is an example of a compensatory strategy in which an overall assessment is arrived at for each alternative by summing over all attribute values (a good rating on one attribute can *compensate* for a poor rating on another attribute). EBA or satisficing would be non-compensatory strategies. On the basis of the information searches used by his subjects, Payne reported a variety of different compensatory and non-compensatory strategies. Interestingly, subjects often used both within the same task, e.g. by using non-compensatory strategies to reduce the number of choices to a small number and then using compensatory strategy to make the final choice. Payne also observed that non-compensatory strategies increased in frequency as task complexity was increased by manipulating the number of alternative apartments and the number of attributes per alternative.

These data, then, indicate that no one descriptive model has a monopoly on the truth about decision making. Rather, it seems as though strategies are adopted that tend to compromise between minimizing cognitive load and maximizing the utility of the outcome chosen. Cognitive load would be minimized by simply choosing at random but the resulting decisions would be very poor. Utility or value would be maximized by assessing all alternatives on all relevant dimensions, integrating the resulting information for all alternatives and selecting the best, but the information processing required would be very demanding. Payne's subjects exhibited a compromise solution: they used simple techniques to reduce the choice set, then analysed the remaining few options more exhaustively.

III. PROCESSING PROBABILITY INFORMATION

In order to choose effectively between options the decision maker often has to reach judgements about the probability of certain outcomes. for instance, a business executive in the US might have to decide whether or not to fly to Europe in a given month. What outcomes might be considered and the probabilities ascribed to those outcomes will be critical in whether a 'go' or a 'no-go' decision is made. If a US plane bound for Europe has recently been hijacked by terrorists, this possible outcome will likely be salient and may deter the executive from the 'go' choice. Since the perceived probability of outcomes is critical in decision making, much research has been aimed at unravelling some of the processes involved in probability judgements. Tversky and Kahneman have been particularly influential in this area and have proposed two major heuristics, *availability* and *representativeness*, which they argue are often used in making probability judgements.

B. Availability

Consider the following question:

> If a word of three letters or more is sampled at random from an English text, is it
> more likely that the word starts with 'r' or has 'r' as its third letter?

Tversky and Kahneman (1974) found a very strong tendency for subjects to report that a word beginning with 'r' was more likely to be picked out by random sampling than a word with 'r' in the third position. However, in fact the reverse is true. Tversky and Kahneman suggest that people tackle this question by comparing how easy they find it to think of words beginning with 'r' as against the words with 'r' as the third letter. Since starting letters usually provide the best cues for word retrieval, subjects are able to think of more words that start with 'r' than they do having 'r' in third place. Therefore, they misjudge the relative frequency of the two types of words.

Reliance on availability of examples to judge frequency is quite reasonable since frequency does affect availability e.g. subjects can readily judge which of two words markedly different in frequency of occurrence are more likely to be selected by chance from a text). However, since availability can also be affected by recency and emotional impact, among other factors, availability is not always a valid guide to objective frequency or probability. Thus a single vivid terrorist incident can deter possible travellers from crossing the Altantic, say, because it makes a highly unlikely outcome very available when the person contemplates travelling. Lichtenstein et al. (1978) have shown how causes of death that have more publicity (e.g. murder) are judged more likely than causes that have less publicity (e.g. suicide), contrary to the true state of affairs.

The availability heuristic can lead to contradictions of the basic laws of probability as well as to the simple inaccuracies indicated above. Tversky and Kahneman (1983) report that subjects were given 60 seconds to list 7-letter words of the form "------ing" and "------n". This is a pure difference in availability since of course, the set of "------n" words includes the set of "------ing" words, and so is considerably larger. Interestingly, Tverksy and Kahneman also found that when subjects were asked to rate the frequencies (in a sample of 2000 words from a novel) with which they would expect "-----ing" and "-----n" words to occur, they rated the former to be much more frequent than the latter. Comparable results were found in a comparison of frequency judgements for words of the forms "-----ly" and "-----l". Those judgements, based on availability, violate a fundamental law of probability, known as the 'extension rule'. If the extension of a set A includes the extension of a set B, then the probability of A must be greater than or equal to the probability of B.

So, use of the availability heuristic can lead to rather gross errors which decision makers should strive to avoid.

B. Representativeness

A second heuristic which Tversky and Kahneman (1983) have identified is that of representativeness. Representativeness is an assessment of the degree of correspondence between an instance and a category. For example, how representative is a particular individual of the category "Hollywood actresses" or how representative is a particular act (e.g. 'murder') of the behaviour of a category of people (e.g. 'law officers')? In the study of conceptual structures (Rosch, 1978) it is well-established that judgements of the representativeness of instances of categories can be made reliably and with high agreement among subjects (e.g. that 'robins' are representative instances of 'birds' but 'penguins' are not). Tversky and Kahneman propose that representative instances tend to be judged more likely to occur than unrepresentative instances and that such judgements can lead to error.

A particular form of error attributed to the representativeness heuristic is that known as the 'conjunction fallacy'. A form of task used by Tversky and Kahneman to demonstrate the conjunction fallacy is as follows. Subjects were first presented with a personality sketch of an imaginary individual and then asked to rate or otherwise judge the likelihood of a number of statements about that individual. Consider the following example:

Linda is 31 years old, single, outspoken and very bright. She majored in philosophy. As a student, she was deeply concerned with issues of discrimination and social justice, and also participated in anti-nuclear demonstrations.

Linda is a teacher in elementary school
Linda works in a bookstore and takes Yoga classes
Linda is active in the feminist movements   (F)
Linda is a psychiatric social worker
Linda is a member of the League of Women Voters
Linda is a bank teller   (T)
Linda is an insurance salesperson
Linda is a bank teller and active in the feminist movement (T *and* F)

The description of Linda was intended to be representative of a feminist (F) and unrepresentative of a bank teller (T). A group of 88 undergraduates ranked the eight statements by 'the degree to which Linda resembles the typical member of that class'. The overwhelmingly chosen order of typicalities for the key statements (F, T and T *and* F) was, F most typical, then T *and* F, then T. Thus Linda was seen as highly typical of the class 'feminist', moderately typical of the class 'feminist bank tellers' and untypical of the class 'bank tellers'. More surprising, and in violation of the extension law of probability, was that nearly all subjects ranked the conjunction "T *and* F" as more probable than either T or F alone. Since the set T includes the set T *and* F, the probability of T must be greater than the probability of T *and* F; similarly, the probability of F must be greater than the probability of T *and* F. Thus, it seems that the representativeness heuristic has led to an error (violation of the extension law), just as the availability heuristic was shown to when subjects judged the probabilities of words ending "ing" or "-n-".

The conjunction fallacy has proved to be a very robust phenomenon and has been replicated under many variations of the task, described by Tversky and Kahneman (1983). Even medically trained subjects were affected by the fallacy when given a brief case history and asked to then say whether the patient was more likely to develop one particular (unusual) symptom (B) or a combination of the unusual symptom (B) and a typical symptom (A). The expert subjects overwhelmingly judged the conjunction A *and* B to be more likely than the single symptom B. Again, this judgement violates the extension law of probability.

Interestingly, use of *extensional* cues seems to virtually remove the fallacy. Consider the following:

> A health survey was conducted on a sample of 100 adult males in British Columbia, of all ages and occupations. Please give your best estimate of the following values.
>
> How many of the 100 participants have had one or more heart attacks?
> How many of the 100 participants both are over 55 years old and have had one or more heart attacks?

Only 25 per cent of 117 statistically naive subjects gave a higher estimate for the second question (Tversky and Kahneman, 1983). When 147 similar subjects were given the same problem but asked to estimate percentages rather than absolute numbers a clear majority gave higher estimates. Using frequencies rather than percentages seems to facilitate correct extensional thinking. Speculatively, it might be that extensional cues lead subjects into forming mental models, similar to those proposed by Johnson-Laird for the case of syllogisms, and that such models help rule out wrong answers and suggest correct answers.

IV. SUMMARY AND CONCLUDING COMMENTS

A. Overview

In this chapter we have reviewed some of the major concepts and research findings in the area of decision making. Although decision making and problem solving are closely intertwined, the foci of the two activities differ. In decision making the focus is on *selecting* between options, in problem solving the focus is on *generating* options.

Decision problems were characterized in terms of a number of dimensions: risky *v.* riskless, single attribute *v.* multi-attribute and single stage *v.* multi-stage. Approaches to decision making were divided into normative and process approaches. Normative models seek to characterize the behaviour of an ideally rational decision maker and vary in the extent to which subjective assessments of value and probability are incorporated. The simplest normative model, the expected value maximization model, clearly does not fit individual behaviour. This is partly because the subjective value (utility) of money, say, is not a simple linear function of money amounts. The rather more plausible subjectively expected utility models fail to handle effects of framing which lead to violation of basic axioms of rationality such as *dominance* and *invariance* (Tversky and Kahneman, 1981), in both risky and riskless decision making.

In the case of multi-attribute decision making, the load of processing differing attributes into an overall value measure leads to sub-optimal but simple strategies such as elimination by aspects (Tversky, 1972) or satisficing (Simon, 1978). Use of elimination by aspects, at least as an initial stage in multi-attribute decision problems, has been shown by Payne (1976).

Since risky decisions require that decision makers take account of probabilities, the question of how people handle probability information has been the object of a number of studies. Tversky and Kahneman (1974, 1983) have provided many demonstrations of inappropriate usage of heuristics such as *availability* and *representativeness* that can lead to misjudgements of likelihood and to violations of the laws of probability, such as the extension rule.

B. Rationality and decision making

Are people rational decision makers? Clearly people do not always behave in accord with a simple expected value maximizing model of rationality, even in situations which are completely well- defined (e.g. simple gambles). To some extent decision behaviour is better explained by models that take subjective values and subjectively assessed probabilities into account (i.e. subjectively expected utility maximizing models).

However, from Tversky and Kahneman's results there are some striking departures from the axioms of subjectively expected utility theory. Examples of such departures occur in problems susceptible to framing effects, in which the invariance and dominance assumptions of rational choice are violated. Furthermore, conjunction effects in the handling of probabilities suggest that typical heuristics lead subjects into error. In the area of multi-attribute decision making, strategies which reduce cognitive load, such as eliminating by aspects and satisficing, lead to sub-optimal and unreliable choices.

As in the study of deductive and inductive inference, then, it appears also to be the case that research on decision making has 'bleak implications for human rationality' (Nisbett and Borgida, 1975). However, Cohen (1981) has urged caution in drawing any sweeping conclusions. First, he points out that the normative theories (e.g. of probability) against which subjects' judgements are compared are themselves founded on human intuitions about assumptions taken to be true (axioms). He argues for a competence/performance distinction in the area of rationality, according to which normal adults are assumed to have some basic competence in reasoning (and this backs up the intuitions underlying normative theories), but their competence is often overshadowed by performance factors (distractions, memory limitations, etc.). Also, he makes the point that when performance is compared against a normative theory, it is not always clear what normative theory applies; there is often more than one applicable normative theory. Macdonald (1986) also points to difficulties in determining which normative theory best applies to a given problem and, in addition, argues that the ordinary assumptions of conversational logic may justify apparent fallacies. For example, in the 'Linda' problem, merely asking how likely Linda is to be a bank teller may raise the credibility of that possibility, since the question would not normally be raised of an individual, unless there were some reason for believing it might be true.

Overall, then, the issue of rationality is a complex one. Simon's (1957) notion of 'bounded' rationality still seems to be a useful compromise between the extremes of imputing complete rationality or irrationality to humans. Simon argued against the notion of "rational man" as used in economic theory, since such a notion implied an infinite capacity for correct information processing, and instead he posited that people would be rational but within the limits imposed by constraints on memory, speed of processing, and available knowledge.

V. FURTHER READING

Kahneman, D., Slovic, P. and Tversky, A. (1982). *Judgement under uncertainty*: *Heuristics and biases*. Cambridge: Cambridge University Press. This is a good collection of readings which gives further detail on the main paradigms used in casting doubt on human rationality.

Wright, G. (Ed.) (1985). *Behavioural decision making*. New York: Plenum Press. Wright has assembled a useful set of papers which together give a broad survey of recent research on decision making.

8

Daydreaming

From early times a distinction has been made between two broad kinds of thinking. According to this distinction, on the one hand, we have thought directed toward some end or goal and, on the other, undirected thought, such as occurs in daydreaming. The English philosopher Thomas Hobbes (1651/1919) expressed the difference over three centuries ago as follows:

> This train of thoughts, or mental discourse, is of two sorts. The first is *unguided, without design,* and inconstant. . . . In which case the thoughts are said to wander, and seem impertinent (unrelated) one to another, as in a dream. . . . And yet, in this wild ranging of the mind, a man may oft times perceive the way of it, and the dependence of one thought upon another . . . the second is more constant, as being regulated by some desire, and design (p. 9).

Much later, a related, influential distinction was made by Freud (1900), between primary and secondary process thinking. Primary process thinking is characterized as wish fulfilling, unfettered by logic or reality, and operating in accord with the *pleasure principle* of immediate gratification (though the gratification obtained may be in the imagination only). This is the earliest form of thought in Freud's view. Secondary process thinking, in contrast, is reality respecting, seeking real rather than imaginary satisfaction and is governed by logic. Secondary process thinking also ultimately serves the pleasure principle but does so with due respect to the *reality principle* of obtaining what is possible and safe, deferring gratification when necessary. In Freud's theory, night dreams are nearly pure representatives of primary process thinking and daydreams predominantly so, while real problem solving would predominantly involve secondary process thinking.

As one might expect, very similar distinctions have been made by many writers. A selection appears in Table 8.1.

Early in the development of psychology as an independent subject there was strong interest in the naturally occurring stream of consciousness, including its undirected flow (e.g. James, 1890). However, post-Watson experimental psychology, in so far as it dealt with thinking at all, focussed on directed thought as exemplified in studies of problem solving and logical

Table 8.1 Classifying thought: a sample of distinctions

Distinction	By whom proposed
Undirected *v*. directed	Many
Passive *v*. active reason	Aristotle
Unregulated *v*. regulated thought	Hobbes (1651)
Primary *v*. secondary process	Freud (1900)
Foreconscious *v*. conscious	Varendonck (1921)
Autistic *v*. reality	McKellar (1957)
Impulsive *v*. realistic	Hilgard (1962)
Autistic *v*. directed	Berlyne (1965)
Multiple *v*. sequential	Neisser (1963b)
Respondent *v*. operant	Klinger (1971)
Type I *v*. Type II	Evans (1980a)

reasoning tasks. Perhaps this was because directed thinking seemed technically easier to investigate behaviourally or perhaps because directed thought was felt to be more educationally and socially useful than undirected daydreaming, which might be judged time-wasting and foolish, if not actually pathological. Interest in daydreams and fantasy generally was kept alive in clinical rather than in experimental psychology until the early 1960s. At that point many psychologists felt ready, technically and theoretically, to try to make sense out of daydreaming, which, after all, is a very common and familiar mental activity. Much of the credit for the revival of scientific interest in this topic must go to Jerome Singer and his colleagues (see Singer, 1975a,b, 1978).

In the next sections of this chapter the empirical work on daydreaming will be reviewed and then its theoretical significance will be considered.

I. PSYCHOMETRIC APPROACHES

A. Descriptive studies

The most basic questions concern the frequency and content of daydreams in the general population. Does everybody daydream? About how often? Are there differences in frequency or in content, depending on age, sex, cultural and personality factors? Some answers can be obtained by questionnaire methods (also called psychometric studies).

First, you may be relieved to learn that daydreaming is extremely widespread. An early survey by Singer and McCraven (1961) sampled 240 normal US adults of whom 96 per cent reported some form of daydream activity every day. This investigation involved a General Daydream Questionnaire in which respondents indicated the frequency on a 6-point scale with which they have experienced each of a series of about 100 daydreams, e.g. 'As a child, I imagined myself as a great detective'; 'I suddenly find I can fly – to the amazement of passers by'; 'I picture an atomic bombing of the town I live in'. The results of this study indicated that daydreams took the form of fairly clear images, mainly of people, objects or events. Items dealing with *planning* for future actions, particularly interpersonal actions, were high in frequency. Daydreaming generally occurred, it was reported, when the person was alone and in a restful state. In addition to such environmental factors it may be noted that studies by Kripke and Sonneschein (1978), in which subjects were asked to report their thoughts at intervals throughout the day, have suggested the existence of an intrinsic cycle, in which daydreaming peaks about every 90 minutes and is associated with heightened alpha waves in EEG and reduced eye movements. This cycle seems to hold both in laboratory studies and in real-life settings.

Most people's high-frequency daydreams involved practical, immediate concerns, with daydreams about sex and unusual good luck also common. Singer suggests that the range of items that have a high frequency do not exactly tally with the notion that daydreaming is purely unrealistic wish ful-filling. Rather, daydreaming often reflects attempts at anticipating possible future events and it is oversimplifying to say that 'daydreams are unrealistic'. It seems that daydreams vary in reality orientation from the practical and plausible through to true fantasies.

More recently, Singer and Antrobus (1972) developed a lengthy question-naire known as the Imaginal Processes Inventory. This involves 400 items that are to be rated on 5-point scales. Example items are 'The pictures in my mind are as clear as photographs'; 'I often have the same daydream over and over'; 'My daydreams have such an emotional effect that I often react with fear'. The items fall into 29 groups of sub-scales dealing with different aspects, such as frequency of daydreaming, degree of acceptance of day-dreaming, fear of failure, sex and hostile–aggressive content, guilty daydreams, visual imagery in daydreams and distractability associated with daydreams, among others.

Using large US student samples, factor analysis of these scales produced three factors, suggesting three different styles of daydreaming. Factor 1 (guilty–dysphoric) high scorers are inclined to 'tortured self-examination', have strong achievement drives and negative fantasies. Subjects high on Factor 2 (anxious–distractable) seem to be very anxious, self-doubting, rather disorganized in thought and lack clear and elaborate daydreams. They are not oriented toward achievement and persistence. The high scorers on Factor 3 have a positive attitude to daydreaming and fantasy and show a high level of 'thoughtfulness'. It appears that Factor 1 and 2 scores decline with age but Factor 3 scores remain steady. Future oriented and sexual daydreams seem to decline with age also.

B. Validity of daydreaming questionnaires

Daydreaming questionnaires, of the type discussed above, exhibit high degrees of test–retest *reliability*. The question of the extent to which they measure something outside of themselves, i.e. the question of their *validity*, has also been investigated with promising results.

One way of validating daydream questionnaires is to see whether subjects whose questionnaire scores put them in high or low daydream frequency categories, differ from one another in various experimental tasks. For such research purposes, daydreaming has often been operationally defined as the report of "thoughts that involve a shift of attention away from an immediately demanding task" (Singer, 1975a, p. 730). An example experiment is that by Antrobus *et al.* (1967) in which subjects who reported themselves to be high or low daydreamers were given a monotonous signal detection task. The high daydreamers indeed reported more thoughts unrelated to the task when 'probed' at intervals throughout. Also, although high and low daydreamers did not differ in efficiency of initial performance, the high daydreamers missed more signals and reported more task-irrelevant thoughts as time went on. It is notable that even although this task involved monetary pay-offs for correct detections, much of the time subjects daydreamed rather than attend to the external stimuli.

An interesting correlation that has turned up is that obese students have significantly lower scores than normal-weight students on daydream vividness as measured by the Imaginal Processes Inventory. Singer (1975a) suggests that this result is consistent with the theory about obesity put forward by Schachter (1968) which says that obese individuals are dominated by external stimulus cues and so, given any amount of food, will continue to eat as long as some food remains. If there is indeed a general tendency on the part of obese individuals to attend to external stimuli rather than to internal stimuli, then lower vividness ratings of daydreams would be expected from such subjects.

During daydreaming, a fixed leftward gaze is often adopted. This leftward orientation of the eyes indicates a predominance of activity in the right cortical hemisphere during daydreaming. Further evidence for the validity of the Imaginal Processes Inventory, then, comes from Meskin and Singer's (1974) observation that high scorers on the Inventory showed more leftward eye-shifts in response to imagery-evoking questions than did low scorers.

Overall, it appears that there is a reasonable amount of evidence for

the validity of daydreaming questionnaires as indices of a style of thinking. Further supporting evidence also emerges in later sections of this
chapter.

II. EXPERIMENTAL APPROACHES TO DAYDREAMING

A. Task demands

As well as individual differences in frequency and style of daydreaming,
situational factors also play a role. Roughly speaking, the more important it
is to attend to the outer environment, the less likely one is to engage in daydreaming. A number of experimental studies support this generalization.

Singer and his colleagues have generally used signal detection tasks. These
have the advantage that the task load can easily be varied in a number of
ways. For example, rate of occurrence of signals (fast v. slow) and complexity
of judgement (judge tone to be high or low v. judge tone to be same or
different to preceding one) were varied in a study by Antrobus et al. (1966).
As dependent measures, in addition to signal detection performance, they
had subjects rate their frequency of task-irrelevant thoughts and obtained
ratings of degree of verbal thinking, visual imagery and auditory imagery at
intervals throughout the task. The major effects were as one might expect.
Task-irrelevant thought declined with an increase in the speed of signals and
with an increase in the complexity of judgement. Overall, the correct response rate was quite high (92.4 per cent) and there was no particular
correlation, in this experiment, between daydreaming frequency and signal
detection performance. Subjects seemed to maintain a fairly stable rate
of correct responses and varied daydreaming up or down depending on
the amount of 'spare mental capacity' left by the demands of the main
task.

A second experiment in the same paper concerned the rate of daydreaming
(i.e. task-irrelevant thought) depending on the rewards and costs of 'hits' and
'misses' in signal detection.

There were four groups of subjects and each group started off with $3, but
the groups differed in the penalties of errors, these being 0¢, 2¢, 4¢, or 8¢
respectively. After each block of 15 trials, the subjects had to make a simple
yes/no report of whether they had had task-irrelevant thoughts or not. The
probability of task-irrelevant thought being reported declined as the penalty
for missing signals increased (see Fig. 8.1). So, it can be shown experimentally that the complexity and importance of a current task affects levels
of daydreaming during performance.

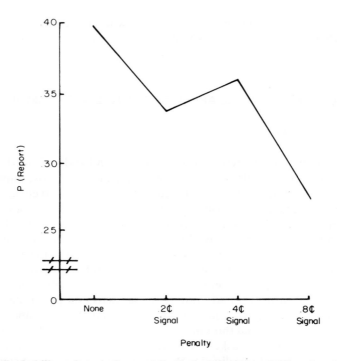

Fig. 8.1 Probability of reporting task-irrelevant thoughts during signal detection task as a function of penalty for missing signals. Reprinted with permission of the authors and publisher from Antrobus, J.S., Singer, J.L. and Greenberg, S. (1966). Studies in the stream of consciousness: Experimental enhancement and suppression of spontaneous cognitive processes. *Perceptual and Motor Skills* **23**, 399–417.

B. 'Bad news'

It was mentioned earlier that, according to survey data, much daydreaming is concerned with anticipating or planning for future events. Antrobus *et al.* (1966) explored this experimentally, by giving a group of subjects some information, which, if true, would have seriously affected their futures. This experimental group were then compared with controls in the amount of task-irrelevant thinking they reported during a signal detection task.

The 'information' was given in the form of a special radio news bulletin that the experimental subjects overheard while in a waiting room before the signal detection task got under way. Imagine you were an American male student in June 1965 and you heard the following:

High military aides in Saigon have conceded that heavy damage has been inflicted upon our air base at Da Nang after the surprise massive air and ground attack earlier today. This action, in addition to last night's sinking of two Navy aircraft carriers by Chinese jets, has served to weaken seriously our offensive air postures in Southeast Asia . . . Meanwhile, the Associated Press reports that Defense Secretary McNamara has placed all active military units on emergency alert status . . . Allegedly, the communique also instructed the local (draft) boards to call in for physical examination as soon as possible, all unemployed youths over 18 and all eligible college graduates.*

As might be expected the experimental group reported much higher levels of task-irrelevant thought throughout the 150 signal detection trials (see Fig, 8.2). Experimental subjects were also more likely to miss signals.

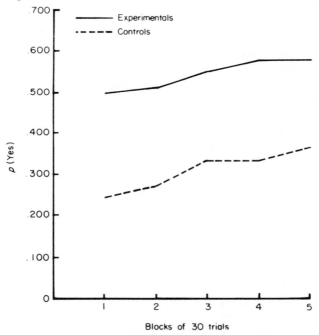

Fig. 8.2 Probability of reporting task-irrelevant thinking as a function of time within the detection session for experimental ('bad news') subjects and control subjects. Reprinted with permission of the authors and publishers from Antrobus, J.S., Singer, J.L. and Greenberg, S. (1966). Studies in the stream of consciousness: Experimental enhancement and suppression of spontaneous cognitive processes. *Perceptual and Motor Skills* **23**, 399–417.

---

*Reprinted with the permission of the authors and the publisher from Antrobus, J.S., Singer, J.L. and Greenberg, S. (1966). Studies in the stream of consciousness: Experimental enhancement and suppression of spontaneous cognitive processes. *Perceptual and motor skills* **23**, 399–417.

After the experiments the subjects wrote down examples of their task-irrelevant thoughts. These generally concerned implications of the news for their future, e.g. possibilities of themselves or their friends being drafted, possibilities of escaping to Canada, etc. Another class of thoughts concerned images of the Vietnam war or war in general. Thus, by introducing a rather drastic change in subjects' expectancies about the future, the 'stream of thought' was diverted toward making adjustments and anticipations in order to deal with the change. Of course, the subjects were 'debriefed' after the experiment – no doubt to their relief!

C. Stress effects

Horowitz and colleagues have reported a number of experiments concerning the effects of stress on cognitive responses (as contrasted with physiological responses). The clinical literature suggested that after traumatic stress, 'intrusive' thoughts that involve 'stimulus repetition' are common reactions. These reactions are sometimes labelled 'repetition compulsion' and involve repeated thoughts about the traumatic experience despite attempts to avoid such thoughts. Horowitz hypothesized that this 'repetition compulsion' was an extreme version of a general tendency that occurs in normal populations even after relatively mild stresses.

In the study carried out by Becker *et al.* (1973), subjects did signal detection tasks after seeing a 6-minute stressful film and after a 6-minute neutral film. The signal detection tasks were split into three periods between which the subjects wrote down what they could recall of their mental contents during the preceding task period. It was expected that the stressful film would produce more signs of 'repetition compulsion' than the neutral film. The stressful film was entitled *Subincision*. It shows repeated scenes of circumcision rites among Australian bushmen and it features old men inflicting pain on young adolescents, nudity, injury, blood and anguished expressions. Prior studies have shown that this film is indeed stressful in terms of physiological measures. The neutral film was entitled *The Runner* and consists of a man running through the town he grew up in, having flashbacks along the way. It is said to be quietly interesting without being very exciting.

After the experiment, the subjects' mental reports were content-analysed by three independent judges for intrusions, film references and task-irrelevant thoughts. Inter-judge reliability correlations were high ($r = 0.94$). An intrusive thought was defined as "any thought the subject experiences as (a) non-volitional; (b) hard to dispel; (c) something to be avoided, or (d) a repetition of the identical thought." (The other thought categories are self-evident). The main results were that the stressful film significantly increased the number of intrusive thoughts and film references but did not significantly affect the total number of task-irrelevant thoughts compared to the neutral film. Both films increased the number of irrelevant thoughts above a baseline level established before the films were shown.

It is interesting that in this experiment the stressful material did not have any direction implications for the subjects' futures, unlike Antrobus *et al.*'s (1966) 'bad news' study, and yet similar effects were obtained. Perhaps because the *Subincision* film presented material very discrepant from the subjects' prior conceptions about human behaviour, cognitive work had to be done to adjust existing schemata to accommodate such events.

Whatever the explanation, it would seem that Singer and Horowitz and their colleagues, have produced experimental analogues of certain real-life experiences, *viz.* compulsive mulling over of 'bad news' in the Antrobus *et al.* experiment and mental replaying of disturbing scenes from films or TV (even if they do not have any personal relevance) in the Horowitz *et al.* study.

D. Analysing daydream protocols

The daydreaming reports obtained in the earlier studies of daydreaming, discussed above, were typically retrospective and/or incomplete. Fuller report methods should produce finer-grain information on the structure of daydreaming sequences. Eric Klinger (1971, 1978), at the University of Minnesota, has experimented with a variety of thought sampling methods. One of these methods – '*thinking out loud*' – requires the subject to talk continuously for a period of 5–30 minutes. The subject is seated in a chair and simply asked to keep talking aloud. The utterances are tape recorded for further analysis. An example 2-minute protocol is given below (from Klinger, 1971, p.97; reprinted by permission of author and publisher):

> Oh, I also think about how I wanted to die. I don't want to die you know, like ahm, by living in a hospital for six months, kept on by drugs. I don't want to die, um, on the golf course on the 9th hole, being struck by lightning or doing my daily jogging – Ahh, being hit by a car or something like that just being free . . . and be still young at heart. I don't know, I don't want to have to sit in a room like that, seeing my family watch me die, I don't know, that's, its ridiculous. Isn't there some way we can say hell and let me die? How can people do that to other people? It's just like an old folks home. Can't stand to go there and watch. It scares me half to death seeing people like that. Usually. . . . Almost like . . . T. and another couple, they're ahm just look at them and you could almost get hypnotized. I think one of the major things is. . . . No, that's, where did I hear that? Oh. D. told me. Told him to quit smoking all you have to do is to go and get hypnotized for a cost of $50 or something but completely, completely quit smoking. No desire to smoke. All you do is get hypnotized. Hmm,

my stomach's growling. Ha I think mmm. . . . You know that one little dot right there seems so funny. Reminds me of a graba I saw in a, from a horror movie. Yeah, creepy films series again for this fall going to be. Consists of um, Frankenstein, King Kong, oh, all those really goodies, man.

Klinger has found that coders can reliably analyse such sequences into 'main routines' or 'themes' (e.g. 'Dying' in above protocol), and further into 'sub-routines' or 'sub-themes' (e.g. 'Dying on golf course' in above). Main routines define an area of concern, while sub-routines either go to finer and finer levels, drift from one sub-topic to another within a given level, return to the main theme or apparently stimulate new themes. Most routines are fragmented and are interrupted before a natural conclusion is reached by some new routine.

Klinger (1974) compared thinking aloud protocols from problem-solving sessions with thinking aloud protocols obtained under daydreaming instructions. In the problem-solving protocols there were many more utterances containing progress evaluations (e.g. 'yep', 'Dammit', 'Now wait . . .'). At the least, these results indicate that the general method of obtaining and analysing thinking aloud records has some validity.

However, it must be acknowledged that the 'thinking aloud' method has some possible drawbacks. The requirement to verbalize may slow down the apparent rate of the flow of thought and may make thinking seem more verbal than it is. A study discussed by Pope and Singer (1978) indicates that verbalization does affect the apparent nature of the stream of consciousness. Subjects were asked to report on shifts in thought by releasing a key each time a change in topic or direction of thinking occurred. These data suggested that thought shifts occurred every 5 or 6 seconds on average. In contrast, data from subjects who had been thinking aloud produced an average rate of one shift per 30 seconds. Thus, thinking aloud methods may produce a biased picture. In view of this point, *thought sampling* methods may be a useful option, in that they can yield fairly detailed data without affecting the flow as much as continuous verbalization. In thought sampling methods the subjects are cued at irregular intervals and describe their most recent thoughts, often by means of rating scales that can be completed quickly. This technique has been used to good effect by Klinger in some studies outlined below.

E. Thought sampling studies

1 Normal thought flow

Klinger (1978) reported a large-scale, quantitative study of normal conscious thought that used thought sampling techniques both in and out of the laboratory. In both settings, subjects were periodically interrupted and asked to report their thoughts in terms of the 15 scales that comprise the 'Thought Sampling Questionnaire'. The scales were as follows:

(1) Estimated duration of the latest thought segment.
(2) Estimated duration of the previous segment.
(3) Vagueness v. specificity of the imagery.
(4) Amount of directed thought.
(5) Amount of undirected thought.
(6) Amount of detail in imagery.
(7) Number of things going on simultaneously.
(8) Visualness of imagery.
(9) Auditoriness of imagery.
(10) Attentiveness to external stimuli.
(11) Recall of recent stimuli.
(12) Degree to which imagery felt controllable.
(13) Degree of trust in accuracy of memory.
(14) Familiarity v. unfamiliarity or bizarreness of the latest experience.
(15) Time of life associated with the experience.

In the out-of-the-laboratory setting, scale 14 was divided into Usualness and Distortedness scales.

In the study conducted in the laboratory the subjects listened to dichotic tapes and were required to indicate by means of a toggle switch the channel that they were attending to. The tapes were interrupted at irregular intervals by a tone that signalled the subjects to report on their thoughts using the questionnaire. A total of 936 thought samples were obtained in the laboratory setting from a sample of 20 subjects.

Outside the laboratory, the subjects carried with them an alarm device (a 'beeper') that emitted a soft tone at random intervals having a mean of 40 minutes. On hearing the tone, the subjects filled in a similar thought sampling questionnaire to that used in the laboratory studies. The beeper could be switched off if the subject felt that its activation might prove embarrassing! This study yielded a total of 285 real-life thought samples from 12 subjects.

Klinger proposed certain *a priori* dimensions in terms of which thoughts could be characterized, and used these in interpreting his thought sampling data. The first dimension is the familiar one of 'directed v. undirected'. The second is that of 'stimulus independent v. stimulus bound'. As Klinger points out, these two dimensions are conceptually independent. A person may think in a very directed way about a problem which does not relate to his or her current stimulus field (e.g. a student trying to solve a maths problem mentally while riding in a bus). At the other extreme, a person might free associate to the stimuli in the immediate environment. Some of the earlier studies of day-dreaming assumed that 'stimulus independent' equalled 'undirected', but this is not necessarily true. A further dimension is that of 'fanciful-realistic'. Again, fanciful thinking about improbable events may or may not be directed. In some problem-solving techniques (e.g. brain storming, discussed in Chapter 9), the person deliberately tries to think of fanciful combinations and events. A fourth dimension is that of 'integrated *v.* fused or degenerate'. In normal waking thought, images and ideas remain intact, separate wholes, while in dream-like thought, images tend to flow together and merge. This latter sort of thinking can also occur in the waking state, especially under the influence of some drugs and during sleep deprivation. Nor are such thoughts at all uncommon, at least fleetingly, during normal waking states.

The main results from Klinger's thought sampling study may be summarized as follows:

(1) The median judged duration of thought segments was 5 seconds and the mean was around 10 seconds. These results agree quite well with other studies that have used toggle-switching to indicate change of thought topic.

(2) Thoughts rated as 'directed' were also rated as more specific, more related to external cues and more controllable than undirected thoughts. 'Directedness' was not related to duration of the thought segment, amount of detail, presence of visual or auditory imagery, familiarity or time of life associated with the thoughts.

(3) Stimulus-bound thoughts tended to be 'directed' but the connection was not a strong one. Degree of fancifulness of thought segments was not strongly related to their directedness (presumably because undirected thought can easily be either fanciful or realistic).

(4) There was a detectable baseline of 'strange' or 'degenerate' thoughts, indeed 22 per cent of out-of-laboratory thoughts were so rated. "Strangeness" was negatively related to thought specificity, to relatedness to external cues and to controllability. 'Strange' thoughts did occur during both directed and undirected segments.

(5) In general, compared with in-laboratory thoughts, out-of-laboratory thoughts were more specific, more directed, more related to external cues, more oriented to the present and led to better recall of external cues.

(6) Visual imagery was reported considerably more frequently than auditory imagery in both in- and out-of-laboratory settings.

These results, especially those obtained outside the laboratory, give a broad picture of the normal thought stream and indicate that thought sampling is a useful technique.

A further thought sampling study of 29 subjects in out-of-laboratory settings generated a total of 1425 thought samples (Klinger *et al.*, in press). Analyses of ratings of these samples corroborated the findings of Klinger (1978) and confirmed the independence of the dimensions of directedness, stimulus independence and fancifulness.

2 The induction principle

It seems apparent from thought sampling and protocol studies that the topic of thought changes quite rapidly in the normal course of events. What determines which topic will be taken up next?

Psychologists have generally assumed that moment-to-moment thoughts are determined by a combination of motivational factors and cues interacting with memory contents.

The motivational concept of a 'current concern' has been found useful in considering the determinants of thought content. A 'current concern' is defined as the state of an organism between the time it becomes committed to pursuing a goal and the time it either obtains the goal or abandons it. Another label for essentially the same concept as 'current concern' is 'unfinished business'. Any individual is typically beset by many current concerns – most of which will not be in consciousness at a given time. However, it is proposed that the contents of consciousness at a particular time will tend to reflect one or other current concerns or pieces of unfinished business.

As well as current concerns, cues related to these concerns are also likely to play a role in steering thought. Klinger (1978, p. 250) proposed an 'induction principle' as follows:

> At any given moment, the next thematic content of thought is determined by the combination of a current concern and a cue related to that concern.

The cue may be of external origin or be a symbolic event in the individual's own stream of thought. Also, it is surmised that people may be more perceptually sensitive to cues bearing on current concerns. Such 'attention tuning' would be of obvious utility.

Taking the induction principle as a starting point, Klinger (1978) carried out the following experiment. First, the subjects were interviewed and from these interviews four current concerns were extracted for each subject. One or two days later the subjects were presented with dichotic tape messages. These consisted of literary extracts in which, at intervals, material relating to a current concern was introduced on one channel while material relating to a non-current concern was introduced into the other channel. The inserted passages lasted 25 seconds. Throughout the experiment, the subjects indicated by means of a switch the channel to which they were attending. Ten seconds after each inserted passage, a signal was given, whereupon the tape stopped and the subjects reported their latest thoughts in accordance with the Thought Sampling Questionnaire. They also reported their recollections of the most recent taped passages.

As would be predicted on the induction principle, the concern-related passages received more attention than the non-concern passages. The subjects switched to them sooner and spent longer listening to them. Furthermore, the concern-related passages had more effect on subsequent thought contents and were recalled better. It seems, then, that people's current concerns dispose them to attend to and to retain and reflect in their thoughts, cues related to those concerns, as the induction principle predicts.

Further research (Hoelschler et al., 1981) indicates that the induction principle even operates on thought content during sleep. Subjects were presented with concern- and non-concern-related words at low volumes during rapid eye movement (REM) sleep. There was significantly more incorporation of concern stimuli than of non-concern stimuli in dream reports obtained shortly after stimulus presentation. Since people might be expected to dream more about concern than non-concern topics irrespective of any cues, the authors checked that the probability of a dream related to a particular concern was indeed higher immediately after the concern stimulus than after other stimuli. These results suggest that the induction principle is descriptive of a powerful tendency that affects cognitive processes both in waking and sleeping.

As it has been described so far, the induction principle is non-committal with respect to the degree of influence that a person's various current concerns will have on thought flow. Most of the research has dealt with the role of cues rather than with the effects of concern attributes. Klinger et al. (1980) have remedied this deficiency to some extent. Questionnaires were used to elicit topics thought about with varying degrees of frequency and the resulting topics were then rated by the subjects on a variety of scales (such as positive value of thing thought of; negative value; anticipated future effort; nearness in time, and so on). Real-life thought sampling (beeper studies) supported the validity of the questionnaires as measures of topic frequency in thought.

The main results may be summarized as follows. The frequency of thoughts about particular goals was predicted best by the person's self-reported commitment to the goal, the value of the goal, the subjective probability of achieving the goal and the time left before action was required. Thoughts related to threatened personal relationships and unexpected difficulties were notably high in frequency. Although the particular thought contents reported in this study probably largely reflect the concerns of undergraduate students, the general conclusions should be widely applicable.

F. Functions of daydreaming

Given the frequency of daydreaming in everyday thought, an obvious question to ask is 'what *functions* does this activity serve?'

As Singer (1975b, Ch. 5) points out, on Freud's psychoanalytic theory, daydreams are always connected, although sometimes indirectly, to drives considered to be basic (such as sex and aggression) and serve a temporary drive-reducing function. The psychoanalytic theory proposes that daydreaming starts in infancy, when the hungry baby, in the absence of immediate gratification, automatically engages in 'primary process' thinking and hallucinates an image of breast or bottle. These images are presumed to have temporary drive-reducing effects.

A label used for such drive reduction brought about by imagery, fantasy or vicarious means is *catharsis*. Freud borrowed this term from Aristotle's theory of tragedy. Watching a play in which a character (Oedipus) discovers that he has murdered his father and married his mother is considered, on the psychoanalytic view, to help the audience to discharge repressed sexual and aggressive tendencies relating to their parents. On this approach, then, daydreams act as safety valves, permitting the partial reduction of drives whose overt expression would be unacceptable. According to this catharsis view, the regular presentation of sex and violence in the mass media should be encouraged in order to help reduce the rates of actual rape and murder.

Alternatively, it can be argued that the witnessing of 'pre-packaged fantasies' on television or films has a stimulating effect on the relevant drives and that such stimulating effects might also hold for self-generated fantasies in daydreaming. Indeed, it seems from the general run of results from a number of studies by Berkowitz (1969), in which subjects were shown aggressive film scenes and then given opportunities to act aggressively, that those who witnessed the aggressive scenes showed an increase in aggressive activity, rather than the decrease that catharsis would suggest.

More directly related to daydreaming is a complex study by Paton, reported in Singer (1975b, pp. 113-114). A group of college student subjects took the Imaginal Processes Inventory and then later in the session were insulted while performing a task. Immediately after the insulting episode, one group were given pictures of aggressive material (such as battle scenes) to look at. A second group that had also been insulted were shown interesting non-violent pictures. Both groups then daydreamed and reported their thoughts. Next, they were given questionnaires which yielded measures of how angry and aggressive they felt about the person who had insulted them. There were also two control groups. One control group had no opportunity for fantasy activity after being insulted, and the other control group was not insulted at all. These control groups made it possible to show that the insults really did anger the subjects. The insulted group without an opportunity to daydream showed a higher level of subsequent anger than did the group that had not been insulted.

The main question in this experiment was whether the opportunity to daydream after becoming angry would lead to a reduction in the amount of anger felt about the insulter. If there is an aggressive drive that is aroused and if daydreams related to the aggressive drive reduce that drive, then one would expect the greatest drop in aggression to occur if the subject has produced angry and hostile thoughts rather than non-violent thoughts. Alternatively, it might be that the effect of daydreaming after being insulted, would be mainly to divert the subject and produce an alternative mood that would reduce anger. In that case, one would expect that the subjects who produced non-violent daydreams would show a greater drop in subsequent aggressive tendencies toward the insulter than would those who produced aggressive fantasies. It would also be consistent with this view if both kinds of daydreams produced greater reductions in anger than did no opportunity for daydreaming.

The results supported the 'diversion' hypothesis. Both groups who daydreamed showed less anger toward the insulter than the group who had no daydream opportunity. However, there was a large difference in the effect between the conditions. Subjects who produced mainly neutral daydreams showed a greater drop in anger than those whose daydreams were aggressive. From this study it seems, then, that the motivational effect of daydreaming is mainly one of diversion and mood shifting. The view that daydreaming brings about automatic reductions of the relevant drives was not supported.

If daydreams do not serve as simple drive-reducing safety-valves, what functions might they serve? On the basis of the existing literature, Singer (1975b, 1978) suggests that daydreams may serve functions of (1) anticipation and planning, (2) reminding us of 'unfinished business' which we may be trying to suppress, and (3) maintaining arousal in dull environments.

Whatever functions daydreams may serve, Singer suggests that their occurrence follows from widespread and continuous activity in the brain. His model is described in the following section.

III. A CONCEPTUAL MODEL OF DAYDREAMING

Singer (1975a; Pope and Singer, 1978) has proposed a simple model that can handle much of the data regarding daydreaming. This model claims that (a) there are two continuously available sources of stimulation, one internal and one external, and (b) that there is a limited capacity central processor that attends to only one of these sources at a time. The external source is the outside environment. The internal source that Singer proposes is a continuously active long-term memory in which information is not stored in some inert form but rather through continuous representational activity. Similar notions of an active long-term memory have also been put forward by other authors (e.g. Neisser, 1963b; Reitman, 1965). Daydreaming, Singer suggests, involves attending to the normally unnoticed ('underground') flows of activity in long-term memory. Some support for the notion of continuous unconscious activity can be drawn from the occurrence of intrusive thoughts (as in Becker *et al.*, 1973) and from personal reports by scientists and artists of incubation and inspiration experiences (see Chapter 9). These phenomena suggest the existence of internal parallel processes than can occasionally 'seize' attention. Of course the existence of such processes would be contrary to the serial activity assumption of the standard information processing approach to thinking.

Whatever the merits and problems of the 'active long-term memory' notion, there is much support for the view that daydreaming and external attending are incompatible and that a selection of one or the other form of activity has to be made on the basis of task demands. Daydreaming frequency drops as task complexity and the costs of errors go up (Antrobus et al., 1966). On the other hand, if external inputs are severely restricted, as in sensory deprivation experiments, then daydreaming increases very markedly. Increased daydreaming could serve useful arousing functions in dull environments.

As a final point, this model suggests that individual differences in self-reported daydreaming frequency, may be due either to differences in dominant attention strategies or to differences in the amount of unconscious mental activity. Whether these two possibilities could be operationally separated is an open question.

IV. SUMMARY AND CONCLUDING COMMENTS

The material reviewed in this chapter shows that undirected thinking can be studied successfully, although it has not been given the same degree of research attention as directed thought. The question of a definition of 'day-dreaming' was largely by-passed in the foregoing review and deserves some consideration at this point.

As Klinger (1978) has argued, thoughts may be independently, directed or not, realistic or not, related to current external stimuli or not, and so on. Of these characteristics the major feature of daydreaming seems to be a lack of persistent direction. Daydreams are not necessarily unrealistic but tend to drift from one topic to another, whereas thinking in problem solving is checked against feedback concerning progress toward the current goal and attention is 'locked' on to the problem materials (Klinger, 1971). Daydreams are often concerned with anticipating future problems. So, for instance, in anticipating a dinner date with a girl, a boy may be seen as setting up an internal symbolic model representing the meeting, which he then runs in order to anticipate possible outcomes of going to alternative restaurants. To be classed as daydreaming, as against problem solving, we would have to suppose a loose degree of control over the model running process – permitting departures from reality and switches to different, if associated, topics.

From the studies discussed above, daydreaming is a widespread and frequently occurring phenomenon, whose incidence varies with personal characteristics (e.g. obesity) and with external demands (e.g. sitting in drab waiting room *v.* descending a sheer rock face). The moment-to-moment contents of daydreams seem to reflect both immediate and recent internal or external stimuli and the person's list of 'current concerns'. In terms of functions, daydreaming resists attempts to reduce it to a Freudian safety valve. Rather, it seems to serve functions of anticipating, reminding about outstanding concerns and maintaining arousal in uninteresting environments.

The model for daydreaming put forward by Singer (1975a; Pope and Singer, 1978) clashes with the 'seriality' assumption intrinsic to the modal information processing approach to thought (e.g. Newell and Simon, 1972). Singer suggests that there is continuous activity within the long-term memory and that this activity is the source of daydreams. From the data discussed so far, the case for parallel processes in conjunction with the conscious mainstream of thought is perhaps most strongly supported by the occurrence of intrusive and unwelcome thoughts (Becker *et al.*, 1973).

A possible 'serialist' argument would be that the mainstream of thought could be halted every so often and the list of current concerns scanned. This might lead to a switch in the thought stream in order to deal with one of those concerns (e.g. adjust concept of range of human behaviour to incorporate data from *Subincision* film in the case of Horowitz *et al.'s* subjects). The issue of serial *v.* parallel models for thinking will arise again in the next chapter, which deals with creative processes, and it will also be discussed in the final chapter in a broader context.

V. FURTHER READING

Klinger, E., Cox, W.M. and Roudebush, R.L. (in press). Dimensions of thought flow in everyday life. *Imagination, Cognition and Personality* 7. This provides a very detailed account of the results from thought-sampling studies of daydreaming.
Singer, J.L. (1978). Studies of daydreaming. In K.S. Pope and J.L. Singer (Eds), *The stream of consciousness*, pp. 187–223. New York: John Wiley. A brief but comprehensive guide to research results in the area of daydreaming.

9

Creative processes

Before discussing creative processes, it is necessary to consider briefly what is meant by the term 'creative' and its associate 'creativity'. It is perhaps easiest to start by defining creative products. Creative products, whether they are poems, scientific theories, paintings or technological advances, are both novel and acknowledged to be valuable or useful in some way. Whether a product is novel or not is relatively easy to determine, although an element of judgement does enter into it, in that some products are more obviously derived from previous developments than others. The objective measurement of novelty is possible in laboratory settings, since the same task can be given to a large number of people (e.g. "think of ways of improving a doorknob"), and the degree of novelty of proposed solutions can readily be assessed by counting their frequencies of occurrence. In real life, however, only the 'creator' may be working on a given self-set problem [e.g. an author seeking to represent the stream of consciousness of a Stone Age man, as in W. Golding's (1955) *The inheritors*], and so frequency of production is not always available as a criterion. When we turn to the quality of a product, subjective judgement looms still larger than in the case of judging novelty. In science and technology the criteria for quality are clearer than in the arts. A new theory or gadget can be seen to 'work' if it covers more phenomena with no more assumptions than its predecessors (e.g. Einstein's theory compared to Newton's) or meets the function for which it was devised (e.g. the first telephone). Notoriously, there is usually less agreement about the merits of artistic productions, both at the time of their emergence and over history. Initial reactions may well be negative to artistic products that either depart too far from established styles or, at the other extreme, are too conventional. Later generations are more likely to appreciate the boldness of developments that their ancestors decried as 'insane', e.g. Surrealism, Cubism, Expressionism, etc.

It may also be suggested here, that judgements of 'novelty' or 'unusualness' will presumably relate to the degree to which the product can be fitted into an established style (in the arts) or 'paradigm' (in the sciences). Highly creative products signal and exemplify a new style or paradigm. Subsequent work within a given style or paradigm would generally be regarded as less creative than the initial style-defining work.

The above comments should serve to indicate what is meant here by a creative product. What of 'creative processes' and persons blessed with 'creativity'? Although it is a starting point, it is not very informative to say that creative processes are those processes that result in creative products. Later on, I will be reviewing some attempts to be more detailed about such processes. At this stage though, it may be noted that psychologists hold to the belief that creative processes are composed of similar ingredients to those entering into less exalted forms of thinking. It is assumed that creative products result from multitudinous, small steps carried out by limited capacity cognitive systems that suffer from all the normal limitations of cramped working memory and imperfect retrieval from long-term memory. Indeed, most of the approaches to 'small-scale' problem solving (e.g. behaviourist, associationist and information processing) have something to say about creative thinking. It is an article of faith for theories of thinking that creative processes can be explained in terms of their basic processes (whatever the basic processes may be for any particular theory, e.g. associations or production rules) and that supernatural interventions in the form of 'daemons' or 'divine sparks' are ruled out. Turning now to 'creativity', this is an attribute ascribed to those individuals who show a long-term tendency to generate novel products that are also influential (Albert, 1975). With a few extremely rare exceptions (such as Leonardo Da Vinci) most 'creatives' display their valued characteristic within a particular speciality – but within that speciality they are marked for their combination of productivity (e.g. Picasso) and high quality of work (as indexed by its influence). Of course, in real life, for someone to be acknowledged as displaying 'creativity' involves social processes, as well as purely within-individual cognitive processes. To become known, creative individuals must 'promote' their products and convince enough others who control the communication media that these products should be presented to a larger audience (Stein, 1974). Given that wider presentation, further social processes leading to widespread acceptance and influence, or to apathy or rejection can begin.

In the rest of this chapter, I will discuss some of the main approaches and topics that have arisen in the study of creative processes. First, there is the psychometric approach, which considers in what ways individuals acknowledged to be creative might differ in cognitive, personality or biographical characteristics from others. Secondly, there is the approach *via* personal accounts by artists and scientists of how the process seemed to them and this leads on to stage models for creative thinking based on personal accounts. Next, we turn to laboratory-based approaches that have examined ways of stimulating idea production. Then, there will be a discussion of theoretical approaches and, finally, a summing up.

I. STUDIES OF CREATIVE INDIVIDUALS

A. Psychometric studies

A number of studies have been made of people acknowledged to be creative, [e.g. Roe's (1952) study of scientists, MacKinnon (1962) on architects, and Barron (1955) on writers and artists]. These studies were aimed at uncovering any common background or personality characteristics of these unusual groups of people.

In one of the earliest investigations of its kind, Ann Roe (1952) studied 64 American scientists who had been rated as eminent in their fields by expert panels. The 64 were roughly evenly split among physicists, biologists and social scientists. Each individual was subjected to long interviews, projective personality tests (TAT and Rorschach) and a conventional intelligence test. On the basis of this investigation Roe gave the following composite picture of the average eminent scientist.

The average eminent scientist was a first-born son in a middle-class Protestant family, with a professional man as a father. He was likely to have often been ill in childhood or to have lost a parent early. He had a very high I.Q. and began reading avidly at an early age. He felt 'lonely' and different from his school mates, did not have much interest in girls and married late (27 years old on average). He usually decided on his career as a professional scientist as a result of a student project involving individual research. He worked hard and persistently, very often 7 days a week with few holidays.

This general picture seems to have held best for the physicists. The social scientists were on average somewhat more extroverted, and showed more concern for personal relationships. They displayed more aggression in the projective tests than members of the other scientific groups. A large proportion of social scientists came from homes with a dominant mother and they had a very high divorce rate (41 per cent). Though different in these ways, they were also totally absorbed by their work and worked very long hours, as did the other groups of scientists.

Similar evidence on personality characteristics of creative people was gathered by Cattell and his colleagues. Before actually testing any 'live' scientists, Cattell (1959) scanned the biographies of many famous scientists and noted that the typical eminent scientist seemed to be introverted and stable. Although introverted, they were generally independent and self-sufficient.

They also tended to be solemn or restrained and rather dominant in personal relationships.

Cattell and Drevdahl (1955) selected groups of about 45 eminent researchers in physics, biology and psychology and had them complete the 16 Personality Factors (PF) test. Compared with the general population, the eminent researchers were more introverted, intelligent, dominant and inhibited; they were also more sensitive emotionally and more radical. These findings are in line with the suggestion of biographies and with the results of Roe's investigation.

A similar study of artists and writers (Drevdahl and Cattel, 1958) yielded a profile rather similar to that of the scientists. The artistic group were more emotionally sensitive than the scientists and exhibited more inner tension – but were otherwise similar.

Also relevant is Mitroff's (1974) study of scientists engaged in the analysis of lunar samples as part of the Apollo moon project. Mitroff noted a strong tendency toward a style of thinking often labelled 'convergent' (Hudson, 1966). Any open-ended question put to the scientists would be quickly transformed into a narrower, more tightly defined one. This tendency fits in with Hudson's finding that those boys who performed better on convergent (one answer) test questions than on divergent items (multiple possible answers) tended to specialize in science subjects. It was also noted that the lunar scientists strongly identified with the traditionally conceived 'masculine' characteristics. They believed in hard work, dedication, striving, and did not disapprove of a touch of ruthlessness. Intriguingly, and contrary to earlier reports, Mitroff found evidence in his interviews of strongly aggressive tendencies. In discussing other scientists and rival groups, the desire to win glory at the expense of others and a fear of their rivals' over-aggressive tactics (e.g. idea stealing) were evident. Aggressiveness was also clear in their attitude to promoting their own ideas. As one scientist remarked:

> if you want to get anybody to believe your hypothesis, you've got to beat them down with numbers: you've got to hit them again and again over the head with hard data until they're stupefied into believing it (Mitroff, 1974, p. 144).

It is possible that aggressiveness in scientists was not evident in previous studies that had relied on projective tests (e.g. TAT), because such tests are uncongenial to the scientists' preferred convergent style. McLelland (1962) noted the extreme dislike of scientists for the TAT and their tendency to analyse portions of the picture rather than empathizing with the characters and telling a story. In Mitroff's study, with material close to their hearts, few inhibitions were evident regarding aggression. Mitroff suggested that the scientists were somewhat one-sided in emotional expression and he found that they were far less free in displaying soft emotions as against harsh or aggressive ones. The notion that science is an aggressive activity was also expressed in Freud's self-description. He wrote

> I am not really a man of science, not an observer, not an experimenter, and not a thinker. I am nothing but by temperament a *conquistador* – an adventurer, . . . with the curiosity, the boldness, and the tenacity that belong to that type of being (Jones, 1961, p. 227).

Another interesting point emerges from a study of the *ages* at which creative accomplishments tend to occur. Data gathered by Lehman (1953) reveals that in many fields the most highly regarded contributions are produced between 30 and 40 years of age. The average age is younger in some subjects, e.g. in chemistry it is at 25–30 years, and is older in others, such as psychology, philosophy, novel writing and architecture. Although these age trends were detectable it should be noted that good work was evident in all fields at a very wide range of ages. The 32-year-old chemist is not necessarily 'finished' as far as creative work is concerned.

B. Personal accounts of creative problem solving

Many scientists and artists have provided accounts of their experiences in solving complex problems (see, e.g. Ghiselin, 1952; Koestler, 1964; Vernon, 1970). These personal accounts are of interest for evidence they may contain about features common to the creative process in a wide range of difficult tasks. Fairly consistent patterns do seem to emerge and these patterns have served as the bases for various analyses into stages of both creative thinking and more routine problem solving.

It is worth noting that some well-known thinkers have disclaimed any ability to tell us how they solved problems or thought creatively. For example, Bertrand Russell was once asked to contribute to a book on how to think clearly. He replied that he could not help because, for him, thinking was instinctive, like digestion. He said that he simply filled up with relevant information, went about his business, doing other things and later, with time and good luck, he found that the work had been done. Perhaps Russell was too modest on this occasion. His brief account broadly matches those of others who have tried to be more detailed. It is only possible to consider a small number of these more detailed reports here and I have selected accounts by Poincaré, Helmholtz and Tchaikovsky.

1 Poincaré's account

Henri Poincaré was a prominent French mathematician of the nineteenth century. He reported (1908) once struggling for a long time to prove a certain theorem without getting any results. One evening he drank black coffee before going to bed and it seemed to him that ideas of possible ways of solving the problem combined and recombined in one way after another before he finally got to sleep. In the morning, he clearly saw how the problem was to be solved, and after 2 hours had completed the detailed proof. The solution to the initial problem raised further problems and Poincaré noted that these problems were solved as a result of ideas that occurred while he was not actively engaged on them, e.g. while riding in a bus, walking along a street or beach.

2 Helmholtz's account

The nineteenth century scientist Herman Helmholtz who contributed to physics, neurology and psychology, volunteered the following report of his problem-solving experience in a speech made at a dinner in honour of his seventieth birthday in 1896 (Woodworth and Schlosberg, 1954, p. 838):

> So far as my experience goes, 'happy thoughts' never came to a fatigued brain and never at the writing desk. It was always necessary, first of all, that I should have turned my problem over on all sides to such an extent that I had all its angles and complexities 'in my head' and could run through them freely without writing. To bring the matter to that point is usually impossible without long preliminary labour. Then, after the fatigue resulting from this labour had passed away, there must come an hour of complete physical freshness and quiet well being, before the good ideas arrived. Often they were there in the morning when I awoke, just according to Goethe's oft cited verses, and as Gauss also once noted. But they especially liked to make their appearance while I was taking an easy walk over wooded hills in sunny weather.

3 Tchaikovsky's account

Peter Ilich Tchaikovsky attempted to describe his experience of composing in a series of letters [extracts of which are reprinted in Vernon (1970, pp. 57–60)]. Here are three examples:

> Do not believe those who try to persuade you that composition is only a cold exercise of the intellect. The only music capable of moving and touching us is that which flows from the depths of a composer's soul when he is stirred by inspiration. There is no doubt that even the greatest musical geniuses have

sometimes worked without inspiration. This guest does not always respond to the first invitation. We must *always* work, and a self respecting artist must not fold his hands on the pretext that he is not in the mood. If we wait for the mood without endeavouring to meet it half way, we easily become indolent and apathetic. We must be patient, and believe that inspiration will come to those who can master their disclination

Generally speaking, the germ of a future composition comes suddenly and unexpectedly. If the soil is ready – that is to say, if the disposition for work is there – it takes root with extraordinary force and rapidity, shoots up through the earth, puts forth branches, leaves and, finally blossoms. I cannot define the creative process in any other way than by this simile. The great difficulty is that the germ must appear at a favourable moment, the rest goes of itself. It would be vain to try to put into words that immeasurable sense of bliss which comes over me directly a new idea awakens in me and begins to assume a definite form. I forget everything and behave like a madman. Everything within me starts pulsing and quivering; hardly have I begun the sketch ere one thought follows another.

Yesterday, when I wrote to you about methods of composing, I did not sufficiently enter into that phase of work which relates to the working out of the sketch. This phase is of primary importance. What has been set down in a moment of ardour must now be critically examined, improved, extended, or condensed, as the form requires. Sometimes one must do oneself violence, must sternly and pitilessly take part against oneself, before one can mercilessly erase things thought out with love and enthusiasm.

II. STAGE ANALYSES

A. Wallas's stage analysis

On the basis of reports such as those of Poincaré, Helmholtz and others, and on the basis of his own experiences as a university teacher, administrator and writer, Graham Wallas (1926) proposed a four-stage analysis of creative problem solving in a book entitled *The art of thought*. In this book Wallas was concerned with the natural course of thought and with how thinking might be made more effective. So, in addition to proposing certain typical stages, he also offered advice on how these stages could be made more fruitful. The stages extracted by Wallas were as follows.

1 Preparation

In this stage the problem solver familiarizes himself with his problem and engages in conscious, effortful, systematic and usually fruitless work on the problem. Although this stage may well not lead to a solution in itself, it is widely believed to be very important in influencing the likelihood that the next stage will result in a useful idea. Much personal testimony indicates that inspiration will not be forthcoming without this preliminary labour or, as Edison, the prolific inventor, is reported to have said, 'No inspiration without perspiration.'

2 Incubation

This is a period during which the task is set aside. No conscious work is done on the problem during this stage. Poincaré and others have hypothesized that unconscious work is carried out during this phase. On the other hand, it may be that this is simply a necessary rest period which enables a later period of conscious work to proceed more effectively than it would have without the break. Wallas suggested that this phase could be made more or less effective, depending on the intervening activity. Light work on minor problems or duties could be beneficial. Better still, he thought, was complete mental rest, coupled with mild exercise. He felt that the habit of filling every spare minute with reading was especially detrimental.

3 Illumination or inspiration

This is the point when a fruitful idea, or 'happy thought' in Helmholtz's phrase, occurs to us. The inspiration is not usually a complete solution to the problem but points in the direction in which the complete solution may be found.

This phase may be preceded by a vague feeling of 'intimation', a feeling that the solution is nigh. Wallas suggests that if thinkers can recognize this feeling, then they should relax, cut out possible distractions and let the inspiration come. If the intimation feeling is not recognized then the possible inspiration may be lost on account of distracting stimuli.

4 Verification

This stage is much like preparation, in that conscious work must be done in order to develop and test the inspiration.

These four stages are visible in the personal reports of Helmholtz, Poincaré and Tchaikovsky. Their reports, however, do not stress 'intimation' and rather suggest that inspiration come very suddenly and without warning. Wallas suggests that the 'intimation' experience is easily forgotten in the excitement of inspiration. It may also be noted, that Poincaré proposed a four-stage view like Wallas's but with the omission of 'intimation'.

Wallas's stage analysis could be interpreted as proposing a strict 1, 2, 3, 4 order that is gone through once and once only in solving a problem. Such a formulation is open to the criticism of being overly rigid. However, Wallas (1926, p. 81) did not intend such a rigid interpretation. He wrote:

> In the daily stream of thought these four different stages constantly overlap each other as we explore different problems. An economist reading a Blue Book, a physiologist watching an experiment, or a business man going through his morning's letters, may at the same time be 'incubating' on a problem which he proposed to himself a few days ago, be accumulating knowledge in 'preparation' for a second problem, and be 'verifying' his conclusions to a third problem. Even in exploring the *same* problem, the mind may be unconsciously incubating on one aspect of it, while it is consciously employed in preparing for or verifying another aspect.

Some attempts have been made to bring Wallas's stages into the laboratory, notably by Patrick (1935, 1937), whose work is reviewed in the next section. The incubation stage has been singled out as the specific focus of some laboratory studies that will be discussed in a later section.

B. Patrick's laboratory studies of stages

In the 1930s Catherine Patrick attempted to gather more systematic data on the stages of creative problem solving than were available in retrospective reports. Her method involved having subjects produce poems in response to a painting (1935) and sketches in response to a poem (1937). In each case, Patrick recorded all that the subject said and did between presentation and completion of the task. I will discuss here the 1937 study of the sketching task. The 1935 study of poetic composition was similar in method and in results.

Two groups of subjects were tested. One group consisted of 50 experienced painters, all of whom had exhibited their paintings publicly. A comparison or control group consisted of 50 non-artist subjects who had no or only very slight experience of art work. The two groups were similar in ages, sex distribution and intelligence test scores.

The subjects were tested in their own homes. After a brief conversation period to put subjects at their ease and to accustom them to having their words noted down, they were presented with an extract from Milton's poem *L'Allegro* and asked to draw a sketch about the poem or anything it suggested to them. There was no time limit and subjects were encouraged to 'think aloud' throughout. When the sketch was finished the artist subjects were questioned about their normal working methods.

To get objective evidence on stages of thinking, Patrick divided each thinking aloud record (protocol) into four equal time quarters. The protocol quarters were then analysed for (a) the number of *thought changes*, (b) the number of *general shapes drawn for the first time*, and (c) the number of instances of *revision* in each quarter.

Thought changes were taken to indicate *preparation* stage thinking and 75 per cent of thought changes occurred in the first quarter. *Illumination* was taken to be indexed by drawing a general shape for the first time and 66 per cent of such events occurred in the second and third quarters. Revisions were taken to indicate a *verification* stage and 75 per cent of revisions occurred in the third and fourth time quarters. The incidences of these types of events, then, were in accord with Wallas's stage analysis.

Incubation was taken to be indicated if an idea occurred early in the protocol, recurred one or more times while the subject spoke of other things and, finally, appeared as the chief topic of the picture. Approximately 85 per cent of the protocols showed such evidence of incubation.

According to the questionnaire given to the artists after the experiment, about 94 per cent reported using incubation at least some of the time in their *normal* work (76 per cent usually, 18 per cent sometimes). The reported time periods of real-life incubation ranged from days to years.

In the experimental data, there were no differences between the artist and the control subjects in amount of incubation. In fact, there were no differences between artist and non-artist groups in any of the performance measures, except in the rated quality of the sketches. The artist's sketches were rated far higher than those of the control subjects, as one would hope.

Patrick's data are in accord with Wallas's four-stage analysis. However, any incubation that occurred in this study was very brief compared to the retrospective reports by noted thinkers. Furthermore, the main problem was never wholly put aside but, rather, was worked on continuously for an average of 18 minutes. In typical reports by artists and scientists of incubation phenomena, the problem is often set aside for lengthy periods. The one example of incubation that Patrick (1937, pp. 55–56) gives in detail, might be explained by the problem-solving strategy of scanning a number of possibilities first, before returning to the most promising one to develop it further. This 'progressive deepening' (see Chapter 2) strategy has emerged in other protocol studies of problem solving (De Groot, 1965) and could account for the effect that Patrick attributed to incubation. The difficulty here seems to be that the criterion used by Patrick for incubation effects was too weak.

To sum up, Patrick's data are certainly of interest and support the broad stages of preparation (in which possible directions are surveyed), illumination (in which one possibility is decided on) and verification (in which revisions occur). The protocol data are less convincing on incubation effects since at no time was the main task set aside during the average 18 minutes spent on it. However, the artists' questionnaire reports *did* support incubation as a real-life phenomenon, despite the difficulty of trapping it in the confines of the sketching task. Finally, Patrick notes, as did Wallas, that the stages appear to overlap and recur.

C. Laboratory studies of incubation

As we have seen, the notion of incubation plays a prominent role in the recollections of artists and scientists. Despite its importance in personal accounts of creative thinking, incubation has not attracted much experimental study. However, some data are available and will now be discussed.

Murray and Denny (1969) investigated the effects of incubation-opportunity on subjects of high and low problem-solving ability. Subjects were divided into high and low ability on the basis of the Gestalt Transformation Test. This test requires the selection of objects for unusual uses, e.g. "From which object could you make a hose: a tree, cigarette, shirt, bicycle, eye glasses?"

Subjects were also divided into control and experimental groups. Both were given a rather complicated problem devised by Saugstad, in which the subject is given a nail, pliers, a length of string, a pulley, some elastic bands and several newspapers.

A glass containing metal balls and standing on a movable frame was situated 8 feet from the subject. Next to the glass was a steel cylinder. The subject had to find a way of transferring the steel balls from the glass to the cylinder without going nearer than 8 feet to the glass or the cylinder.

The solution involves two stages. First, bend the nail into a hook, attach the hook to the string and throw it into the frame. The frame can then be dragged back to the line and the balls removed. The second stage is to construct a long hollow tube by rolling up the newspapers and connecting them telescope fashion by elastic bands, and then roll the balls down the tube to the steel cylinder.

Control subjects were given 20 minutes continuously to solve the problem, whereas the experimental subjects worked 5 minutes on the task, then had 5 minutes on an unrelated pencil and paper task, and then they were given a further 15 minutes on the main task.

Neither incubation nor ability level significantly affected the frequency of solutions – but there was a significant interaction in that high-ability solvers were *hindered* by incubation-opportunity, whereas low-ability solvers were *aided* by an incubation-opportunity. Murray and Denny interpreted these results by suggesting that low-ability subjects quickly became fixated, and incubation allowed their inappropriate sets to die out, while the high-ability subjects may have been working more systematically through various possibilities, without fixation, but this orderly process was disrupted by an incubation opportunity.

Murray and Denny suggest, then, that incubation will be most effective when the problem is very difficult for the solver – as for their low-ability subjects tackling the tube and balls problem and, presumably, for famous scientists and artists tackling major problems and projects.

Incubation effects appear to be difficult to obtain in the laboratory. Dominowski and Jenrick (1972) carried out a follow-up study of Murray and Denny's results using a different problem involving the manipulation of objects, but found no significant effect of incubation. However, on a divergent task, Fulgosi and Guildford (1968) found significant effects of 20 minutes incubation on the quantity of solutions provided, but no effect on the quality of solutions. Clearly, research remains to be done, e.g. varying problem types, preparation time and length of incubation period. Olton and Johnson (1976) examined possible incubation effects on the solving of chess problems by expert players. Thus, the problems were realistic and familiar for the subjects (unlike the situation in previous studies that used unfamiliar puzzles). However, the chess-playing subjects given an incubation opportunity showed no advantage over subjects who worked continuously on the task.

Assuming that incubation opportunities are sometimes useful, how might any benefits be brought about?

The two main ideas that have been put forward, are those of unconscious work and the decay of inappropriate sets during the incubation.

Poincaré (1980) provided a graphic attempt at describing possible unconscious work during incubation periods. He proposed that the course of unconscious activity would be influenced by prior preparation or conscious work. Imagine ideas to be like hooked atoms, then, Poincaré says, conscious work selects certain atoms/ideas as relevant to the problem and tries to organize them to reach a solution. When the problem is put aside, the atoms continue to move about hooking up with each other and with other atoms not activated during conscious work. Eventually, a solution combination may be reached, but it will generally involve at least one of the atoms/ideas which were selected during conscious work.

In contrast, Woodworth and Schlosberg (1954) suggested that incubation simply involves a decay in misleading tendencies that interfere with problem solution. At present, both the 'decay' and the 'unconscious work' hypotheses remain open.

III. INCREASING IDEA PRODUCTION

Are there any ways of increasing the production of novel ideas? Numerous proposals have been put forward (see Stein, 1974, 1975) for stimulating the idea production stage of creative thinking. Probably the most famous, and certainly the most researched, method is that known as 'brainstorming'.

A. Brainstorming

1 Basic results

In the 1940s and 1950s a practical businessman, Alex Osborn, developed a package of recommendations known as the brainstorming method. This was intended mainly for use in group problem solving and as a means of increasing idea production. The method can be adapted for individual use and is described in Osborn's (1953) book *Applied imagination*. Brainstorming has been taken up quite widely in a variety of organizations and has also been extensively investigated in laboratory settings.

Osborn adopts the standard view that problem solving and creative thinking involve (1) problem formulation, (2) idea-finding and (3) the evaluation of ideas to find a likely solution. Brainstorming aims at facilitating the middle, idea-finding stage and it can be summarized as involving two main principles and four rules.

Principles
(1) Deferment of judgement.
(2) Quantity breeds quality.

Rules
(1) Criticism is ruled out.
(2) Free-wheeling is welcomed.
(3) Quantity wanted.
(4) Combination and improvement sought.

The 'deferment of judgement' principle meant that evaluation of ideas was to be postponed until a set period of idea production had elapsed. The untutored thinker will tend to evaluate each idea as it is produced. Osborn suggests that this can be inhibiting and may lead to premature abandonment of ideas that, although not useful in themselves, may lead on to possible solutions. The 'quantity breeds quality' principle states that the more ideas produced the larger the absolute number of useful ones there are likely to be, even if the proportion is very low. The rules listed above remind 'brainstormers' not to criticize their own ideas or those of others, to freely associate to ideas already produced, to aim for quantity and to combine and improve already generated suggestions.

The method was originally devised for group use but can be adapted for individual applications. A number of questions arise – for example, does the method lead to better productivity (a) for groups and (b) for individuals? Does group brainstorming lead to better results than would be obtained by pooling the ideas produced by the appropriate number of individual brainstormers?

Numerous studies support the hypothesis that groups using brainstorming produce more ideas than similar groups working along conventional lines. Brainstorming instructions strongly affect the quantity of ideas produced and, although effects on *average* quality are not so evident, reports of more high-quality ideas have been obtained (as would be expected by virtue of the 'quantity effect'). An example study is the following by Meadow *et al.* (1959). They compared the effects of brainstorming instructions with the effects of instructions that stressed the quality of ideas produced. The tasks set the subjects were to think of as many uses as they could for a broom and a coathanger. Ideas were rated independently for *uniqueness* (the degree to which the suggested use differed from normal use) and for *value* (social, economic or aesthetic). 'Good' ideas were defined as those rated highly on both uniqueness and value. The results indicated that significantly more good ideas were produced with the brainstorming instructions than with the non-brainstorming instructions.

Favourable results on individual brainstorming have also been reported by Parnes and Meadow (1963). In one study, subjects were individually required to think up possible solutions to problems for 5 minutes. On one problem they operated conventionally, evaluating ideas as they thought of them, whereas on the other problem, they used deferred judgement. The first method produced an average of 2.5 'good' ideas, whereas the second produced an average 4.3 'good' ideas. Parnes estimated that in this case about 72 per cent better productivity resulted from deliberate deferment of judgement during idea production.

2 Brainstorming: real v. nominal groups

Given that both individual and group brainstorming seem to be effective, the question arises whether brainstorming in a group produces better results than would be obtained by pooling results from individual brainstormers? It could be argued either that the group procedure would lead to beneficial mutual stimulation or, alternatively, that participants would be inhibited by fear of implicit criticism even although overt criticism is not permitted.

Taylor *et al.* (1958) tackled this question with an experiment in which 12 groups of four men and 48 individuals followed the basic rules of brainstorming while working on the same three problems. The problems were (a) 'think of as many ways as possible of encouraging European tourists to visit the U.S.A.'; (b) 'what would be the consequences if all future children were born with an extra thumb on each hand?' (a diagram of the new hand structure was provided); and (c) 'how could the education system cope with the effects of a 'bulge' in the school age population?' (as was being experienced at the time of the study).

After the idea production stage, the 48 individual subjects' data were assigned to 12 *nominal* groups of size four. The performance of each such nominal group was then scored as though the members had in fact worked together. The achievement of such nominal groups provided a base line level of performance which would be achieved if group work were neither facilitating nor inhibiting. The nominal groups produced (a) more unique ideas than the real groups and (b) more distinct 'good' ideas – largely by virtue of a quantity effect.

It was concluded from these data that group participation in brainstorming inhibited creative thinking relative to individual brainstorming. Perhaps, then, individuals feared implicit criticism even when open criticism was not permitted. Also, individuals working in a real group are more likely to develop the same set or direction in their thinking than the same number of individuals working alone. Individuals working alone will probably develop 'sets', but these sets are likely to differ from person to person.

The 'nominal group superiority effect' first revealed in Taylor *et al.*'s experiment, has held up over a number of procedural variations. For example, Dunnette *et al.* (1963) used a similar design to Taylor *et al.*, but their subjects were research scientists and advertising people who had extensive prior experience of working with each other. Thus the groups were more like real groups in a working environment than were Taylor *et al.*'s student groups. The same three problems as those in the Taylor *et al.* study were used, plus the so-called 'People' problem (i.e. 'what adjustments and consequences would follow if people's average height increased to 80 inches and their average weight doubled?'). The performance of real brainstorming groups of size four was compared with that of nominal brainstorming groups of four. Again, the nominal groups produced more ideas, and more good ideas, than the real group. This led Dunnette *et al.* to conclude that brainstorming is most effective when undertaken by individuals working *alone* in an atmosphere free from the apparently inhibiting influence of group interaction.

Four-person groups, as in the above two studies, are at the low end of group size. Perhaps larger groups would show an advantage over nominal groups? Bouchard and Hare (1970) addressed this possibility in a study in which 84 male students individually brainstormed the 'thumbs' problem while a further 84 were assigned to groups of five, seven or nine persons. The results indicated that as group size increased, the advantage of the nominal groups also increased, both in terms of quantity and quality.

The problems used in the foregoing studies were rather artificial, or unreal, and possibly not very involving for the subjects. Dillon *et al.* (1972) used a topic that was both real-life and 'hot' at the time. This was, 'How might people influence U.S. foreign policy as a result of the U.S. invasion of Cambodia in 1970?' Once more, nominal groups out-scored real groups on the quantity of ideas for dealing with this question.

The nominal group superiority effect seems to be very robust and, in addition to the manipulations already described, it has withstood variations in sex of experimenter, presence of experimenter, and written *v.* tape-recorded responses (see Stein, 1975, Ch. XIII, for further details).

3 Deferment v. separation of judgement

Whether undertaken by individuals or groups, deferment of judgement is a key tenet of Osborn's description of brainstorming. Some research has considered whether it is really the deferment of judgement or simply the *separation* of judgement from production that is the effective feature. Brilhart and Jochem (1964) compared three different patterns of stages in problem solving. Pattern A was labelled 'ideas–criteria' and conformed to the normal brainstorming sequence of events, i.e. (1) analysis of the problem, (2) brainstorming production of ideas, (3) consideration of criteria, (4) evaluation, and (5) report of best idea. Pattern B ('criteria–ideas') reversed the order of steps 3 (criteria consideration) and 2 (idea production) but was otherwise the same as Pattern A. In Pattern C ('problem–solution') the following three steps were followed: (a) analysis, (2) simultaneous generation and evaluation of ideas, and (3) selection of best solution.

Five-man groups worked on three problems using three different patterns of steps and all group results were scored for quantity and quality of ideas produced. Patterns A and B resulted in many more ideas than Pattern C and Pattern A was best in terms of numbers of good ideas. So, it seems that separation of idea production and criteria consideration is useful in terms of quantity irrespective of the order of these two steps. However, the standard order used in brainstorming (i.e. 'ideas–criteria'), seems most effective in terms of quality of ideas, as compared to the other two patterns.

B. Checklists and morphological synthesis

The brainstorming technique was not very explicit on *how* to generate ideas, apart from urging free association. Warren and Davis (1969) compared three more specific methods that are suitable for individual use. Subjects were set the task of thinking of ideas for changing or improving a particular object, viz. a doorknob. One group of subjects was given a short checklist of general 'idea-spurring' suggestions (e.g. add something; subtract something; change colour; change materials, etc.). A second group was given a long checklist of 73 idea-spurring questions organized into nine categories [e.g. *magnify?* (add what?, time frequency, strength, etc.), *modify?* (meaning, colour, motion, etc.)]. The third group were instructed in a technique known as *morphological synthesis* (Zwicky, 1969). This technique requires the problem solver to list ideas for one aspect of the object in question along one axis and ideas for another aspect of the problem along a second axis. Novel ideas would then be found in the matrix formed by combining the two axes. For example, if the problem was to invent a new type of vehicle, this could be tackled by creating a matrix with ideas for power sources along one dimension (axis) and ideas for the medium of transport along the other dimension (see Fig. 9.1 for a possible morphological synthesis of the 'new vehicle' problem).

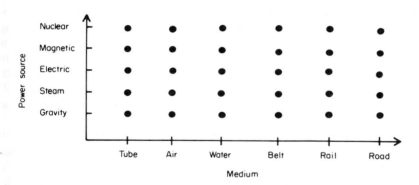

Fig. 9.1 Morphological synthesis applied to the 'new vehicles' problem.

Each point in the matrix (Fig. 9.1) represents some combination of power source and medium. Some are familiar, and some impossible; but others may be new and useful. Evidently, the number of combinations increases rapidly with the number of ideas per dimension. More than two dimensions may be used, leading to further increases in the number of combinations.

A fourth, control, group were given no particular instructions in problem-solving methods. Of the four groups, the short checklist and morphological synthesis groups produced the highest number of ideas and the greatest number synthesis groups produced the highest number of ideas and the greatest number of high-quality ideas. Surprisingly, perhaps, the long check-list produced no improvement over the control conditions. The morphological synthesis instructions produced the greatest number of ideas and had the highest rate of production; and so, when time is taken into account, this method appeared to be the most effective of those studied.

C. Synectics

A method which has been extensively taken up, especially in the United States, by industrial and other organizations that have practical and pressing needs for innovative ideas, is known as synectics (Gordon, 1961). Despite its wide use in practice, it does not seem to have attracted much laboratory investigation. Thus data on its utility are largely in the form of anecdotes. However, it is an interesting and plausible technique and is worth describing here, albeit briefly.

Synectics involves the joining together of different and apparently irrelevant elements by the use of metaphors and analogies. An unfamiliar problem may be better understood when it can be represented by an analogy with something familiar (i.e. 'making the strange familiar'). Conversely, a problem that is overfamiliar, and about which we have difficulty generating fresh ideas, can often be usefully handled by means of an unusual metaphor ('making the familiar strange'). These two uses of metaphor are helpful in developing formulations of problems. Four types of analogy are proposed for use in generating further ideas toward solutions: (1) personal analogy, (2) direct analogy, (3) symbolic analogy, and (4) fantasy analogy. The personal analogy requires that the problem solver identify him or herself with part or all of the problem and its solution (e.g. imagine how it would feel to be a zip fastener, if the problem was to improve on such a device). Direct analogy attempts to find parallel facts in other fields (e.g. considering biological examples of apertures that close up tightly in the zip fastener problem). The symbolic analogy involves a compressed description of the problem or of a possible solution, and may be verbal, or in the form of an image. For example, according to Stein (1974, p. 189), one group used the Indian rope trick as a symbolic analogy in developing a new jacking mechanism. Fantasy analogy allows purely wish-fulfilling and unrealistic proposals to be put forward. For example, on the problem of making a vapour-proof closure for space suits (earlier referred to as the zip fastener problem), one participant expressed a fantasy analogy as follows: ". . . wish fulfilment. Childhood dream . . . you wish it closed, and invisible microbes, working for you, cross hands across the opening and *pull* it tight."

Little work appears to have been published evaluating synectics, apart from anecdotal accounts of successes. However, Bouchard (1972) did find that use of the personal analogy technique led to improved performance in brainstorming as compared to a brainstorming without use of personal analogy. This result then, lends some laboratory support to the use of synectics.

D. Lateral thinking

De Bono (1983) has popularized the notion of *lateral thinking* as an aid to effective creativity and has developed instructional materials aimed at teaching lateral thinking skills. Lateral thinking involves re-representing a problem while, in contrast, normal ("vertical") thinking involves working *within* a given problem representation. Vertical thinking is seen as logical, sequential, predictable and habit-bound, whereas lateral thinking would be characterized by the opposite attributes. De Bono has devised a set of instructional materials known as the CoRT programme (named after de Bono's Cognitive Research Trust). These materials are intended to increase individuals' skills in lateral thinking. The programme involves six units each consisting of ten 35-minute lessons. The six units are outlined in de Bono (1983) and may be summarized as follows:

(1) CoRT1: *Breadth* – stresses thinking about problems in different ways.
(2) CoRT2: *Organization* – aims at effective control of attention.
(3) CoRT3: *Interaction* – focusses on questions of evidence and arguments.
(4) CoRT4: *Creativity* – provides strategies for producing unusual ideas.
(5) CoRT5: *Information and feeling* – considers affective factors related to thinking.
(6) CoRT6: *Action* – presents a general framework for tackling problems.

De Bono suggests that CoRT1 should be taught first, after which the other units can be used in any order. Broadly speaking, the CoRT lessons involve using "operators" which are given to help students retrieve and apply the operators when needed. Sample operators are "consider all factors" (CAF), and "positive, negative and interesting points" (PNI).

De Bono (1976) reports studies in which students who had undergone CoRT instructions produced more ideas than control groups. This certainly suggests a "quantity" effect; whether average quality was improved is unclear. The test questions were similar to the exercises in the training material and so the extent of transfer of training is also unclear. Edwards and Baldauf (1983) carried out an instructional study using CoRT1 and found that various measures of quantity and quality of divergent thinking improved after the CoRT1 course. Transfer of training in CoRT1 to performance in high school physics was investigated, but no clear indication of transfer emerged.

Rather stronger evidence supporting the CoRT programme comes from a Venezuelan study (de Sanchez and Astorga, 1983). Large groups of children received training in a version of the CoRT programme for periods of 1–3 years. Control subjects of similar background did not receive these lessons. Pre- and post-tests with divergent problems similar to those used in training showed significantly larger gains on quantity and quality measures for the experimental subjects compared to the controls. Interestingly, the relative gains increased with the number of years of training.

The results, particularly those of the Venezuelan study, are quite encouraging for the CoRT programme. However, questions regarding transfer to dissimilar tasks and long-term beneficial effects remain open.

IV. THEORETICAL APPROACHES

So far, our discussion of research on creative processes has been somewhat atheoretical. In this section I will consider some attempts to explain creative processes within the frameworks of theoretical approaches established in other areas. The approaches dealt with here are those of associative, Piagetian and information processing theory.

A. Associative theories

1 Mednick

Mednick (1962, p. 221) defines the creative thinking process as the "forming of associative elements into new combinations which either meet specified requirements or are in some way useful". On this view, then, the creative thinker comes up with useful combinations of ideas that are already in the thinker's repertoire but which have not been previously brought together (e.g. Salvador Dali combining the idea of a 'watch' with that of 'softness', producing the novel combination 'a soft watch'). In accord with the standard associative approach, ideas are assumed to be linked to each other, more or less directly and with varying degrees of strength, in a vast associative network. Thus 'watch' and 'clock' would tend to be strongly associated, whereas 'watch' and 'soft' would not be. Mednick suggests that the more weakly or indirectly connected two combined ideas are, the more original is their combination. As he puts it: "The more mutually remote the elements of the new combination, the more creative the process of solution" (1962, p. 221). Three ways are suggested in which 'mutually remote' ideas could be brought together.

(a) Serendipity. This is the accidental occurrence of environmental stimuli that evoke the requisite ideas in close proximity. Accidental events do seem to have played a role in a number of scientific discoveries and inventions, e.g. discovering the vulcanization of rubber, X-rays and penicillin.

Deliberate use of serendipity is not unknown in the arts and sciences. Mednick cites a physicist who keeps in a fishbowl large numbers of slips of paper each having some physical fact written on it. Every so often, he randomly draws pairs of facts from the bowl in the hope of finding new and useful combinations. The avant-garde author William Burroughs made good use of his 'cut up' method, which involved snipping portions from newspapers and randomly arranging and rearranging them until a suitable effect was obtained. Similarly, in painting, collages and *objets trouvés* deliberately involve chance elements.

(b) Similarity. The required elements may be evoked close together by similarity on some dimension. Examples would include rhymes, alliterations and homonyms.

(c) Mediation. The required ideas may be evoked through the mediation of associates that they have in common. For example, the idea of using a vacuum cleaner to remove a cloud of small flies that has settled on the ceiling may come about through an associative sequence such as 'ceiling–floor–vacuum cleaner' where the 'ceiling–vacuum cleaner' connection is mediated by their common associate 'floor'.

Given this view, Mednick proposes explanations of individual differences in creativity principally in terms of differences in associative organization. In particular, it is suggested that individuals may be characterized by the 'steepness' of their 'associative hierarchies'. Take the word 'table'. Two individuals may have the same set of associates to table, ordered in the same way, but one may have a steep hierarchy in which the most associated word ('chair') is much more strongly associated with 'table' than is the second associate ('cloth'). The other person may have a much flatter hierarchy in which the differences in strength between successive associates to 'table' are much less. Figure 9.2 represents two such hierarchies.

Mednick suggests that creative individuals may be characterized by relatively flat associative hierarchies which enable them to connect together remote ideas more readily than people with steep hierarchies. On the basis of this theory, Mednick devised the Remote Associates Test (RAT). In this test, each of the 30 items consists of three words, known to be mutually remote. The subject's tasks is to produce a fourth word which is a common associate of all three remote words. An example item is 'surprise, line, birthday', and the answer is 'party'. People with 'flat' hierarchies should find this test easier

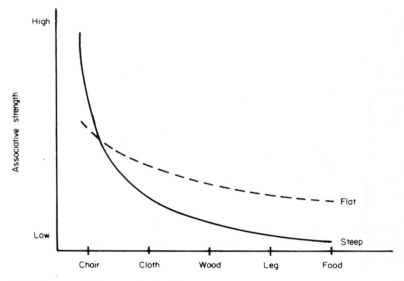

Fig. 9.2 Steep and flat associative hierarchies to the word 'table' (after Mednick, 1962).

than those with 'steep' hierarchies. The test displays satisfactory levels of reliability (around 0.91) and validation studies have been quite encouraging. Mednick reported a correlation of 0.7 between RAT score and rated creativity of design students. Other, weaker, but statistically significant connections were reported between RAT scores and creativity ratings of psychology graduate students, originality assessments of eminent architects and 'nonconformist' tendencies among students. Furthermore, high scorers on the RAT have been found to detect and use incidentally presented information to a greater degree than low RAT scorers (Mendelsohn and Griswold, 1964; Laughlin et al., 1968). This suggests that a broad, less focussed attentional style may underlie the development of the presumed flatter hierarchies of high RAT scorers.

Despite the plausibility of Mednick's theory and the early promise of the RAT, little further development seems to have occurred in this approach since the late 1960s. This may reflect a general disenchantment with simple associative theories of memory and thought. Before moving on to consider some approaches that allow more to mental organization than purely associative links a quite influential associative theory due to Koestler (1964) will briefly be discussed.

2 Koestler

Arthur Koestler (1964) has put forward a somewhat more sophisticated associative theory than Mednick's. However, perhaps because it derives very largely from case studies of numerous 'acts of creation' and has not led to laboratory tests, this theory has had little impact on psychology, although it has been well-received by the lay public. Koestler's *bisociative* theory claims that a creative act involves linking together two previously unconnected 'frames of reference' (also known as 'associative contexts', 'universes of discourse' or 'matrices'). Koestler proposes that, in given associative contexts ideas are connected by fixed rules, and that normal problem solving involves working with the established rules within one context (e.g. applying rules of chess, exploring permissible moves in an 8-puzzle problem, etc.). The (possibly apocryphal) case of Archimedes solving the problem of measuring the volume of an irregular object (a crown) serves to illustrate the bisociation of different associative contexts. None of the rules in Archimedes' habitual 'frame of reference' for measuring volume would yield the volume of a valuable crown without damaging it (e.g. by melting it down or by hammering it into a regular shape). Presumably, all the time, Archimedes also had rules relating to the 'bathing' context. One of the bathing rules would be that if one got into a full bath, the water would spill out. The volume-measuring 'frame of reference' and the bathing 'frame of reference' were suddenly linked when Archimedes noticed the water level rise as he stepped into a bath after thinking about the volume problem for a considerable time. It became clear that immersion of a body in a full container (as in bathing) would displace liquid whose volume could then be measured by the rules already well-established in the volume-measuring 'frame of reference'.

Koestler interpreted as cases of bisociation numerous other examples of scientific creativity (e.g. the discovery or invention of vaccination, printing, the notions of elliptical planetary orbits and evolution by natural selection). However, no predictions that could be tested in laboratory settings, or possible measures of individual differences that might be relevant to predicting creativity, have arisen from this theory. Indeed, Perkins (1981) has argued that Koestler's 'theory' of bisociation is essentially a redescription of creative products rather than a process explanation. Perkins's point is that a creative product is bound to involve a novel combination of ideas and thus can be described as 'bisociative'. It is not then helpful to say that there is a special process of bisociation that results in bisociative products. On this argument, Koestler's 'theory' is not a testable theory.

B. Gruber's Piagetian approach

Gruber (1980) has painstakingly analysed the case of Charles Darwin's development of evolutionary theory from a Piagetian point of view. Piagetian theory is, of course, mainly concerned with the development of concepts (e.g. that of the conservation of mass) in children, but Gruber shows that the approach can be usefully applied to conceptual growth in adults. Gruber points to the long time periods involved in developing significant new ideas. The emphasis on 'acts of creation' and 'moments of insight' has, perhaps, been misleading and diverted attention from the long-term growth-like processes in which moments of insight are embedded. Analysis of Darwin's notebooks indicates a series of changes in his 'system of ideas' concerning the relationship of biological and geological phenomena. Initially, the dominant conceptual scheme was that the physical world and the species inhabiting it were fixed at creation. However, evidence from geology more and more indicated a changing physical world. This led to a conceptual conflict. How could species fixed at creation remain adapted to changing environments? Darwin's first theory – the monad theory – suggested that simple living forms (monads) appeared through spontaneous generation from inanimate matter and then evolved to match the environment. This was fairly quickly abandoned and Darwin then sought other ways in which species could change. Hybridization seemed possible and led Darwin to a study of plant and animal breeding which increased his knowledge of artificial selection. The transmission of acquired characteristics was another possible solution and led Darwin into a study of mental processes and behaviour in animals and humans. Although this approach did not produce the desired answer to the question of heritable variation, it produced much evidence that would influence the final theory. Studying the evolution of mental processes also raised forcibly the issue of materialism. This was a somewhat suspect and dangerous idea at the time and Darwin expressed fear of persecution on account of his materialist notions. After many years of prior study and experience, Darwin read Malthus's *Essay on Population* on 28 September 1838, and this seems to have led him to realize that natural selection could work in favour of variants that were better suited to their environment than their ancestors had been. The idea of natural selection as a 'conservative' force, weeding out weak or maladapted variants was well known, but the positive aspects of natural selection, favouring the best adapted variants, had not been emphasized before Darwin's insight.

Darwin was not quite satisfied with the theory because it did not explain variation but rather took variation and heredity as unexplained assumptions. A further 20 years work and the stimulus of Wallace's independent conception of 'evolution by natural selection' were required before Darwin finally published his evolutionary theory.

Gruber emphasizes the slowness of the changes in Darwin's system of ideas and he interprets the process of change in terms of Piaget's notions of 'assimilation' and 'accommodation'. 'Assimilation' involves the incorporation of new information into existing conceptual structures, while 'accommodation' involves changes in conceptual structure brought about by new information. Gruber argues that what appear to be dramatic breaks with the past, can also be seen as the culmination of numerous small changes. This approach, then, places 'moments of insight' within their long-term context and would suggest that little understanding of high-order creativity will result from laboratory studies of small-scale problem solving.

C. The information processing approach

Simon (1966) indicated how the information processing approach might tackle the topic of creativity in science. He pointed out that high-level creativity in science is a very rare event and that scientific discovery is a very slow process (as Gruber has also argued). A theory of scientific creativity, therefore, should account not only for the occurrence of major conceptual advances but also for their rarity of occurrence. Simon proposed that the information processing theory of small-scale problem solving can be applied usefully to highly creative scientific thinking. The information processing theory of problem solving is basically that outlined in Chapters 2 and 3 of this book. Thinking is seen as a hierarchical organization of elementary processes carried out one at a time. Considerable search is postulated, limited by selective heuristics, such as means–end analysis.

Scientific biographies generally reveal considerable trial-and-error search through a vast space of alternative hypotheses before breakthroughs occur. Persistence and strong motivation are marked characteristics of successful scientists. Some scientists apparently have better heuristics than others and can reach solutions more rapidly on that account. A prime source of heuristics are good representational or observational methods. For instance, many advances followed the inventions of telescopes and microscopes. These devices presumably helped in formulating the nature of the relevant problems more clearly and in ruling out possible alternative hypotheses more decisively than had been possible previously.

Simon's outline of how scientific discovery might be accounted for in information processing terms has been vindicated by the development of computer program models capable of inducing laws such as Kepler's Third

Law of planetary motion (Langley *et al.*, 1987). The program BACON, reported by Langley *et al.*, uses simple heuristics to search through the space of possible laws that might interrelate quantitative data. For example, consider Kepler's Third Law. This says that the cube of a planet's distance from the sun is proportional to the square of its period.

Symbolically, the Law can be expressed as $D^3/P^2 = c$, where D is the distance, P is the period and c is a constant. Three heuristics aid in discovering such laws:

(1) If the values of a term are constant, then infer that the term always has that value.
(2) If the values of two numerical terms increase together, then consider their ratio.
(3) If the values of one term increase as those of another decrease, then consider their product.

Suppose data are available for three planets, as follows:

	P	D
Planet A	1.0	1.0
Planet B	8.0	4.0
Planet C	27.0	9.0

Heuristic 2 can be applied; since D increases with P, consider their ratio and call it Term 1. Applying the heuristic gives the following data:

	P	D	Term 1 (D/P)
Planet A	1.0	1.0	1.0
Planet B	8.0	4.0	0.5
Planet C	27.0	9.0	0.333

Now, D increases as Term 1 decreases. Thus, Heuristic 3 applies. Take the product of D and Term 1 and define it as Term 2 $(D(D/P) = D^2/P)$. Carrying out Heuristic 3 we now have the following:

	P	D	Term 1	Term 2 (D^2/P)
Planet A	1.0	1.0	1.0	1.0
Planet B	8.0	4.0	0.5	2.0
Planet C	27.0	9.0	0.333	3.0

Since Term 1 increases as Term 2 decreases, Heuristic 3 applies again. Define Term 3 as the product of Term 1 and Term 2 $((D/P)(D^2/P) = D^3/P^2)$. The data are now as follows:

	P	D	Term 1	Term 2	Term 3 (D^3/P^2)
Planet A	1.0	1.0	1.0	1.0	1.0
Planet B	8.0	4.0	0.5	2.0	1.0
Planet C	27.0	9.0	0.333	3.0	1.0

Term 3 is constant, so Heuristic 1 applies and we assert $D^3/P^2 = c$, which is Kepler's Third Law. Using the types of heuristics outlined in this example, Langley *et al.*'s discovery program, BACON, was able to discover a number of quantitative laws starting from tables of 'raw' data (e.g. Ohm's Law, Coulomb's Law).

What of incubation and possible unconscious processes in discovery and invention? Simon (1966) argued that incubation and inspiration phenomena could be explained in terms of two mechanisms he labelled *familiarization* and *selective forgetting*. Familiarization is a slow process of building up a representation of the problem and relevant data in long-term memory. It is assumed, that, in seeking information, the person is guided by a goal tree that is stored and developed in working memory. In the course of pursuing goals, information is obtained and added to the long-term memory. This information in turn is used in constructing new goals and sub-goals. Thus there is a continuous interaction between goal information in working memory and problem information in the long-term memory. When the problem is set aside the goal information is lost and has to be reconstructed again. However, when the problem is taken up again, there is more information about the task in the long-term memory than there was before, so a different set of goals and sub-goals will likely be erected and these may lead to a quick solution where the previous goals did not.

There is no need for parallel processing in this theory. Inspiration would be explained by a switch of attention to the problem, followed by rapid solution. Attention-switching could be accomplished by a time-sharing scheme that checked on outstanding goals or tasks at regular intervals and decided whether the current task should continue to occupy attention or whether to switch for a while to a different task. Such systems are common in computer installations and ensure that all outstanding claims on processing time get a fair share of attention. Further discussion of this topic will be found in the next chapter, where the issue of parallel *v.* serial thought processes is considered in the general context of research on thinking.

To sum up, Simon's (1966) analysis foreshadowed detailed computer models such as BACON which show concretely how the information processing approach can tackle creative processes in science.

V. SUMMARY AND CONCLUDING COMMENTS

This chapter has concerned the kinds of thinking involved in generating creative products, where a creative product was defined as being both novel and valuable, in some way. Studies of individuals acknowledged to be creative (i.e. to have a tendency to make creative products), noted tendencies towards dominance, radicalism and high intelligence as conventionally measured (Cattell and Drevdahl, 1955). In the sciences, creative individuals tended to be first-born or only sons (Roe, 1952). Aggression was not far below the surface, especially in connection with rival scientists. However, aggressive tendencies usually did not show up in projective test responses, probably because such tests were not congenial to the scientists' preferred 'convergent' style of thinking (Mitroff, 1974; Hudson, 1966).

Personal accounts by scientists and artists suggested four broad phases in creative work that Wallas (1926) labelled 'preparation', 'incubation', 'illumination' and 'verification'. Patrick's (1935, 1937) laboratory studies indicated some support, at least for the conscious phases or stages of preparation, illumination and verification. Her results on incubation were less clear, perhaps because the problems were too small-scale in terms of the times involved. Incubation has largely resisted capture in the laboratory, although Murray and Denny (1969) and Fulgosi and Guilford (1968) did find some beneficial effects of incubation opportunities. Even if incubation opportunities do facilitate later solution, the mechanisms involved are not clear. Both unconscious work and selective forgetting are viable explanatory candidates and will remain so until the appropriate experiments have been devised.

Various schemes for increasing idea-production have been promoted. Many studies have focussed on Osborn's brainstorming method, which involves deferment of idea evaluation until after a period of free-wheeling idea production. Brainstorming seems to be beneficial on many problems and appears to work both for groups and for individuals. However, from many experiments, it seems that the group version of the method is inhibiting compared to individual brainstorming (Stein, 1975). Other individual-oriented techniques, such as short idea-spurring checklists and Zwicky's (1969) morphological synthesis, appear to be useful (Warren and Davis, 1969). Although they have been widely adopted in practice, there has been little experimental evaluation of Gordon's (1961) synectics techniques, which are based on using various forms of analogy (personal, direct, symbolic and fantasy). Bouchard (1972) did find results in favour of using the personal analogies technique in brainstorming sessions. Some support has been reported for de Bono's (1983) lateral thinking programme.

A number of theoretical approaches were considered . Associative theory, as developed by Mednick (1962), gained some empirical support from the apparent validity of the Remote Associates Test, which was constructed on the basis of the theory. However, perhaps because of a general disenchant- ment with associative theories of thinking, this approach has not been further developed. Koestler's (1964) bisociative theory allows more complexity to mental organization than Mednick's associative theory and postulates 'asso- ciative contexts' or 'frames of reference'. He proposed that normal, non- creative, thought proceeds *within* particular contexts or frames and that the creative act involves linking together previously unconnected frames. Although Koestler's ideas are attractive they remain unexplored in the labo- ratory or by computer modelling. Like Koestler, Gruber (1980) has based his analysis on case studies. He has focussed especially on Darwin's development of the Theory of Evolution. Using Piagetian notions, such as assimilation and accommodation, Gruber shows how Darwin's system of ideas changed very slowly over a period of many years. 'Moments of insight', in Gruber's analysis, were the culmination of slow long-term processes. If this approach is accepted, laboratory analysis of high-level creativity would seem to be ruled out in favour of meticulous case studies. Finally, the information pro- cessing approach, as represented by Simon (1966) and Langley *et al.* (1987) was considered. Simon indicates how the apparent phenomena of incubation and inspiration could be explained in information processing terms by using the notions of 'familiarization' and 'selective forgetting'. No parallel pro- cessing is required by Simon's scheme. He points out the importance of good problem representations – both to ensure search is in an appropriate prob- lem space and to aid in developing heuristic evaluations of possible research directions. As Simon notes, many advances in science have followed improved representational technology (e.g. microscopes and telescopes). Also, he reminds us that the rate of progress in science is generally slow and this fact fits well with the information processing notion of the thinker as a limited-capacity, serial system, slowly searching for solutions in a vast space of possibilities. The work of Langley *et al.* (1987) demonstrates how such search processes, realized in computer programs, can indeed discover many basic laws of science from tables of raw data.

VI. FURTHER READING

Perkins, D.N. (1981). *The mind's best work*. Cambridge, Mass.: Harvard University Press. Perkins reviews the main theories and common beliefs about creativity and argues strongly in favour of the view that creative processes are essentially the ordinary processes of attention, memory and problem solving, suitably orchestrated.

Langley, P., Simon, H.A., Bradshaw, G.L. and Zytkow, J.M. (1987). *Scientific discovery: Computational explorations of the creative process.* Cambridge, Mass.: MIT Press. Langley *et al.* explain very clearly their impressive working models of scientific discovery as heuristically-guided search.

10
Thinking: theoretical overview, progress and prospects

In this book thinking has been taken to be a form of information processing and, on this view, models of thinking should fit in with more general frameworks for understanding human information processing. A number of broad frameworks have been proposed, and until the early 1980s certain assumptions were widely accepted by different theorists [from Broadbent (1958) to Anderson (1983)]. These common assumptions formed an important part of what I have referred to as the 'modal model' for thinking. According to the modal model, individuals have a vast long-term memory and a small-capacity working memory. These two memories are supplemented in the overall system by high-capacity but short-lived sensory memories (e.g. Sperling, 1960) which are not usually regarded as very important for thinking and may be ignored for our present purposes. In the modal model, thinking is seen as the manipulation of symbols both within working memory and between long-term and working memory. The manipulations are assumed to be in accord with rules stored in long-term memory. At a given time, the rule selected from long-term memory will depend on which goals are current and on the contents of the working memory. It is assumed that only one thinking step occurs at a time (the *seriality* assumption). This modal model of thinking, just outlined, was consistent with many broader frameworks for the whole human information processing system. However, recent approaches, such as connectionism, have been developed in which both the symbol manipulation assumptions *and* the seriality assumption are abandoned. Somewhat 'in between' positions have also been promoted in which symbol manipulation is assumed, although strict seriality is abandoned. These non-modal approaches will be considered shortly. But first, it is still worth asking "How well does the modal model of thinking cope with the experimental data?"

We will then consider a second question: "What implications do developments in our general understanding of human information processing have for models of thinking?"

In addition to these questions, this chapter will also suggest likely research trends in the thinking area.

I. MODAL MODEL ASSUMPTIONS

A. Memory and symbol manipulation

First, the memory assumptions of the modal model do not appear to be directly challenged by the data. Quite sharp limits on mental search were indicated by the data from both adversary and non-adversary problems. Thus, working memory can only sustain a limited size of symbol structure representing sequences of possibilities. These working memory limitations quite likely underlie the preference for depth-first searches, in which memory load grows slowly, compared to breadth first searches. The 'progressive deepening' strategy observed in chess play (De Groot, 1965) may reflect a familiarization process that builds up a structure in long-term memory to represent explored paths (Simon, 1966). Through a process of 'chunking', ultimately quite long paths can be represented by single symbols in working memory. Ericsson (1985) has shown that practice in chunking can lead to very large digit spans. Presumably experts could similarly increase their effective memory span, e.g. for chess move sequences. Differences in long-term memory contents between individuals are important in explaining skill differences in many areas of problem solving. For example, the data from studies of expertise indicate that the experts' advantage in many areas resides in vast collections of familiar patterns in long-term memory rather than in any quantitative superiority in working memory capacity beyond average levels. It was very notable that De Groot's (1965) chess masters searched to about the same depth as did less skilled players and this result suggests essentially equal working memory capacities in both groups. The greater effectiveness of the master players' mental explorations reflected the superior structuring they imposed on the initial problem configuration, compared to that of the good, but amateur, players. Similar results have been found with experts in other domains, such as physics problem solving (Chi *et al.*, 1982).

The notion that thinking is goal directed is non-controversial, at least in the case of problem solving. However, difficulties for the modal model do arise in connection with goal scheduling and with urgent interruptions to single-minded goal seeking, that demand attention in real time (Neisser, 1963b; Simon, 1967). These questions relate to the serial *v.* parallel thinking issue and will be discussed in the next section. Even the apparently undirected thoughts involved in daydreaming are in fact often related to goals (or 'current concerns'), although the thought sequence is not constrained by higher-level goals of 'keeping to the topic' or 'sticking to practical possibilities'. However, the occurrence of 'intrusive thoughts', reported in the daydreaming literature, is a possible problem for the modal serial model, in that such thoughts suggest parallel processes 'breaking through' into consciousness.

The view of thinking as symbol manipulation is fundamental to the information processing approach and is not challenged directly by the research results that have been reviewed here. However, the assumption that thinking can be fully described as symbol manipulation according to rules, has been questioned on philosophical grounds by John Searle (1984). Searle has argued that since thought is meaningful and meaning cannot reside merely in symbols, then thinking cannot be fully understood simply as symbol manipulation. In Searle's view, then, a robot equipped with an impeccable natural language understanding program would not truly "understand" language because it would only be manipulating symbols. The argument is bolstered by inviting the reader (assumed not to know Chinese language) to consider him or herself hand-simulating such a program to deal with Chinese inputs and produce Chinese outputs. Would the hand-simulator truly understand Chinese? Intuitively, it would seem not. However, a counter argument is that the broader context of processing must be considered, in that symbols relate to sensory inputs and motor outputs, as well as to each other. Meaning, it may be argued, resides in systems as wholes not in surgically isolated symbols or symbol strings.

Assuming that thinking is symbol-manipulating, the further specification of the modal model that manipulations are either within working memory (e.g. rearranging letters in a short anagram) or between working memory and long-term memory (e.g. in mental arithmetic, retrieving an intermediate sum from long-term memory and placing it in working memory) discounts manipulations occurring purely within long-term memory. On this point, the modal model clashes with notions of spontaneous activity within long-term memory as proposed by Freud (1900), Neisser (1963b), Singer (1975a) and Gestalt memory theorists (see Baddeley, 1976, Ch. 4) among others. Theorists who have postulated activity within long-term memory have usually also considered that this activity could occur in parallel with the main stream of conscious thinking. Since the notion of within long-term memory activity thus also clashes (potentially at least) with the seriality assumption, this matter will be discussed more fully in a later section on the issue of parallelism.

From this brief survey, then, the assumption of serial processing emerges as a very problematic aspect of the modal model. Hence, the seriality issue will now be considered in more detail.

B. Serial or parallel thought processes?

This question is very important for modelling thought in that the answer chosen influences the model maker's treatment of many other topics, e.g. interpretation of 'incubation' data, daydreaming (especially intrusive thoughts), goal scheduling and goal interruptions. This issue also impinges on the utility of verbal reports. If all thinking is serial, then verbal reports could give a good view of, at least, that large portion of thought which is in a verbal code or readily translatable into verbal terms (Ericsson and Simon, 1980, 1984). However, if parallel streams of thought exist and people can only report on that stream going through working memory, then much thought could not be reported and less direct methods would be needed to tap the 'underground' thought streams. Of course, the seriality assumption is simpler, more parsimonious and more testable than the alternative and has the advantage of leading to models for particular tasks that can readily be explored on existing computer systems which are completely serial devices. So, there is much to be said for adopting the seriality assumption as an initial hypothesis. Also, as Newell has argued (1962), an awkward possibility arises when parallel activities are permitted, in that information processing may become like an "Alice in Wonderland croquet game, with porcupine balls unrolling themselves and wandering off, and flamingo mallets asking questions at inopportune times" (p. 398). Here, Newell is pointing to the chaotic possibilities of parallel systems; however, other theorists have not been so deterred, and although some have willingly embraced chaos (e.g. as a potential source of novel ideas), yet others have striven to show how order and parallel activity can co-exist within a single system. Consideration of some of these proposals and of the 'serialist' treatment of the relevant data is now in order.

1 Neisser and Simon on the 'multiplicity' of thought

In a paper entitled 'The imitation of man by machine', Neisser (1963a) argued that thought is intimately linked with emotions and usually serves more than one goal at a time. He charged that information processing models cast in the form of computer programs lack any representation of emotion and are overly single minded in seeking relentlessly for a single top-level goal. Simon (1967) replied with suggestions for incorporating some emotional phenomena and for dealing with multiple goals. In the case of emotion, Simon proposed that emotion is associated with interruption of the current activity sequence by an urgent stimulus demanding real-time attention (e.g. shouts of 'Fire' while working on an algebra problem). However, to handle 'interruptions' Simon did allow that a low-level monitoring process may take place along with the main stream of thought. In his own words:

A certain amount of processing must go on continuously or almost continuously, to enable the system to *notice* when conditions have arisen that require ongoing programs to be interrupted. The noticing processes will be substantially in parallel with the ongoing goal attaining program of the total system, although this parallelism may be realized in fact, by the high frequency time sharing of a single serial processor (1967, p. 34, Simon's italics).

Thus, Simon raised the possibility of parallel 'noticing' processes that scan for 'danger' signals, but he kept open the serialist option of 'time sharing'. The notion of 'time sharing' is simply that the system rapidly switches from one program to another and so gives the appearance of doing two things at once without true simultaneity. Time sharing requires a higher-level program to determine which lower-level program should take over next and for how long. Time sharing is one way in which real computer systems allocate processing to the various jobs that come in and queue for attention. So, it is a method of known utility for serial systems.

Neisser's point about humans having multiple goals and being other than single minded is more easily tackled without parallelism. Simon showed that multiple goals can be readily generated in computer game playing, for instance, and that current goals can be set aside for other goals on the basis of time – and effort – limits put on the search for goal states.

Thus Neisser's anti-serialist points in his 1963a paper were acknowledged and largely 'defused' by Simon, but in a second paper in the same year, Neisser (1963b) espoused the radical notion of multiple simultaneous thought processes, and this concept cannot be accommodated within a serial framework.

Neisser proposed that a number of more or less independent trains of thought co-occur but that there is a 'main sequence' corresponding to the ordinary flow of consciousness. The main sequence, except perhaps in pathological cases, has control of motor activity. It was suggested that the unconscious trains of thought might generally follow the rules of Freud's primary process thinking and interact together in a chaotic way. However, when the main sequence is not too demanding the unconscious sequences may attain high degrees of complexity and do useful 'unconscious work' – the results of which can later be made available to consciousness. Accounts of incubation and inspiration in creative thinking were taken by Neisser as supporting these ideas. Serialist rejoinders (Simon, 1966; Ericsson and Simon, 1980, 1984) have tended to (a) play down the solidity of reports of incubation, and (b) to propose alternative explanations for any apparently well-founded claims of incubation phenomena. So, for instance, Ericsson and Simon pointed out that reports of incubation have frequently been given many years after the supposed events occurred. It could be that the scientists, inventors or artists concerned did start to consciously muse on their problems but, on the critical occasion of 'inspiration', rapidly solved, forgot the details of their own thought processes and then reported the event as one of sudden insight occurring without warning (Woodworth and Schlosberg, 1954). The occurrence of a rapid solution on trial $n + 1$ after n failures may be attributed (Simon, 1966) to beneficial forgetting of misleading sub-goals in the rest period between trial n and $n + 1$. The topic of 'incubation' is clearly very important for theories of thinking but unfortunately the supposed phenomenon has proven difficult to capture in the laboratory. Apart from a very few published experimental studies (e.g. Patrick, 1937; Murray and Denny, 1969; Fulgosi and Guilford, 1968; Dominowski and Jenrick, 1972; Olton and Johnson, 1976) there are only anecdotal data on which to rely. Of course, if incubation is a real phenomenon but is only associated with high-level creativity, psychologists are unlikely to be able to observe it with the usual laboratory tools of small-scale, often artificial, puzzles presented to normal subjects for short periods. Intuitively, incubation does seem to play a role in less exalted, more everyday forms of problem solving, and it may yet be possible to get leads on this elusive process, either in laboratory settings or perhaps through naturalistic 'diary' studies using more ordinary people than those whose recollections fill the anthologies on creative thinking experiences (e.g. Ghiselin, 1952). However, at present, the very existence of the phenomenon, let alone its explanation, is uncertain.

The question of 'intrusive' thoughts also arises in connection with the 'parallelism' issue. Becker *et al.* (1973) and Antrobus *et al.* (1966) found that unwelcome thoughts appear to intrude onto consciousness following exposure to disturbing information. This phenomenon is certainly consistent with Neisser's multiple thinking scheme. The rival serial position could propose, along with Simon's (1967) reply to Neisser (1963a), that goals of "assimilating the disturbing information" are set up and given high priority. Thus, a time sharing system could switch from external task goals to the 'intrusive' goals quite frequently. It is conceivable that a longstanding high-level goal will process disturbing information even if it is painful, and that this goal is not easily ignored.

2 Dissociations between verbal reports and behaviour?

If the important thought processes involved in problem solving are serial then it is reasonable to hope that verbal reports could be informative about the course of those processes. On the other hand, if parallel thought streams are importantly involved, the best verbal reports can only be very incomplete, being restricted to the main conscious stream. Thus, the status of verbal reports on mental processes is relevant to the serial *v.* parallel issue.

The question of the accuracy of verbal reports of mental activity has generated considerable controversy, since the era of the Introspectionists until the present time. A major critique of verbal reports as a source of information on cognitive processes was presented by Nisbett and Wilson (1977), which stimulated a reply from Ericsson and Simon (1980, 1984) who attempted to detail the circumstances under which the 'modal model' of thinking would expect verbal reports to be valid.

Nisbett and Wilson (1977) reviewed a dauntingly large collection of studies, mainly from the social psychological literature. The experiments reviewed by Nisbett and Wilson involved such varied topics as subjects changing their opinions (Goethals and Leckmann, 1973), coming to eat grasshoppers (Zimbardo *et al.*, 1969b), taking electric shocks (Zimbardo *et al.*, 1969a) and selecting which of four pairs of stockings they preferred. When subjects in these various studies were asked about the cognitive processes that had led them to make their responses, their verbal reports did not refer to the stimuli that the experimenters could demonstrate to be influencing their behaviour. In view of the very low accuracy of the verbal reports in these studies, Nisbett and Wilson concluded that reports on cognitive processes are not based on genuine 'privileged' information of a type only available to introspection but, rather, are based on implicit and widely held causal theories of which stimuli could cause given responses. This latter point draws its support from studies in which control subjects are asked to say which factors they think will be effective in particular experiments. Control groups' predictive judgements of the effectiveness of experimental variables were highly correlated with experimental subjects' judgements – but both sets of judgements were equally inaccurate. Nisbett and Wilson qualify their condemnation of verbal reports and allow that such reports may be accurate if confined to mental *contents* (e.g. contents of focal attention, current sensations, plans, etc.) but they maintain that verbal reports will be woefully inaccurate regarding mental *processes*. Thus, they are claiming that the most important processes underlying behaviour in a variety of tasks are unavailable to consciousness and that the conscious thought stream is largely epiphenomenal.

Even if Nisbett and Wilson's (1977) conclusions are accepted, a serial model could still be tenable, if the unreportable processes could be seen as not using working memory but as being run off in a 'ballistic' or 'compiled' mode, such as has been postulated for highly practised actions (e.g. Anderson, 1983). However, this explanatory escape route seems implausible, in view of the unfamiliar nature of many of the tasks in which inaccurate verbal reporting has been claimed. Ericsson and Simon (1980, 1984) take a different tack and, on the basis of the modal, serial model, they propose conditions under which accurate verbal reports should and should not occur. In particular they suggest that verbalization can only be expected to be accurate to the degree that the report is made *concurrently* with the task-related cognitive activity. Furthermore, for maximum validity the report should be made in a free manner, i.e. in the subject's own words, not confined to some experimenter-set categories which may not match the subject's own representational schemes. The basic notion put forward by Ericsson and Simon is that only information in focal attention can be verbalized. This principle limits 'verbalizable' information to that in working memory and, further, it predicts that information about the inputs and outputs of current processes will receive priority in free concurrent verbal reports. Ericsson and Simon point out that almost all the studies discussed by Nisbett and Wilson involved retrospective reports, often some considerable time after the behaviour concerned has occurred. The serial modal model would not predict accurate reports in such circumstances since the contents of working memory during processing are very transitory, and so subjects asked to give retrospective reports have to fall back on inferences based on their implicit causal theories of behaviour. Under more favourable conditions, such as in Newell and Simon's (1972) study of cryptarithmetic problem solving, Ericsson's (1975) studies of 8-puzzle performance and De Groot's (1965) studies of chess play, concurrent verbal reports appear quite consistent with behaviour and lead to coherent models of underlying processes.

From Ericsson and Simon's analysis, it follows that processes not using working memory will not be reportable. This would be true for highly practised sequences of operations. Beginners at writing, say, would perhaps be able to report how they wrote a 't', at least to the level of 'draw vertical' then 'put cross bar through vertical', whereas skilled writers would probably not be able to say with confidence which operation has been carried out first. Highly practised motor sequences become 'automatic' and seem to run off as wholes without reference to working memory. Of course, this is a generally useful development, though it can contribute to accidents since intermediate steps are not monitored and may be based on assumptions that no longer hold (see, e.g. Reason, 1979, and Norman, 1981a, on behavioural slips and accidents). On this view, the depth of detail with which processes can be verbally reported will depend on their degree of automaticity. Where sub-processes have not been 'compiled' or automatized into larger wholes, extensive detail would be expected. A further point of contention lies in Nisbett and Wilson's claim that although mental *processes* can never be reported, mental *contents* can sometimes be reported. This may be disputed. For example, if we set people the task of multiplying 11 × 15 while thinking aloud, the labels of various processes are likely to be mentioned, e.g. '*multiply* 5 × 11' or *add* 15 to 150'. Reports will tend to mention inputs, outputs *and* process labels. Admittedly, if we ask 'how did you multiply 5 × 11' the answer will likely be 'I don't know how – I just know its 55.' The relevant 'look up' or retrieval process from long-term memory is automatized in the practised numerate person. It seems that processes *can* be reported, down to the level of those component sub-processes that have been automatized.

Overall, then, it seems that much information on mental contents and processes can be accurately reported, in the proper conditions, up to the point at which automatized sub-processes come into play. The proper conditions include both the conditions of the main task and of the verbalization task. For accurate reports the task must not be too highly practised and free concurrent verbalization should be used since this will be much more likely to yield valid introspective reports than delayed retrospections to vague or inappropriate probes.

Thus, on the issue of serial *v.* parallel processing, it appears that the data from studies of subjective report validity are not absolutely decisive. In certain circumstances, detailed by Ericsson and Simon, and summarized above, valid reports of working memory contents, including process labels, can be given, in accord with the serialist position. A parallel model would interpret cases of valid verbal reporting to mean that, in the appropriate circumstances, behaviour is controlled by the introspectible main sequence. What of inaccurate verbal reports? The serialist position could account for many of these cases in terms of delays in reporting short-lived working memory contents, leading to retrospective rationalizations rather than to valid introspections, since the relevant information may have been lost before the query was made. Also, failures to report accurately may be due to the relevant processes being automatized and so not using working memory. The parallel alternative would propose that the effective processes were unconscious in the cases of inaccurate verbal reports and so were never available even for concurrent reports. In the face of the controversy over verbal report accuracy, it may be noted that an obvious research possibility is to carry out the relevant experiments reported by Nisbett and Wilson, but to obtain verbal reports in accord with the conditions that Ericsson and Simon deem ideal for valid introspective reports. If the results remained as before (i.e. inaccurate reports), then the view that important thought processes can be unconscious and parallel to the conscious stream would be upheld. In the absence of such experiments, perhaps a resolution of the serial *v.* parallel issue might be obtained by looking at the broader context of human information processing? Within this wider area a number of theorists have proposed schemes that incorporate parallel processes, yet still possess a degree of orderliness. The serialist position in thinking has generally derided the parallel alternative as being a recipe for chaos, while the opposite insult is that serial models are mechanistically single-minded. In conflicts like this, compromise positions are worth exploring and I will next consider some possible mergers of parallel and serial views.

3 Hierarchical parallelism

A popular analogy for an orderly parallel system is probably that of the hierarchical bureaucracy. In such systems, upper levels decide on broad forms of action while lower levels attend to the details. The various levels intercommunicate information and instructions. Most interestingly, the sub-systems at each level can work simultaneously and largely independently of each other.

So, while the chief executive of a large company is pondering the next 5-year plan, numerous shop-floor workers, clerks and intermediate level managers pursue their own functions. The levels must interact, of course, to avoid chaos developing. Thus, the upper levels have to monitor lower-level performance, send instructions down the line and receive information from below. Instructions from above are only as detailed as need be since they can be unpacked by lower-level specialists. So if the top level decrees "increase production of Brand Y and phase out Brand X", lower-level specialists will attend to the details of, say, increasing orders of some raw materials and reducing others, shifting workers and changing equipment, etc.

Indeed the upper levels do not need to know how the lower levels actually execute their orders ('principle of executive ignorance' – Becker, 1975). Similarly, on this type of model, within an individual person an upper-level process may initiate an action sequence (e.g. picking up a cup), but no information about the lower-level, detailed sensory-motor processes that execute the sequence is available to the upper levels. Johnson-Laird (1983) has developed a computational model, incorporating hierarchical parallel processes. This is similar to the 'bureaucratic' model but without the homuncular overtones. The top level of this system is identified with computer operating systems that govern the behaviour of sub-processes rather than with human executives.

The motivation for hierarchical or multi-level parallel models of human information processing becomes more apparent if one steps back from the 'thinking' domain and looks more broadly at human behaviour. The 'thinker', after all, may be driving a car, walking or carrying out any other routine activity at the same time as mentally exploring a chess problem. These abilities to carry out two or more tasks simultaneously can readily be explained in terms of different levels and types of processing which can proceed simultaneously as long as they do not require the same input and output channels. The multi-level approach explains why some task combinations are easier than others (i.e. those not requiring the same input and output channels) and also helps explain why drugs and stress may have unexpected effects, e.g. depressants, such as alcohol, may knock out an upper level and lead to increased activity by lower-level processes normally controlled by the upper level (see Broadbent, 1977, for a very relevant general discussion), producing the apparent paradox of a depressant drug increasing overt activity rather than decreasing it. These points about task compatibility and differential (and unexpected) effects of drugs, stress, fatigue, brain damage, and so on, do not seem to be so readily met by the thorough-going serialist proposal that *all* appearances of parallel activity are due to the 'time sharing' of a single central processor.

4 Parallel production systems

Approaching the question from the neuropsychological angle, a number of theorists have put forward possible schemes of parallel neural activity (e.g. Arbib, 1972; Shallice, 1972, 1978). The brain, of which thought is a product, appears to be highly parallel in its operations, and Allport (1980a) has recently argued strongly in favour of the view that processing is distributed throughout the brain. On the bases of neurological data, of experiments on divided attention (e.g. Spelke *et al.*, 1976), and of production systems notions in AI, Allport proposes that the human information processing system can best be represented by a highly parallel model in which productions can 'fire' independently and simultaneously. On this scheme no central processor is required. A 'withering away' of the executive is attractive in view of the unfortunate homuncular properties of the 'central processor/executive' in most prior models. Conflicts between productions calling for the same output systems could be handled by means of other productions which are triggered by conflict states and which specialize in resolving conflicts. Thus a special executive or decision maker does not need to be postulated, since the decision-making functions can be taken over by production rules identical in form to all the other production rules stored in long-term memory. [Many of these ideas have been developed, apparently independently, in Holland *et al.*'s (1986) model for induction, which is discussed in Chapter 4.]

What limits might there be on parallel mental activity? Allport (1980b) suggests that various forms of inter-process interference impose limitations. Physically incompatible actions cannot occur simultaneously and so must be 'queued' or alternated. Slightly more subtly, on the production system approach, if two activities have similar conditions, there is a grave risk of 'cross-talk', such that the stimuli meant to be dealt with by activity 1 actually elicit activity 2 and vice versa. Such 'data-specific' limitations would clearly restrict the degree to which the activities concerned could be carried out effectively in parallel with each other.

How might these limitations affect thinking? In the case of problem solving, it may well be that data-specific limitations would restrict parallel, mental exploration of alternative courses of action within a single problem. If

parallel exploration was attempted then the productions involved in generating and assessing the different alternatives would be in danger of calling on
similar data (i.e. the task definitions) and so interfere with one another.
Therefore, simultaneous exploration of different lines of attack on the same
problem seems unlikely. However, when a problem has been thoroughly
familiarized and can be explored mentally without references to outside
sensory channels or to external memories *and* the mainstream of thought is
concerned with some other goal, it is possible that some work could take
place on the familiarized problem in parallel with the mainstream. These conditions for successful parallel streams of thought are essentially those
reported for successful incubation. So, although this particular parallel processing approach does not predict simultaneous thought streams on the *same*
problem, it would be compatible with some parallel thinking on *different*
problems. Thus, it seems that a broad range of data favours a parallel or distributed processing approach to human information handling, but there are
severe limits on the degree of parallelism in thinking. Thus, in many cases,
especially of directed thinking, a serial model will be consistent with the data.

5 The connectionist approach

Connectionist approaches differ from the parallel models discussed so far in
that they postulate massively parallel processing carried out by *sub-symbolic*
units. Holland *et al.*'s (1986) model, for example (discussed in Chapter 4),
proposes a relatively modest degree of parallel activity at the symbolic level of
production rules. Connectionist theorists argue that production systems lack
psychological reality and that although such systems may summarize mental
processes in a rather approximate way, a more accurate characterization of
mental processes will be given by analyses in terms of densely interconnected
units which fluctuate in activation level and pass excitatory and inhibitory
signals among themselves. The units are taken to represent micro-features
and recognition of a single symbol is assumed to involve cooperative activity
among a large network of relevant units. For example, recognition of the
symbol "A" is interpreted as due to the response of a network of micro-
featural units which respond maximally to the constituent features of the
graphemic input "A", while other networks do not respond so strongly to
this input. (See McClelland *et al.*, 1986b, for a more detailed overview of the
connectionist approach). Connectionist models have proven fruitful in
studies of letter and word recognition (Rumelhart and McClelland, 1982),
associative learning (McClelland and Rumelhart, 1986) and in learning past
tenses of verbs (Rumelhart and McClelland, 1986). The models are fairly
readily computable (even on strictly serial machines) and often deliver
surprisingly human-like performance. For many years cognitive models

have been guided by the "(serial) computer metaphor"; the connectionist approach offers an alternative, "brain metaphor" (Rumelhart *et al.*, 1986b).

At first sight, the notion of massively parallel activity in sub-symbolic units would not appear to be applicable to sequential thinking. However, Rumelhart *et al.* (1986c) and Smolensky (1986) have indicated possible applications. Rumelhart *et al.* suggest that thinking involves a succession of states of consciousness in which the stable states last about 500 milliseconds and the transitions require in the order of 100 milliseconds. They then argue that the stable states of consciousness reflect stable states of activation in the underlying network of sub-symbolic units and that about 100 milliseconds is a reasonable estimate of the time required for a new activation pattern to become established. Since the network can only be in one state at any one time, an appearance of seriality holds when the time-scale of study is in terms of seconds or minutes, as is usually the case in studies of problem solving, for example. With shorter time-scales, up to 100 milliseconds or so, parallel processes of interpretation emerge into theoretical view. Rumelhart *et al.* (1986c) further propose that much problem solving involves a cyclical process of creating a representation (i.e. a stable state of the network), processing that state to produce a new representation (network state) and so on, until a goal state is recognized. The account has plausibility for routine types of problem solving such as adult mental arithmetic. Rumelhart *et al.* also indicate how their approach could lead to a model for playing the game known as tic-tac-toe in the United States and as noughts-and-crosses in Britain. The model incorporates a representation of both the player and his or her opponent, and essentially "imagines" a whole game of moves and counter-moves. Although Rumelhart *et al.* do not discuss the notion of a working memory in their treatment of thinking, some such notion seems needed for those cases where a subject thinks ahead through a tree of alternative moves before selecting one (Holding, 1985, reports considerable relevant data on search in chess, for example). However, McClelland (1986) describes a 'programmable blackboard model' which offers a possible treatment of working memory in a connectionist scheme. Perhaps, therefore, this aspect of thinking will also be dealt with in later developments of the theory.

Norman (1986) suggests that a dual model, with a connectionist approach to lower-level cognition and a serial approach to higher-level cognition, may be a good theoretical combination. The next few years should make clearer how far connectionist analyses can be pushed into the realms of higher mental processes and how much will be left for Norman's proposed higher-level "overseeing" serial system to accomplish.

II. THEORETICAL PROGRESS?

Has the information processing approach to thinking led to genuine progress in our understanding of thought? Certainly, within the framework of the modal model, H.A. Simon and his colleagues at Carnegie-Mellon University have succeeded in interpreting an ever widening range of thinking tasks over the last 30 years or so. Their task analyses have ranged from symbolic logic (Newell *et al.*, 1958), cryptarithmetic, chess (Newell and Simon, 1972), understanding task instructions (Simon and Hayes, 1976) and the accuracy of introspective data (Ericsson and Simon, 1980, 1984) to scientific discovery (Langley *et al.*, 1987). Therefore, it would seem that steady progress has been demonstrated by this research team. However, as indicated in the previous sections of this chapter, there is some dissatisfaction with the limited, rather one-dimensional, perspective of the modal model. Richer models are under development, but it seems likely that the serial model will survive as a component of a broader scheme which also includes a large degree of distributed processing.

Despite the good example of the Carnegie-Mellon group, it must be admitted that the thinking field of research could still be accused with some justice, of being excessively 'phenomenon-driven' and not sufficiently concerned with general theory (as Newell, 1973, charged of cognitive psychology in general). It is quite easy to list a string of phenomena that have attracted research, e.g. 'state-action problems', 'expert and novice memory', 'atmosphere effect', 'matching bias', 'verification set', 'intrusive thoughts', 'incubation', 'brainstorming', 'introspective accuracy' and 'analogy-use', among others. Unfortunately, a truly general theory that would tie all these topics together convincingly is lacking. Although some theoretical progress has been made, particularly by the Carnegie-Mellon group, and parallel distributed processing notions look promising, the overall problem of accounting for thought in all its manifestations still stands as a challenge to future researchers and theorists.

III. RESEARCH TRENDS?

Will future research be essentially 'more of the same'? Recent research has shown a change in emphasis away from laboratory settings toward more real-life tasks (e.g. Isenberg's, 1987, study of senior managers' thinking). This trend is likely to continue.

It is notable that many of the earlier studies reviewed in this book used very artificial tasks (e.g. missionaries-and-cannibals; Wason's four-card task). Arguments for using simple, artificial materials are generally in terms of equating subjects' prior task experience and helping to ensure uniform interpretations of task materials. Of course, experimenters hoped that the artificial tasks would reflect aspects of real-life problem solving, such as 'looking ahead' or 'testing hypotheses'. In Neisser's (1976) terminology, 'ecological validity' was hoped for – but rarely demonstrated. A recent research trend has been to focus on real-life skills expertise, although often studied in artificial settings, as against the real contexts in which the skills are exercised. To complement laboratory studies, it is very worthwhile to examine cases of real-life problem solving. For instance, Mitroff's (1974) study of moon scientists indicated that 'verification' tendencies were by no means limited to artificial laboratory conditions. This study also helped to explain why verification tendencies arise in view of the positive, motivating functions of a personal commitment to a hypothesis. Furthermore, Mitroff highlighted the long-term and social dimensions of much real-life problem solving – factors which are generally still ignored in laboratory investigations. Therefore, it would seem desirable for more effort to go into studies of real-life problem solving and thinking in the future.

Csikszentmihalyi's (1975) research on the experience of self-motivated problem solving suggests other reasons for studying real-life problem solving. Csikszentmihalyi found that people reported very enjoyable 'flow' experiences when totally absorbed in self-set problems that matched their skill levels. So, the mountaineer, the chess player and the surgeon, for instance, find enormous satisfaction when they are working on problems just within their skill limits. If the problems are too easy, boredom results, and if they are too difficult, anxiety is produced. A better understanding of motivation for problem solving may come from such out-of-the-laboratory studies. In the laboratory, the motivation is supplied by an outside agent, the experimenter. It may be that the levels of performance obtained (e.g. depth of look-ahead) would be much greater with self-motivation and when the problem is enjoyed for its own sake. That problem solving is often enjoyable is evident from the reports cited by Csikszentmihalyi and also from the high circulation figures of puzzle magazines, the enduring popularity of crossword puzzles and the recent successes of Rubik's cube and its derivatives and descendants.

IV. CONCLUDING COMMENTS

I will finish by summarizing very briefly my conclusions about the recent past and the possible future of studies of thinking. Although the serial model of human thinking has coped with a wide range of data, there are anomalies (e.g. incubation, intrusive thoughts), that tax the serial scheme. These, together with difficulties for the general serialist framework (e.g. Allport, 1980a, b; Rumelhart *et al.*, 1986a; McClelland *et al.*, 1986a) suggest that there will be an increasing trend toward parallel distributed processing models. In terms of research techniques, more out-of-laboratory studies seem likely and would be very useful complements to laboratory methods.

V. FURTHER READING

McClelland, J.L., Rumelhart, D.E. and Hinton, G.E. (1986). The appeal of parallel distributed processing. In D.E. Rumelhart, J.L. McClelland and the PDP Research Group (Eds), *Parallel distributed processing*, Vol. 1, pp. 3–44. Cambridge, Mass.: MIT Press. An excellent introduction to the connectionist approach by three of its leading protagonists.

Rumelhart, D.R., Smolensky, P., McClelland, J.L. and Hinton, G.E. (1986). Schemata and sequential thought processes in PDP models. In J.L. McClelland, D.E. Rumelhart and the PDP Research Group (Eds), *Parallel distributed processing*, Vol. 2, pp. 7–57. Cambridge, Mass.: MIT Press. Connectionism applied to thinking; this approach is likely to be very influential in the study of thought processes in the next few years.

References

Adamson, R.E. and Taylor, D.W. (1954). Functional fixedness as related to elapsed time and set. *Journal of Experimental Psychology* **147**, 122–126.

Adelson, B. (1981). Problem solving and the development of abstract categories in programming languages. *Memory and Cognition* **9**, 422–433.

Albert, R.S. (1975). Toward a behavioral definition of genius. *American Psychologist* **30**, 140–151.

Allport, D.A. (1980a). Patterns and actions: Cognitive mechanisms are content-specific. In G. Claxton (Ed.), *Cognitive psychology*, pp. 26–64. London: Routledge and Kegan Paul.

Allport, D.A. (1980b). Attention and performance. In G. Claxton (Ed.), *Cognitive psychology*, pp. 112–153. London: Routledge and Kegan Paul.

Anderson, J.R. (1978). Arguments concerning representations for mental imagery. *Psychological Review* **86**, 249–277.

Anderson, J.R. (1983). *The architecture of cognition*. Cambridge, Mass.: Harvard University Press.

Antrobus, J.S., Singer, J.L. and Greenberg, S. (1966). Studies in the stream of consciousness: Experimental enhancement and suppression of spontaneous cognitive process. *Perceptual and Motor Skills* **23**, 399–417.

Antrobus, J.S., Coleman, R. and Singer, J.L. (1967). Signal detection performance by subjects differing in predisposition to daydreaming. *Journal of Consulting Psychology* **31**, 487–491.

Anzai, Y. and Simon, H.A. (1979). The theory of learning by doing. *Psychological Review* **86**, 124–140.

Arbib, M. (1972). *The metaphorical brain*. New York: John Wiley.

Atwood, M.E. and Polson, P.G. (1976). A process model for water jug problems. *Cognitive Psychology* **8**, 191–216.

Atwood, M.E., Masson, M.E.J. and Polson, P.G. (1980). Further exploration with a process model for water jug problems. *Memory and Cognition* **8**, 182–192.

Baddeley, A.D. (1976). *The psychology of memory*. New York: Basic Books.

Baddeley, A.D. (1986). *Working memory*. Oxford: Oxford University Press.

Barron, F. (1955). The disposition toward originality. *Journal of Abnormal and Social Psychology* **51**, 478–485.

Baylor, G.W. and Gascon, J. (1974). An information processing theory of aspects of the development of weight seriation in children. *Cognitive Psychology* **6**, 1–40.

Becker, J.D. (1975). The formal representation of behaviour. In D.G. Bobrow and A. Collins (Eds), *Representation and understanding*. London and San Diego: Academic Press.

Becker, S., Horowitz, M. and Campbell, L. (1973). Cognitive responses to stress: Effects of changes in demand and sex. *Journal of Abnormal Psychology* **82**, 519–522.

Begg, I. and Denny, J.P. (1969). Empirical reconciliation of atmosphere and conversion interpretations of syllogistic reasoning errors. *Journal of Experimental Psychology* **81**, 351–354.

Bell, A.G. (1978). *The machine plays chess?* Oxford: Pergamon Press.

Berkowitz, J.(1969). *The roots of aggression*. New York: Lieber-Atherton.

Berlyne, D.E. (1965). *Structure and direction in thinking*. New York: John Wiley.

Bernoulli, D. (1954). Exposition of a new theory on the measurement of risk. *Econometrika* **22**, 23–26. (Originally published, 1738.)

Bhaskhar, R. and Simon, H.A. (1977). Problem solving in semantically rich domains: An example from engineering thermodynamics. *Cognitive Science* **1**, 193–215.

Birch, H.G. (1945). The relation of previous experience to insightful problem solving. *Journal of Comparative Psychology* **38**, 367–383.

Birch, H.G. and Rabinowitz, H.S. (1951). The negative effect of previous experience on productive thinking. *Journal of Experimental Psychology* **41**, 122–126

Boden, M.A. (1987). *Artificial intelligence and natural man*, 2nd edition. Cambridge, Mass.: MIT Press.

Bouchard, T.J., Jr (1972). A comparison of two group brainstorming procedures. *Journal of Applied Psychology* **56**, 418–421.

Bouchard, T.J., Jr and Hare, M. (1970). Size, performance, and potential in brainstorming groups. *Journal of Applied Psychology* **54**, 51–55.

Bourne, L.E. (1966). *Human conceptual behavior*. Boston, Mass.: Allyn and Bacon.

Bracewell, R.J. (1974). Interpretation factors in the four card selection task. Paper presented at the Selection Task Conference, Trento, Italy, 17–19 April.

Bracewell, R.J. and Hidi, S.E. (1974). The solution of an inferential problem as a function of stimulus materials. *Quarterly Journal of Experimental Psychology* **26**, 480–488.

Brilhart, J.K. and Jochem, E.M. (1964). Effects of different patterns on outcomes of problem solving discussions. *Journal of Applied Psychology* **48**, 175–179.

Broadbent, D.E. (1958). *Perception and Communication*. Oxford: Pergammon Press.

Broadbent, D.E. (1977). Levels, hierarchies, and the locus of control. *Quarterly Journal of Experimental Psychology* **29**, 181–201.

Broadbent, D.E. (1987). Simple models for experimentable situations. In P. Morris (Ed.), *Modelling cognition*, pp. 169–186. New York: John Wiley.

Brown, J. (1958). Some tests of the decay theory of immediate memory. *Quarterly Journal of Experimental Psychology* **10**, 12–21.

Brown, R. (1973). *A first language*. Cambridge, Mass.: Harvard University Press.

Bruner, J.S. (1957). On going beyond the information given. In H.E. Gruber *et al.* (Eds) *Contemporary approaches to cognition*, pp. 41–69. Cambridge, Mass.: Harvard University Press.

Bruner, J.S., Goodnow, J.J. and Austin, G.A. (1956). *A study of thinking*. New York: John Wiley.

Burnham, C.A. and Davis, K.G. (1969). The 9-dot problem – beyond perceptual organization. *Psychonomic Science* **17**, 321–323.

Cattell, R.B. (1959). The personality and motivation of the researcher from measurements of contemporaries and from biography. In C.W. Taylor (Ed.), *The 1959 University of Utah Research Conference on the Identification of Creative Scientific Talent*. University of Utah Press.

Cattell, R.B. and Drevdahl, J.E. (1955). A comparison of the personality profile (16PF) of eminent researchers with that of eminent teachers and administrators, and of the general population. *British Journal of Psychology* **46**, 248–261.

Ceraso, J. and Provitera, A. (1971). Sources of error in syllogistic reasoning. *Cognitive Psychology* **2**, 400–410.

Chalmers, A.F. (1978). *What is this thing called science?* Milton Keynes: Open University Press.

Chapman, J.L. and Chapman, J.P. (1959). Atmosphere effect re-examined. *Journal of Experimental Psychology* **58**, 220–226.

Charness, N. (1976). Memory for chess positions: Resistance to interference. *Journal of Experimental Psychology: Human Learning and Memory* **2**, 641–653.

Charness, N. (1979). Components of skills in bridge. *Canadian Journal of Psychology* **33**, 1–16.

Charness, N. (1981a). Aging and skilled problem solving. *Journal of Experimental Psychology: General* **110**, 21–38.

Charness, N. (1981b). Search in chess: Age and skill differences. *Journal of Experimental Psychology: Human Perception and Performance* **7**, 467–476.

Charness, N. (1981c). Visual short term memory and aging in chess players. *Journal of Gerontology* **36**, 615–619.

Chase, W.G. and Simon, H.A. (1973a). Perception in chess. *Cognitive Psychology* **4**, 55–81.

Chase, W.G. and Simon, H.A. (1973b). The mind's eye in chess. In W.G. Chase (Ed.), *Visual information processing*, pp. 215–282. London and San Diego: Academic Press.

Cheng, P.W. and Holyoak, K.J. (1985). Pragmatic reasoning schemas. *Cognitive Psychology* **17**, 391–416.

Chi, M.T.H., Glaser, R. and Rees, E. (1982). Expertise in problem solving. In R.J. Sternberg (Ed.), *Advances in the psychology of human intelligence*, Vol. 1, pp. 7–75. Hillsdale, N.J.: Lawrence Erlbaum Associates.

Clancey, W.J. (1984). Methodology for building an intelligent tutoring system. In W. Kintsch, H. Miller and P. Polson (Eds), *Methods and tactics in cognitive science*, Hillsdale, N.J.: Lawrence Erlbaum Associates.

Clement, J. (1982). Analogical reasoning patterns in expert problem solving. Paper presented at the 4th Annual Conference of the Cognitive Science Society, August 1982 Ann Arbor.

Cohen, L.J. (1981). Can human irrationality be experimentally demonstrated? *Behavioral and Brain Sciences* **4**, 317–331.

Craik, K.J.W. (1943). *The nature of explanation.* Cambridge: Cambridge University Press.

Csikszentmihalyi, M. (1975). *Beyond boredom and anxiety.* San Francisco: Jossey-Bass.

De Bono, E. (1976). *Teaching thinking.* London: Temple Smith.

De Bono, E. (1983). The Cognitive Research Trust (CoRT) thinking program. In W. Maxwell (Ed.), *Thinking: the expanding frontier*, Philadelphia, Pa.: The Franklin Institute Press.

De Groot, A.D. (1965). *Thought and choice in chess.* The Hague: Mouton.

De Sanchez, M.A. and Astorga, M. (1983). *Projecto aprendar a pensor.* Caracas: Ministerio de Educacion.

Dillon, P.C., Graham, W.K. and Aidells, A.L. (1972). Brainstorming on a 'hot' problem: Effects of training and practice on individual and group performance. *Journal of Applied Psychology* **56**, 487–490.

Dominowski, R.L. (1981). Comment on "An examination of the alleged role of 'fixation' in the solution of several insight problems" by Weisberg and Alba. *Journal* of Experimental Psychology: General **110**, 193–198.

Dominowski, R.L. and Jenrick, R. (1972). Effects of hints and interpolated activity on solution of an insight problem. *Psychonomic Science* **26**, 335–338.

Doran, J.W. and Michie, D. (1966). Experiments with the graph traverser program. *Proceedings of the Royal Society* **A294**, 235–259.

Drevdahl, J.E. and Cattell, R.N. (1958). Personality and creativity in artists and writers. *Journal of Clinical Psychology* **14**, 107–111.

Duncker, K. (1945). On problem solving. *Psychological Monographs* **58** (270), 1–113.

Dunnette, M.D., Campbell, J. and Jaastad, K. (1963). The effects of group participation on brainstorming effectiveness for two industrial samples. *Journal of Applied Psychology* **47**, 10–37.

Edwards, J. and Baldauf, R.B. (1983). Teaching thinking in secondary science. In W. Maxwell (Ed.), *Thinking: the expanding frontier*, Philadelphia, Pa.: The Franklin Institute Press.

Edwards, W. (1977). Use of multiattribute utility measurement for social decision making. In D.F. Bell, R.L. Keeney and H. Raiffa (Eds), *Conflicting objectives in decisions*. Chichester: John Wiley.

Egan, D.W. and Greeno, J.G. (1974). Theories of rule induction: Knowledge acquired in concept learning, serial pattern learning, and problem solving. In L.W. Gregg (Ed.), *Knowledge and cognition*, pp. 43–104. New York: John Wiley.

Eisenstadt, M. and Kareev, Y. (1977). Perception in game playing. In P.N. Johnson-Laird and P.C. Wason (Eds), *Thinking*, pp. 548–564. Cambridge: Cambridge University Press.

Ellen, P. (1982). Direction, past experience and hints in creative problem solving: reply to Weisberg and Alba. *Journal of Experimental Psychology*: *General* **111**, 316–325.

Elstein, A.S., Shulman, L.S. and Sprafka, S.A. (1978). *Medical problem solving: an analysis of clinical reasoning*. Cambridge, Mass.: Harvard University Press.

Engle, R.W. and Bukstel, L. (1978). Memory processes among bridge players of differing expertise. *American Journal of Psychology* **91**, 673–689.

Erickson, J.R. (1974). A set analysis theory of behavior in formal syllogistic reasoning tasks. In R. Solso (Ed.), *Theories of cognitive psychology*: *The Loyola Symposium*. Hillsdale, N.J.: Lawrence Erlbaum Associates.

Erickson, J.R. (1978). Models of formal reasoning. In R. Revlin and R. Mayer (Eds), *Human reasoning*. Washington, D.C.: V.H. Winston.

Ericsson, K.A. (1975). Instruction to verbalize as a means to study problem solving processes with the 8-puzzle: A preliminary study. Report No. 458, Department of Psychology, The University of Stockholm, Stockholm.

Ericsson, K.A. (1985). Memory skill. *Canadian Journal of Psychology* **39**, 158–231.

Ericsson, K.A. and Simon, H.A. (1980). Verbal reports as data. *Psychological Review* **87**, 215–251.

Ericsson, K.A. and Simon, H.A. (1984). *Protocol analysis*. Cambridge, Mass.: MIT Press.

Erlich, K. and Soloway, E. (1984). An empirical investigation of tacit plan knowledge in programming. In J.C. Thomas and M.L. Schneider (Eds), *Human factors in computing systems*, Norwood, N.J.: Ablex.

Ernst, G.W. and Newell, A. (1969). *GPS: A case study in generality and problem solving*. London and San Diego: Academic Press.

Evans, J. St. B.T. (1980a). Current issues in the psychology of reasoning. *British Journal of Psychology* **71**, 227–239.

Evans, J. St. B.T. (1984). Heuristic and analytic processes in reasoning. *British Journal of Psychology* **75**, 451–458.

Evans, J. St. B.T. and Lynch, J.S. (1973). Matching bias in the selection task. *British Journal of Psychology* **64**, 391–397.

Evans, J. St. B.T. and Wason, P.C. (1976). Rationalization in a reasoning task. *British Journal of Psychology* **67**, 479–486.

Findler, N. (1978). Computer poker. *Scientific American* **239**, 112–119.

Freud, S. (1900). The interpretation of dreams. In *Standard Edition*, Vols IV and V. London: Hogarth Press, 1953. (First German edition, 1900.)

Frey, P.W. and Adesman, P. (1976). Recall memory for visually presented chess positions. *Memory and Cognition* **4**, 541–547.

Frijda, N.H. and De Groot, A.D. (1981). *Otto Selz: His contribution to psychology*. The Hague: Mouton.

Fulgosi, A. and Guilford J.P. (1968). Short term incubation in divergent production. *American Journal of Psychology* **81**, 241–246.

Gardner, H. (1985). *The mind's new science: A history of the cognitive revolution*. New York: Basic Books.

Ghiselin, B. (1952). *The creative process*. Berkeley, CA., University of California Press.

Gick, M.L. (1986). Problem solving strategies. *Educational Psychologist* **21**, 99–120.

Gick, M.L. and Holyoak, K.J. (1980). Analogical problem solving. *Cognitive Psychology* **12**, 306–355.

Gick, M.L. and Holyoak, K.J. (1983). Schema induction in analogical transfer. *Cognitive Psychology* **15**, 1–38.

Gilhooly, K.J. (1987). Mental modelling: A framework for the study of thinking. In D.N. Perkins, J. Lochhead and J.C. Bishop (Eds), *Thinking*, pp. 19–32. Hillsdale, N.J.: Lawrence Erlbaum Associates.

Gilhooly, K.J. and Falconer, W. (1974). Concrete and abstract terms and relations in testing a rule. *Quarterly Journal of Experimental Psychology* **26**, 355–359.

Glucksberg, S. and Danks, J.H. (1968). Effects of discriminative labels. *Journal of Verbal Learning and Verbal Behaviour* **7**, 72–76.

Glucksberg, S. and Weisberg, R.W. (1966). Verbal behavior and problem solving. *Journal of Experimental Psychology* **71**, 659–664.

Goethals, G.R. and Leckmann, R.F. (1973). The perception of consistency in attitudes. *Journal of Experimental Psychology* **9**, 491–501.

Golding, W. (1955). *The inheritors*. London: Faber and Faber.

Goodwin, R.Q. and Wason, P.C. (1972). Degrees of insight. *British Journal of Psychology* **63**, 205–212.

Gordon, W.J. (1961). *Synectics*. New York: Harper.

Gorman, M.E. (1986). How the possibility of error affects falsification on a task that models scientific problem solving. *British Journal of Psychology* **77**, 85–96.

Gorman, M.E., Gorman, M.E., Latta, R.M. and Cunningham, G. (1984). How disconfirmatory, confirmatory and combined strategies affect group problem solving. *British Journal of Psychology* **75**, 65–80.

Griggs, R.A and Cox, J.R. (1982). The elusive thematic-materials effect in Wason's selection task. *British Journal of Psychology* **73**, 407–420.

Griggs, R.A. and Cox, J.R. (1983). The effects of problem content and negation on Wason's selection task. *Quarterly Journal of Experimental Psychology* **35A**, 519–534.

Gruber, H.E. (1980). *Darwin on man: A psychological study of scientific creativity*, 2nd edition. Chicago: University of Chicago Press.

Guyote, M.J. and Sternberg, R.J. (1981). A transitive-chain theory of syllogistic reasoning. *Cognitive Psychology* **13**, 461–525.

Hayes, J.R. and Simon H.A. (1977). Understanding written problem instructions. In L.W. Gregg (Ed.), *Knowledge and cognition*, pp. 167–200. Hillsdale, N.J.: Lawrence Erlbaum Associates.

Hearst, E. (1977). Man and machine: Chess achievements and chess thinking. In P.W. Frey (Ed.), Chess skill in man and machine, pp. 167–200. New York: Springer-Verlag.

Henle, M. (1962). On the relation between logic and thinking. *Psychological Review* **69**, 366–378.

Henle, M. (1978). Foreword. In R. Revlin and R.E. Mayer (Eds), *Human reasoning*, pp. xiii-xviii. New York: John Wiley.

Hesse, M. (1975). Bayesian methods and the initial probabilities of theories. In G. Maxwell and R.M. Anderson, Jr (Eds), *Induction, probability and confirmation*. Minneapolis, Minn.: University of Minnesota Press.

Hilgard, E.R. (1962). Impulsive versus realistic thinking: An examination of the distinction between primary and secondary processes in thought. *Psychological Bulletin* **59**, 477–489.

Hillis, D. (1985). *The connection machine*. Cambridge, Mass.: MIT Press.

Hobbes, T. (1651). *Leviathan*, 1919 edition. London: J.M. Dent.

Hoelscher, T.J., Klinger, E. and Barta, S.G. (1981). Incorporation of concern and nonconcern related verbal stimuli into dream content. *Journal of Abnormal Psychology* **90**, 88–91.

Holding, D.H. (1979). The evaluation of chess positions. *Simulation and Games* **10**, 207–221.

Holding, D.H. (1985). *The psychology of chess*. Hillsdale, N.J.: Lawrence Erlbaum Associates.

Holding, D.H. and Reynolds, J.R. (1982). Recall or evaluation of chess positions as determinants of chess skill. *Memory and Cognition* **10**, 237–242.

Holland, J.H. Holyoak, K.J., Nisbett, R.E. and Thagard, R.R. (1986). *Induction: processes of inference, learning and discovery*. Cambridge, Mass.: MIT Press.

Holyoak, K.J. (1984). Mental models in problem solving. In J.R. Anderson (Ed.), *Tutorials in learning and memory*, pp. 193–218. San Francisco: W.H. Freeman.

Holyoak, K.J. and Koh, K. (in press). Surface and structural similarity in analogical transfer. *Memory and Cognition*.

Hudson, L. (1966). *Contrary imaginations*. London: Methuen.

Hull, C.L. (1934). The concept of the habit-family hierarchy and maze-learning. *Psychological Review* **41**, 33–52, 134–152.

Humphreys, P.C. and Humphreys A.R. (1975). An investigation of subjective preference orderings for multi-attributed alternatives. In D. Wendt and C. Vlek (Eds), *Utility, probability and human decision making*. Dordrecht: Reidel.

Isenberg, D.J. (1987). Inside the mind of the senior manager. In D.N. Perkins, J. Lochhead and J.C. Bishop (Eds), *Thinking*. Hillsdale, N.J.: Lawrence Erlbaum Associates.

James, W. (1890). *The principles of psychology*. New York: Henry Holt.

Jeffries, R., Polson, P.G., Razran, L. and Atwood, M.E. (1977). A process model for missionaires–cannibals and other river crossing problems. *Cognitive Psychology* **9**, 412–420.

Johnson, P.E., Duran, A.S., Hassebrock, F., Moller, J., Prietula, M., Feltovich, P.J. and Swanson, D.B. (1981). Expertise and error in diagnostic reasoning. *Cognitive Science* **5**, 235–283.

Johnson-Laird, P.N. (1975). Models of deduction. In R.C. Falmagne (Ed.), *Reasoning: Representation and process*, pp. 7–54. Hillsdale, N.J.: Lawrence Erlbaum Associates.

Johnson-Laird, P.N. (1983). *Mental models.* Cambridge: Cambridge University Press.

Johnson-Laird, P.N. and Bara, B.G. (1984). Syllogistic inference. *Cognition* **16**, 1–61.

Johnson-Laird, P.N. and Steedman, M. (1978). The psychology of syllogisms. *Cognitive Psychology* **10**, 64–99.

Johnson-Laird, P.N. and Wason, P.C. (1970). A theoretical analysis of insight into a reasoning task. *Cognitive Psychology* **1**, 134–148.

Johnson-Laird, P.N., Legrenzi, P. and Legrenzi, M.S. (1972). Reasoning and a sense of reality. *British Journal of Psychology* **63**, 395–400.

Jones, E. (1961). *The life and work of Sigmund Freud.* Edited by L. Trilling and S. Marcus. London: Hogarth.

Kahneman, D. and Tversky, A. (1984). Choices, values and frames. *American Psychologist* **39**, 341–350.

Karat, J. (1982). A model of problem-solving with incomplete constraint knowledge. *Cognitive Psychology* **14**, 538–559.

Keane, M. (1988). *Analogical problem solving.* Chichester:Ellis Horwood/New York: John Wiley.

Klinger, E. (1971). *Structure and function of fantasy.* New York: John Wiley.

Klinger, E. (1974). Utterances to evaluate steps and control attention distinguish operant from respondent thought while thinking out loud. *Bulletin of the Psychonomic Society* **4**, 44–45.

Klinger, E. (1978). Modes of normal conscious flow. In K.S. Pope and J.L. Singer (Eds), *The stream of consciousness*, pp. 225–258. New York: John Wiley.

Klinger, E., Barta, S.G. and Maxeimer, M.E. (1980). Motivational correlates of thought content frequency and commitment. *Journal of Personality and Social Psychology* **39**, 1222–1237.

Klinger, E., Cox, W.M. and Roudebush, R.L. (in press). Dimensions of thought flow in everyday life. *Imagination, Cognition and Personality* **7**.

Kochen, M. and Badre, A.N. (1974). Questions and shifts of representation in problem solving. *American Journal of Psychology* **87**, 369–383.

Koestler, A. (1964). *The act of creation.* London: Hutchinson.

Kohler, W. (1925). *The mentality of apes.* New York: Harcourt, Brace.

Kosslyn, S.M. (1981). The medium and the message in mental imagery: A theory. *Psychological Review* **88**, 46–66.

Kosslyn, S.M. and Pomerantz, J.R. (1977). Imagery, propositions, and the form of internal representations. *Cognitive Psychology* **9**, 52–76.

Krechevsky, I. (1935). Brain mechanisms and 'hypotheses'. *Journal of Comparative Psychology* **19**, 425–462.

Kripke, D.F. and Sonnenschein, D. (1978). A biologic rhythm in waking fantasy. In K.S. Pope and J.L. Singer (Eds), *The stream of consciousness,* pp. 321–332. New York: John Wiley.

Kuhn, T. (1970). *The structure of scientific revolutions*, 2nd edition. Chicago: University of Chicago Press.

Lachman, R. (1973). Uncertainty effects on time taken to access the internal lexicon. *Journal of Experimental Psychology* **99**, 199–208.

Lakatos, I. (1970). Falsification and the methodology of scientific research programmes. In I. Lakatos and A. Musgrave (Eds), *Criticism and the growth of knowledge*. Cambridge: Cambridge University Press.

Langley, P., Simon, H.A., Bradshaw, G.L. and Zytkow, J.M. (1987). Scientific *discovery: Computational explorations of the creative processes*. Cambridge, Mass.: MIT Press.

Larkin, J.H. (1978). Problem solving in physics: Structure, process and learning. In J.M. Scandura and C.J. Brainerd (Eds), *Structural/process models of complex human behavior*. The Netherlands: Sijthoff and Noordhoff.

Larkin, J.H. (1979). Information processing models and science instructions. In J. Lochhead and J. Clement, (Eds), *Cognitive process instructions*. Philadelphia, Pa.: Franklin Institute Press.

Larkin, J.H., McDermott, J., Simon, D.P. and Simon, H.A. (1980). Models of competence in solving physics problems. *Cognitive Science* **4**, 317–345.

Laughlin, P.R., Doherty, M.A. and Dunn, R.F. (1968). Intentional and incidental concept formation as a function of motivation, creativity, intelligence and sex. *Journal of Personality and Social Psychology* **8**, 401–409.

Legrenzi, P. (1971). Discovery as a means to understanding. *Quarterly Journal of Experimental Psychology* **23**, 417–422.

Lehman, H.C. (1953). *Age and achievement*. Princeton. N.J.: Princeton University Press.

Lesgold, A.M. (1984). Acquiring expertise. In J.R. Anderson (Ed.), *Tutorials in learning and memory*, pp. 31–60. San Fransisco: W.H. Freeman.

Lesgold, A.M., Rubinson, H., Feltovich, P., Glaser, R. and Klopfer, D. (1988). Expertise in complex skills: Diagnosing X-ray pictures. In M. Chi, R. Glaser and M. Farr (Eds), *The nature of expertise*. Hillsdale, N.J.: Lawrence Erlbaum Associates.

Levy, D. (1978). Computers are now chess masters. *New Scientist* 27 July, 256–258.

Lewis, C. (1981). Skill in algebra. In J.R. Anderson (Ed.), *Cognitive skills and their acquisition*. Hillsdale, N.J.: Lawrence Erlbaum Associates.

Lichenstein, S., Slovic, P., Fischhoff, B., Layman, M. and Coombes, B. (1978). Judged frequency of lethal events. *Journal of Experimental Psychology: Human Learning and Memory* **4**, 551–578.

Lopes, L. (1976). Model based decision and inference in stud poker. *Journal of Experimental Psychology: General* **105**, 217–239.

Luchins, A.W. (1942). Mechanization in problem solving: The effect of Einstellung. *Psychological Monographs* **54** (248).

Luger, G.F. (1976). The use of the state-space to record the behavioural effects of subproblems and symmetries on the Tower of Hanoi problem. *International Journal of Man–Machine Studies* **8**, 411–421.

Lung, C.T. and Dominowski, R.L. (1985). Effects of strategy instructions and practice on nine-dot problem solving. *Journal of Experimental Psychology: Learning, Memory and Cognition* **11**, 804–811.

McClelland, J.L. (1986). The programmable blackboard model of reading. In J.H. McClelland, D.E. Rumelhart and the PDP Research Group (Eds), *Parallel distributed processing*, Vol. 2. Cambridge, Mass.: MIT Press.

McClelland, J.L. and Rumelhart, D.E. (1985). Distributed memory and the representation of general and specific information. *Journal of Experimental Psychology: General* **114**, 159–188.

McClelland, J.L. and Rumelhart, D.E. (1986). A distributed model of human learning and memory. In J.L. McClelland, D.E. Rumelhart and the PDP Research Group (Eds), *Parallel distributed processing*, Vol. 2. Cambridge, Mass.: MIT Press.

McClelland, J.L., Rumelhart, D.E. and the PDP Research Group (Eds) (1986a). *Parallel distributed processing*, Vol. 2. Cambridge, Mass.:MIT Press.

McClelland, J.L., Rumelhart, D.E. and Hinton, G.E. (1986b). The appeal of parallel distributed processing. In D.E. Rumelhart, J.C. McClelland and the PDP Research Group (Eds), *Parallel distributed processing*, Vol. 1. Cambridge, Mass.: MIT Press.

McCloskey, M. (1983). Intuitive physics. *Scientific American* **24**, 122–130.

McCloskey, M. and Kaiser, M.K. (1984). Children's intuitive physics. *The Sciences* **24**, 40–45.

MacDonald, R.R. (1986). Credible conceptions and implausible probabilities. *British Journal of Mathematical and Statistical Psychology* **39**, 15–27.

McKeithen, K.B., Reitman, J.S., Rueter, H.H. and Hirtle, S.C. (1981). Knowledge organization and skill differences in computer programmers. *Cognitive Psychology* **13**, 307–325.

McKellar, P. (1957). *Imagination and thinking*. New York: Basic Books.

MacKinnon, D.W. (1962). The personality correlates of creativity: A study of American architects. In *Proceedings of the 14th Congress of Applied Psychology*, Vol. 2, pp. 11–39, Munksgaard. Excerpts reprinted in P.E. Vernon (Ed.), *Creativity*. Harmondsworth: Penguin Books, 1970.

McLelland, D.C. (1962). On the dynamics of creative physical scientists. In H.E. Gruber *et al.* (Eds), *Contemporary approaches to creative thinking*, pp.141–174. New York: Atherton.

Maltzman, I. (1955). Thinking: From a behavioristic point of view. *Psychological Review* **62**, 275–286.

Manktelow, K.I. and Evans, J. St. B.T. (1979). Facilitation of reasoning by realism: Effect or non-effect? *British Journal of Psychology* **70**, 477–488.

Mawer, R.F. and Sweller, J. (1982). Effects of subgoal density and location on learning during problem solving. *Journal of Experimental Psychology: Learning, Memory and Cognition* **8**, 252–259.

Meadow, A., Parnes, S.J. and Reese, H. (1959). Influence of brainstorming instruction and problem sequence on a creative problem solving test. *Journal of Applied Psychology* **43**, 413–416.

Mednick, S.A. (1962). The associative basis of the creative process. *Psychological Review* **69**, 431–436.

Mendelsohn, G.A. and Griswold, B.B. (1964). Differential use of incidental stimuli in problem solving as a function of creativity. *Journal of Abnormal and Social Psychology* **68**, 431–436.

Meskin, B.B. and Singer, J.L. (1974). Daydreaming, reflective thought and laterality of eye movements. *Journal of Personality and Social Psychology* **30**, 64–71.

Mill, J.S. (1875/1967). *A system of logic*. London: Longmans.

Millenson J.R. (1967). *Principles of behavioral analysis*. New York: MacMillan.

Miller, G.A. (1956). The magical number seven, plus or minus two: Some limits on our capacity for processing information. *Psychological Review* **63**, 81–87.

Miller, G.A. (1960). *Psychology: The science of mental life*. Harmondsworth: Penguin.

Miller, G.A., Galanter, E.H. and Pribram, H.H. (1960). *Plans and the structure of behavior*. New York: Holt.

Mitroff, I.I. (1974). *The subjective side of science*. Amsterdam: Elsevier.

Murdock, B.B., Jr (1971). Short term memory. In G. Bower (Ed.), *The psychology of learning and motivation*, Vol. 5, pp. 67–127. London and San Diego: Academic Press.

Murray, H.G. and Denny, J.P. (1969). Interaction of ability level and interpolated activity in human problem solving. *Psychological Reports* **24**, 271–276.

Mynatt, C.R., Doherty, M.E. and Tweney, R.D. (1977). Confirmation bias in a simulated research environment: An experimental study of scientific inference. *Quarterly Journal of Experimental Psychology* **29**, 85–95.

Mynatt, C.R., Doherty, M.E. and Tweney, R.D. (1978). Consequences of confirmation and disconfirmation in a simulated research environment. *Quarterly Journal of Experimental Psychology* **30**, 395–406.

Neisser, U. (1963a). The imitation of man by machine. *Science* **139**, 193–197.

Neisser, U. (1963b). The multiplicity of thought. *British Journal of Psychology* **54**, 1–14.

Neisser, U. (1976). *Cognition and reality*. San Francisco: W.H. Freeman.

Newell, A. (1962). Some problems of basic organization in problem solving programs. In M.C. Yovits, G.T. Jacobi and G.D. Goldstein (Eds), *Self Organizing Systems*. Washington, D.C.: Spartan Books.

Newell, A. (1973). You can't play 20 questions with nature and win. In W.G. Chase (Ed.), *Visual information processing*, pp. 283–302. London and San Diego: Academic Press.

Newell, A. and Simon, H.A. (1972). *Human problem solving*. Englewood Cliffs, N.J.: Prentice Hall.

Newell, A., Shaw, J.C. and Simon, H.A. (1958). The processes of creative thinking. In H.E. Gruber, G. Terrell and M. Wertheimer (Eds), *Contemporary approaches to creative thinking*, pp. 63–119. New York: Atherton.

Nilsson, N.J. (1971). *Problem solving methods in artificial intelligence*. New York: McGraw-Hill.

Nisbett, R.E. and Borgida, D. (1975). Attribution and the psychology of prediction. *Journal of Personal and Social Psychology* **32**, 932–943.

Nisbett, R.E. and Wilson, T.D. (1977). Telling more than we can know: Verbal reports on mental processes. *Psychological Review* **84**, 231–259.

Norman, D.A. (1981a). Categorization of action slips. *Psychological Review* **88**, 1–15.

Norman, D.A. (1986). Reflections on cognition and parallel distributed processing. In D.E. Rumelhart, J.L. McClelland and the PDP Research Group (Eds), *Parallel distributed processing*, Vol. 2, pp. 531–546. Cambridge, Mass.: MIT Press.

Oldfield, R.C. (1966). Things, words and the brain. *Quarterly Journal of Experimental Psychology* **18**, 340–353.

Olton, R.M. and Johnson, D.M. (1976). Mechanisms of incubation in creative problem solving. *American Journal of Psychology* **7**.

Osborn, A.F. (1953). *Applied imagination*. New York: Scribners.

Parnes, S.J. and Meadow, A. (1963). Development of individual creative talent. In C.W. Taylor and F. Barron (Eds), *Scientific creativity: Its recognition and development*. New York: John Wiley.

Patrick, C. (1935). Creative thought in poets. *Archives of Psychology*, **26**, 73.
Patrick, C. (1937). Creative thought in artists. *Journal of Psychology*, **4**, 35–73.
Payne, J. (1976) Task complexity and contingent processing in decision making: An information search and protocol analysis. *Organizational Behavior and Human Performance* **16**, 366–387.
Pearl, J. (1983). On the nature of pathology in game searching. *Artificial Intelligence* **20**, 427–453.
Perkins, D. (1981). *The mind's best work*. Cambridge, Mass.: Harvard University Press.
Peterson, C.R. and Peterson, M.J. (1959). Short-term retention of individual verbal items. *Journal of Experimental Psychology* **58**, 193–198.
Pfau, H.D. and Murphy, M.D. (in press). The role of verbal knowledge in chess skill. *American Journal of Psychology*.
Platt, J.R. (1964). Strong inference. *Science* **146**, 347–353.
Poincaré, H. (1908). *Science et methode*. Paris: Flammarion.
Pollard, P. and Evans, J. St. B.T. (1981). The effects of prior beliefs in reasoning: An associational interpretation. *British Journal of Psychology* **72**, 73–82.
Polson, P.G. and Jeffries, R. (1982). Problem solving as search and understanding. In R.J. Sternberg (Ed.), *Advances in the psychology of human intelligence*. Hillsdale, N.J.: Lawrence Erlbaum Associates.
Polya, G. (1957). *How to solve it*. Princetown, NJ.: Princetown University Press.
Pope, K.S. and Singer, J.L. (1978). Regulation of the stream of consciousness: Toward a theory of ongoing thought. In G.E. Schwartz and D. Shapiro (Eds), *Consciousness and self-regulation*, Vol. 2, pp. 101–138. New York: John Wiley.
Popper, K.R. (1959). *The logic of scientific discovery*. London: Hutchinson.
Pylyshyn, Z.W. (1973). What the mind's eye tells the mind's brain: A critique of mental imagery. *Psychological Bulletin* **80**, 1–24.
Pylyshyn, Z.W. (1981). The imagery debate: Analogue media versus tacit knowledge. *Psychological Review* **88**, 16–45.
Pylyshyn, Z.W. (1984). *Computation and cognition*. Cambridge, Mass.: MIT Press.
Raphael, B. (1976). *The thinking computer*. San Francisco: W.H. Freeman.
Reason, J. (1979). Actions not as planned: The price of automatization. In G. Underwood and K. Stevens (Eds), *Aspects of consciousness*, Vol. 1, pp. 67–90. London and San Diego: Academic Press.
Reitman, J. (1976). Skilled perception in Go: Deducing memory structures from inter-response times. *Cognitive Psychology* **8**, 336–356.
Reitman, W.R. (1965). *Cognition and thought*. New York: John Wiley.
Restle, F. and Davis, J.H. (1962). Success and speed of problem solving by individuals and groups. *Psychological Review* **69**, 520–536.
Roe, A. (1952). A psychologist examines sixty-four eminent scientists. *Scientific American* **187**, 21–25.
Rosch, E. (1978). Principles of categorization. In E. Rosch and B.B. Lloyd (Eds), *Cognition and categorization*. Hillsdale, N.J.: Lawrence Erlbaum Associates.
Ruger, H. (1910). The psychology of efficiency. *Archives of Psychology (New York)* **15**.
Rumelhart, D.E., (1980). Schemata: The building blocks of cognition. In R.J. Spiro, B.C. Brue and W. F. Brewer (Eds), *Theoretical issues in reading comprehension*. Hillsdale, N.J.: Lawrence Erlbaum Associates.
Rumelhart, D.E. and McClelland, J.L. (1982). An interactive activation model of context effects in letter perception: Part 2. The contextual enhancement effect and

some tests and extensions of the model. *Psychological Review* **89**, 60–94.

Rumelhart, D.E. and McClelland, J.L. (1986). On learning the past tenses of English verbs. In J.L. McClelland, D.E. Rumelhart and the PDP Research Group (Eds), *Parallel distributed processing*, Vol. 2. Cambridge, Mass.: MIT Press.

Rumelhart, D.E., McClelland, J.L. and the PDP Research Group (Eds) (1986a). *Parallel distributed processing*, Vol. 1. Cambridge, Mass.: MIT Press.

Rumelhart, D.E., Hinton, G.E. and McClelland, J.L. (1986b). A general framework for parallel distributed processing. In D.E. Rumelhart, J.L. McClelland and the PDP Research Group (Eds), *Parallel distributed processing*, Vol. 1. Cambridge, Mass.: MIT Press.

Rumelhart D.E., Smolensky, P., McClelland, J.L. and Hinton, G.E. (1986c). Schemata and sequential thought processes in PDP models. In J.L. McClelland, D.E. Rumelhart and the PDP Research Group (Eds), *Parallel distributed processing*, Vol. 2. Cambridge, Mass.: MIT Press.

Savage, L.J. (1954). *The foundation of statistics.* New York: John Wiley.

Schachter, S. (1968). Obesity and Eating, *Science*, **161**, 751–6.

Scheerer, M. (1963). Problem-solving. *Scientific American* **208**(4), 118–128.

Schoenfeld, A.H. and Hermann, D.J. (1982). Problem perception and knowledge structure in expert and novice mathematical problem solvers. *Journal of Experimental Psychology: Learning, Memory and Cognition* **8**, 484–494.

Searle, J. (1984). *Minds, brains and science.* London: British Broadcasting Corporation.

Sells, S.B. (1935). The atmosphere effect: An experimental study of reasoning. *Archives of Psychology* **200**, 1–72.

Sells, S.B. and Koob, H.F. (1937). A classroom demonstration of "atmosphere effect" in reasoning. *Journal of Educational Psychology* **72**, 197–200.

Shallice, T. (1972). Dual functions of consciousness. *Psychological Review* **79**, 383–393.

Shallice, T. (1978). The dominant action system: An information-processing approach to consciousness. In K.S. Pope and J.L. Singer (Eds), *The stream of consciousness*, pp. 117–158. New York: John Wiley.

Shannon, C. (1950). Programming a computer to play chess. *Philosophy Magazine* **41**, 256–275.

Shapiro, D. (1971). 'Representativeness', structure and content in a reasoning problem. *Bulletin of the British Psychological Society* **24**, 43–44.

Shepard, R.N. and Metzler J. (1971). Mental rotation of three-dimensional objects. *Science* **171**, 701–703.

Simon, H.A. (1957). *Models of man: Social and rational.* New York: John Wiley.

Simon, H.A. (1966). Scientific discovery and the psychology of problem solving. In R.G. Colodny (Ed.), *Mind and cosmos: Essays in contemporary science and philosophy*, Pittsburgh: University of Pittsburgh Press.

Simon, H.A. (1976). Motivational and emotional controls of cognition. *Psychological Review* **74**, 29–39.

Simon, H.A. (1975). The functional equivalence of problem solving skills. *Cognitive Psychology* **7**, 268–288.

Simon, H.A. (1978). Rationality as process and product of thought. *American Economic Association* **68**, 1–16.

Simon, H.A. (1981). Cognitive science: The newest science of the artificial. In D.A. Norman (Ed.), *Perspectives on cognitive science*, pp. 13–26. Norwood, N.J.: Ablex.

Simon, H. and Barenfeld, M. (1969). Information-processing analysis of perceptual processes in problem-solving. *Psychological Review* **76**, 473–483.

Simon, H. and Gilmartin, K. (1973). A simulation of memory for chess positions. *Cognitive Psychology* **5**, 29–46.

Simon, H.A. and Hayes, J.R. (1976). The understanding process: Problem isomorphs. *Cognitive Psychology* **8**, 165–190.

Simon, H.A. and Reed, S.K. (1976). Modelling strategy shifts on a problem solving task. *Cognitive Psychology* **8**, 86–97.

Singer, J.L. (1975a). Navigating the stream of consciousness: Research in daydreaming and related inner experience. *American Psychologist* **30**, 727–738.

Singer, J.L. (1975b). *Daydreaming and fantasy*. London: Allen and Unwin.

Singer, J.L. (1978). Studies of daydreaming. In K.S. Pope and J.L. Singer (Eds), *The stream of consciousness*, pp. 187–223. New York: John Wiley.

Singer, J.L. and Antrobus, J.S. (1972). Daydreaming, imaginal processes, and personality: A normative study. In P. Sheehan (Ed.), *The function and nature of imagery*. London and San Diego: Academic Press.

Singer, J.L. and McCraven, V. (1961). Some characteristics of adult daydreaming. *Journal of Psychology* **51**, 151–164.

Skinner, B.F. (1985). Cognitive Science and Behaviourism, *British Journal of Psychology* **76**, 291–301.

Slate, D.J. and Atkin, C.R. (1977). Chess 4.5. The Northwestern University chess program. In P.W. Frey (Ed.), *Chess skill in man and machine*. New York: Springer-Verlag.

Slovic, P., Fischhoff, B. and Lichtenstein, S. (1982). Response mode, framing, and information processing effects in risk assessment. In R.Hogarth (Ed.), *New directions for methodology of social and behavioral science: question framing and response consistency*. San Francisco: Jossey-Bass.

Smalley, N.S. (1974) Evaluating a rule against possible instances. *British Journal of Psychology* **65**, 293–304.

Smolensky, P. (1986). Information processing in dynamical systems: Foundations of harmony theory. In D.E. Rumelhart, J.L. McClelland and the PDP Research Group (Eds), *Parallel distributed processing*, Vol. 1. Cambridge, Mass.: MIT Press.

Spelke, E., Hirst, W. and Neisser, U. (1976). Skills of divided attention. *Cognition* **4**, 215–230.

Spence, K.W. (1936). The nature of discrimination learning in animals. *Psychological Review* **43**, 427–449.

Sperling, G.A. (1960). The information available in brief visual presentation. *Psychological Monographs* **74**, (498).

Stein, M. (1974). *Stimulating creativity*, Vol. 1. London and San Diego: Academic Press.

Stein, M. (1975). *Stimulating creativity*, Vol. 2. London and San Diego: Academic Press.

Sternberg, R.J. (1987). Coping with novelty and human intelligence. In P. Morris (Ed.), *Modelling cognition*. Chichester: John Wiley.

Sternberg, R.J. and Davidson, J.E. (1982). Componential analysis and componential theory. *Behavioral and Brain Sciences* **53**, 352–3.

Sweller, J. and Levine, M. (1982). Effects of goal specificity on means–ends analysis and learning. *Journal of Experimental Psychology: Learning, Memory and Cognition* **8**, 463–474.

Sweller, J. Mawer, R.F. and Ward, M.R. (1983). Development of expertise in mathematical problem-solving. *Journal of Experimental Psychology: General* **112**, 639–661.

Taylor, D.W., Berry, P.C. and Block, C.H. (1985). Does group participating when using brainstorming facilitate or inhibit creative thinking? *Administrative Science Quarterly* **3**, 23–47.

Thomas, J.C. Jr (1974). An analysis of behavior in the hobbits–orcs problem. *Cognitive Psychology* **6**, 257–269.

Thorndike, E.L. (1898). *Animal intelligence*. New York: Macmillan.

Thouless, R.H. (1953). *Straight and crooked thinking*. London: Pan Books.

Tolkien, J.R.R. (1966). *The hobbit*, 3rd edition. London: Allen and Unwin.

Tukey, D.D. (1986). A philosophical and empirical analysis of subject's modes of inquiry in Wason's 2–4–6 task. *Quarterly Journal of Experimental Psychology* **38A**, 5–34.

Tulving, E.C. (1983). *Elements of Episodic Memory*. Oxford, Oxford University Press.

Tversky, A. (1972). Elimination by aspects: a theory of choice. *Psychological Review* **79**, 281–299.

Tversky, A. and Kahneman, D. (1974). Judgment under uncertainty: Heuristic and biases. *Science* **125**, 1124–1131.

Tversky, A. and Kahneman, D. (1981). The framing of decisions and the psychology of choice. *Science* **211**, 453–458.

Tversky, A. and Kahneman, D. (1983). Extensional versus intuitive reasoning: the conjunction fallacy in probability judgement. *Psychological Review* **90**, 293–315.

Van Duyne, P.C. (1974). Realism and linguistic complexity in reasoning. *British Journal of Psychology* **65**, 59–69.

Van Duyne, P.C. (1976). Necessity and contingency in reasoning. *Acta Psychologica* **40**, 85–101.

Varendonck, J. (1921). *The Psychology of daydreams*. New York: Macmillan.

Vernon, P.E. (1970). *Creativity*. Harmondsworth: Penguin.

Von Neumann, J. and Morgenstern, O. (1944). *Theory of games and economic behavior*. Princeton, N.J.: Princeton University Press.

Voss. J.F., Greene, T.R., Post, T.A. and Penner, B.C. (1983). Problem solving skill in the social sciences. In G.Bower (Ed.), *The psychology of learning and motivation*, Vol. 17, pp. 165–213. London and San Diego: Academic Press.

Wagner, D.A. and Scurrah, M.J. (1971). Some characteristics of human problem solving in chess. *Cognitive Psychology* **2**, 451–478.

Wallas, G. (1926). *The art of thought*. London: Jonathan Cape.

Warren, T.F. and Davis, G.A. (1969). Techniques for creative thinking: An empirical comparison of three methods. *Psychological Reports* **25**, 207–214.

Wason. P.C. (1960). On the failure to eliminate hypotheses in a conceptual task. *The Quarterly Journal of Experimental Psychology* **12**, 129–140.

Wason. P.C. (1966). Reasoning. In B.M. Foss (Ed.), *New horizons in psychology*. Harmondsworth: Penguin.

Wason, P.C. (1968). Reasoning about a rule. *Quarterly Journal of Experimental Psychology* **20**, 273–281.

Wason, P.C. (1969). Regression in reasoning? *British Journal of Psychology* **60**, 471–480.

Wason, P.C. and Evans, J. St. B.T. (1975). Dual processes in reasoning? *Cognition* **3**, 141–154.

Wason, P.C. and Johnson-Laird, P.N. (1970). A conflict between selecting and evaluating information in an inferential task. *British Journal of Psychology* **61**, 509-515.

Wason, P.C. and Johnson-Laird, P.N. (1972). *Psychology of reasoning: Structure and content*. London: Batsford.

Wason, P.C. and Shapiro, D. (1971). Natural and contrived experience in a reasoning problem. *Quarterly Journal of Experimental Psychology* **23**, 63-71.

Watson, J.B. (1913). Psychology as the behaviorist views it. *Psychological Review* **20**, 158-177.

Weisberg, R.W. (1986). *Creativity*: Genius and other myths. San Francisco: W.H. Freeman.

Weisberg, R.W. and Alba, J.W. (1981a). An examination of the alleged role of 'fixation' in the solution of several 'insight' problems. *Journal of Experimental Psychology: General* **110**, 169-192.

Weisberg, R.W. and Alba, J.W. (1981b). Gestalt theory, insight and past experience: Reply to Dominowski. *Journal of Experimental Psychology: General* **110**, 193-198.

Weisberg, R.W. and Alba, J.W. (1982). Problem solving is not like preception: More on Gestalt theory. *Journal of Experimental Psychology: General* **111**, 326-330.

Wertheimer, M. (1945). *Productive thinking*. New York: Harper and Row.

Wetherick, N.E. (1970). On the representativeness of some experiments in cognition. *Bulletin of the British Psychological Society* **23**, 213-214.

Wetherick, N.E. (1971). 'Representativeness' in a reasoning problem: A reply to Shapiro. *Bulletin of the British Psychological Society* **24**, 213-214.

Wetherick, N.E. (1979). The foundations of psychology. In N. Bolton (Ed.), *Philosophical Problems in Psychology*, pp. 89-100. London: Methuen.

Wickelgren, W. (1974). *How to solve problems*. San Fransisco: W.H. Freeman.

Wilkins, M (1928). The effect of changed material on ability to do formal syllogistic reasoning. *Archives of Psychology* **16**, 83.

Winston, P.H. (1984). *Artificial intelligence*, 2nd edition. New York: Addison-Wesley.

Woodworth, R.S. and Schlosberg, H. (1954). *Experimental psychology*, 3rd edition. London: Methuen.

Woodworth, R.S. and Sells, S.B. (1935). An atmosphere effect in formal syllogistic reasoning. *Journal of Experimental Psychology* **18**, 451-460.

Wright, G. (1984). *Behavioural decision theory*. Harmondsworth: Penguin.

Young, R. (1974). Production systems as models of cognitive development. *Bionics Research Reports*, No. 22. Bionics Research Laboratory, School of Artificial Intelligence, University of Edinburgh, Edinburgh.

Zangwill, O.L. (1980), Kenneth Craik: The man and his work. *British Journal of Psychology* **71**, 1-16.

Zimbardo, P.G., Cohen, A., Weisenberg. M., Dworkin, L. and Firestone, I. (1969a). The control of experimental pain. In P.G. Zimbardo (Ed.), *The cognitive control of motivation*. Glenview, Ill.: Scott, Foresman.

Zimbardo, P.G., Weisenberg, M., Firestone, I. and Levy, B. (1969b). Changing appetites for eating fried grasshoppers with cognitive dissonance. In P.G. Zimbardo (Ed.), *The cognitive control of motivation*. Glenview, Ill.: Scott, Foresman.

Zwicky, F. (1969). *Discovery, invention, research*. New York: Macmillan.

Author index

Subject index